TIMBER COUNTRY
REVISITED

The peace and quiet of a forest grove is exemplified in this grove of coastal redwoods near Pepperwood. Some of these trees were growing at the time of the Crusades and were already two hundred feet tall when Columbus made his epic journey. They survive to this day as a priceless heritage.

TIMBER COUNTRY REVISITED

BY
EARL ROBERGE

Edited By
William Pickell
Ellen C. Pickell

WASHINGTON CONTRACT LOGGERS ASSOCIATION
OLYMPIA, WASHINGTON
1991

International Standard Book Number 0-9631295-0-3
Library of Congress Catalog Card Number 91-067222
Copyright© 1991 by
Washington Contract Loggers Association
P.O. Box 2168•Olympia•Washington 98507-2168

DEDICATON

**This book is respectfully dedicated
to the North American Logger, an Endangered Species determined to survive.**

Balanced on a springboard a dozen feet above a steep slope, Earl Marcellus, one of the few remaining practitioners of what used to be common art, uses his precarious position to make an otherwise impossible cut on this double-boled old ponderosa.

CONTENTS

LIST OF ILLUSTRATIONS

ACKNOWLEDGEMENTS

My mother, of blessed memory, long ago taught me that when someone gives you a lift along the road of life, good manners, if nothing else, require that due acknowledgement be given to that person. That is the task facing me now, for without the help and support I have received from numerous involved people, this book would still be an unrealized dream. I approach that task willingly, for it gives me a chance to vicariously revisit with some very nice people whose path touched mine along the way, and thereby greatly enriched my life.

There were many, and I cannot pretend to name them all, so for all of you good people out there who helped fill in the potholes that abound along the highway of life, please accept this blanket "thank you" and know that your help was very much appreciated, even though you are not mentioned by name. It may have been sharing your nosebag with me, when my stay in the woods extended into lunchtime, or drawing a map to guide me to some out-of-the-way logging show, but these are the small courtesies that have helped to make this book a very rich, fulfilling human experience.

My first and very sincere thanks go to Bill Pickell, Managing Director of the Washington Contract Loggers' Association, and his able assistant, Bob Davison. They assured me that I would have a completely free hand in writing my book, and such help as they would give me would be only that which I requested. It has been a pleasure to work with these two men, who were always quick to ferret out some odd piece of information, verify some obscure fact, or take me out to a good lunch. Believe me, you both have my sincere gratitude for a job well done.

My first contact with a gyppo logger was so pleasant that if I were superstitious, I would say that it presaged the way the whole book would go. I am not superstitious, believing rather that one makes his own luck, but the warm welcome I got from Bob and Joy Gardner at Chewelah certainly got me off to a roaring good start, even if Joy had to give me a four-wheel drive assist up their icy driveway! Visiting with these warm, friendly folks made me realize that the qualities I had come to admire so greatly in loggers eighteen years ago had not been diluted over the years but were alive and well in Chewelah. If I were to get nothing else out of this book other than the pleasure of launching what I sincerely hope will be a lifetime friendship with Bobcat and Joy, I would consider it reward enough, but these two, being excellent business people, will see to it that I get much, much more! My sincere thanks to you, Bob, and a big warm hug to your Joy.

My next foray was into the redwood country of California, and here Ed Lewis Sr. and his logger son, Ed

Jr., took me under their wings and initiated me into the mysteries of redwood logging. This was the first of several trips to the Redwood Country, and I couldn't have asked for more competent or congenial guides. On subsequent visits, Dan McLoughlin, Logging Supervisor for Pacific Lumber Company, took me in tow, introduced me to Robert Stephens, Forest Manager for PALCO, and generally was not only a font of information but also a very pleasant traveling companion. Steve Kerns, wildlife biologist, who seemingly knows hundreds of spotted owls by their first names, coaxed one of them within range of my lenses, and filled me in on the life style of this much maligned but quite nice bird. My sincere thanks and gratitude to all of you folks who made my stay in California so pleasant.

On the other side of the Coast Range, Tom Nelson and Tom Harrington, foresters for Sierra Pacific Industries, took me in tow and filled me in on the reasons why California is the largest producer of forest products in the United States. The days I spent with these dedicated, highly competent men I count as golden. You will always have a cherished spot in my book of memories, as well as my gratitude for the help you gave me.

On the Olympic Peninsula, my old friends Nat and Barbara Vale solaced me with the kind of hospitality that always leaves a warm glow in my heart. The chance to break bread and pull a few corks with these old friends is not one that I will ever willingly forego, and as usual, the meeting was warm, friendly, and all too short. With old friends such as these, formal thanks aren't necessary, but you have them anyway.

Bill Hermann is a busy, successful contract logger on the Peninsula, but he took time from his full day to show me some of the latest innovations in logging and reforesting. My thanks to you, Bill, and please know that your kindness is remembered with gratitude.

No book on logging in the Northwest would be complete without the help and active participation of the Weyerhaeuser Company, and help they gave me...in spades! John Keatly and Ross Gilchrist of the Longview Branch were my guides into the wilds of the Weyerhaeuser domain, an area as big as some states, and showed me any and all aspects of logging and reforestation on their extensive acres. Both are delightful men and wonderful guides, whose love for the forest they tend so lovingly shines through their eyes, whether it be in a fifty-year-old grove almost ready for harvest, or a ten-year-old plantation whose placement they supervised. To these men and to Jim Mason who so willingly filled the need whenever I needed a good model, my thanks and sincere appreciation. Weyco bills itself as "The Tree Growing Company" and the slogan is not misplaced. At the Mima Nursery and the Rochester Reforestation Center, I saw how millions of choice seedlings are raised, which will eventually clothe harvested acres in yet another generation of sturdy trees. My thanks to Jim Byran and Mike Pfaff for arranging very rewarding visits on short notice. Also on extremely short notice, Joan Ruthford of the Centralia Research Laboratory arranged for some badly needed photography. My thanks to you exceptional people to whom the impossible is only something that takes a little time. My sincere thanks and appreciation for a job well done also go to Pat Stack, who has a way with helicopters, especially when flying near active volcanoes. Pat, you can fly me anywhere!

Another helicopter pilot whose skill and general knowledge of the region is much appreciated is Cliff Kamm, who showed me some aspects of Prince of Wales Island that were new to me, even though I had become reasonably familiar with this big island years ago. Don Finney, Manager of the Alaska Forest Association pulled the necessary strings for this flight. I should have been prepared for this "tour de force" for Don had already accomplished the impossible: on short notice, he got me hotel accommodations in Ketchikan at the height of the tourist season. To you, Don, for answering all my questions and for a job well done, and to Louisiana-Pacific, for making a chopper available, I give a tip of my battered hard hat and a sincere "thank you."

It seems most of my helpers on this project are people to whom the impossible is routine. Even though springboards are seldom used nowadays, they still are a very picturesque relic of a colorful past, and I was determined to find someone, somewhere, who still practiced this ancient art. Earl Marcellus came to my rescue. He personally reconnoitered a large tract of hilly land to find the right tree, then took me on a half-mile hike (straight up!) to the spot so that I could record a vanishing art. Meeting Earl and his charming family was a high spot in my month, even if his son Jared beat me at chess, and his daughters, Jenny, Joy and Jessica, stole my heart. And how can I say "thank you" enough to his pretty wife, Linda, who made me feel like part of the family? Getting paid for writing a book is only part of the reward that accrues to a writer.

The world, I find, is full of charming, helpful people, but would you believe a lady logger is one of them? That's right. Betty Walker, along with three stalwart sons runs a very successful logging operation in the Blue Mountains of Washington, and the day that I spent with this gracious logger I simply must class as pure enjoyment. The day was warm, the soft drinks were cold, the sandwiches delicious and the company delightful. Oh, yes, we even got some good pictures! Thanks, Betty, for a delightful memory, and let's do it again!

The Blues have no monopoly on good intermountain logging. Over in Montana, John Hansen, Safety Man for the Montana Loggers' Association took me into some spectacular country and showed me logging, Montana style. Even a midsummer hailstorm that pelted us with marble-sized stones couldn't dampen the fun we had that day. The next day, in a big new Christofferson log truck driven by Bill Walters, was equally enjoyable. My thanks to the Christoffersons who made this possible, even though our only contact was by telephone. Believe me, I will take up your invitation and come back to Missoula and thank you personally for a wonderful adventure. To all of you wonderful people who made my Montana stay so enjoyable, a sincere and heartfelt vote of thanks.

British Columbia is not about to be outdone in hospitality. I have a soft spot in my heart for this beautiful province, and it became even softer after meeting Colin Wood of Forestry Canada in Victoria. The information and tips he gave me as to where I could find the pictures I needed were invaluable, but most of all, I enjoyed him and his associate, Dr. Robert De Boo. Here are two people whose acquaintance I intend to foster, but in the meantime, please know that my appreciation runs deeply. Oregon is not about to be left out of this picture. Peter Quast, Director of Woods Operations for Roseburg Lumber, was instrumental in making it possible to get some needed photography, and Jim Churchill of the Coquille operation did some very impressive detective work in pinpointing the desired site. To both these good men, I owe a vote of thanks. It would have been impossible without your help. I like "can do" types, and that definitely fits you two.

The men and women of the Forest Service do a work that is often not sufficiently appreciated by the general public but not by this writer. Whenever I needed help or information, they were there, and the help was unstinting. To these men and women, especially to Carl Maass, Timber Sales Administrator for the Umatilla National Forest, my thanks and appreciation.

It has often been said, and often very truly, that behind every man who ever accomplishes anything, there is a woman behind him telling him how to do it. In my case, the woman stands not behind me, but beside me, for she is not only my right arm but the center of my universe. To my little Irish bride, my beloved Gadget, I give my heartfelt thanks for the gentle, loving assistance that only a loving wife who is always in your heart can give.

To you, Gadget, my thanks and my pledge...plus qu'hier, moin que demain.

GLOSSARY

The following is a list of words common in the logging fraternity, but not generally known to the general public. It is only a very small part of a large, colorful, often lusty and always expressive vocabulary which to the uninitiated sounds vaguely like English, but may be completely unintelligible. Listed here is a sanitized list of words that appear in the text plus a few others that I just couldn't resist including, simply because they are so colorful.

BEAVER BAIT	Trash logs and debris. A log drive term.
BLOCK CUT	A small or partial clearcut, in which some trees are left standing.
BLOWDOWN	A tree felled by the wind or some other natural cause.
BOOM BOAT	A small, powerful, almost circular and highly maneuverable boat used to herd logs, usually in a mill pond.
BRAIL	In water logging, a system whereby the outermost of several floating logs is held in place with a pike pole and the whole pod moved into the current by the jet boat.
BRUSH APE	A logger, usually a chokerman. You'd better be smiling when you call a logger this name or be a very good friend.
BUCKER	The logger who cuts the felled logs to size to get the most scale.
BUCKSKIN	A log which has lost its bark.
BULLBLOCK	An oversized, massive block hung from the spar tree and carrying the mainline. In redwood logging, some of these monsters weighed over a ton.
BULL COOK	A cook's assistant, who does all of the dirty work.
BULL OF THE WOODS	The person in charge of the woods operation. In the old days, the toughest man on the crew; nowadays still a pretty tough logger.
BUTT CUT	The first and largest diameter cut, directly above the stump.
BUTT RIGGING	The heavy metal knobs and rings suspended from the mainline to which chokers are attached.
CALKS	The logger's classic, high-topped, steel-spiked boot, which gives him steady footing on a fallen log. Not usually worn socially.
CAMPER'S BLIGHT	A gradual deterioration of the woods due to overuse by people. Generally prevalent in areas accessible by car and characterized by compacted soil, scarred trees and litter.
CAMP INSPECTOR	An itinerant logger. Also "timber tramp."

CANT	A log which has had a slab taken off each of four sides. Also known as a "Japanese square" if intended for export.
CHASER	A person who unhooks the chokers from the logs at the landing.
CHOKER	A small length of cable with a knob and fitting bell, used to attach logs to the butt rigging of cable systems or to skidders. Chokerman say a choker is an instrument of torture invented by people who hate loggers.
CHOKERMAN	Also "choker setter." A person who attaches chokers to logs. Usually the first (and toughest) job a logger gets.
CHOPPER	A helicopter. Also, in Northern California, the man who cuts down the tree.
CLEARCUT	A method of harvesting wherein all trees, regardless of size, are cut. Also the area where this has been done.
COLD DECK	A pile of stored logs which will be moved at a later date.
COMMERCIAL THINNING	Usually the second or third thinning on a stand of trees. So called because the wood taken out is large enough to have commercial value.
CONK	A fungus disease characterized by a conchoidal growth on the outside of a tree, evidence of heart rot and a cull tree.
COSMETIC LOGGING	Logging done mostly for aesthetic reasons.
CRUMMY	A logger's bus. Also an adjective meaning "no good" or "undesirable."
CULL	Applied to a log. It means rotten, rejected. Applied to a person, it means pretty much the same thing. A logger's strong insult.
DONKEY PUNCHER	Not a man who is cruel to mules but the operator of the heavy diesel that powers loaders and yarders. The name is a relic from the days of steam.
DIRT HIDER	A road grader.
DOG HAIR	A thick growth of small, suppressed trees.
FALLER	The person who cuts down the tree on a logging show. Also called cutter, chopper, busheler, and in the Intermountain, sawyer.
FLUNKY	A cook's assistant who waits on tables.
GAY CAT	A timber tramp who is also a criminal. The name was in use many years before the current usage of the word "gay" to denote homosexuality, so no slur is indicated.
GRAPPLE	A heavy set of metal tongs with teeth on the inside edge, which can be opened and shut at will by the operator.
GRAPPLE SHOW	A method of logging in which a grapple, rather than chokers, is used to haul in logs.
GROUSE LADDER	A tree with many limbs, especially on the lower part. Also called a "Wolf Tree" in Alaska.
GUT ROBBER	A camp cook, especially one of dubious ability. Fortunately, now a threatened species.
HAULBACK	A cable which is used to carry the butt rigging back to the work site.
HAYWIRE	The essential baling wire which is used for a thousand impromptu repairs on a logging show. Also an adjective meaning "patched up" or "no good." Also describes

	a light cable used to pull a heavier cable.
HEATHEN	A logger not particularly noted for social graces.
HIGHBALLER	A logger in a hurry. A fast, energetic worker.
HIGH CLIMBER	A person who tops a spar tree and hangs the butt rigging.
HIGH GRADING	Taking only the best logs, or the best cut of a tree, and leaving the rest to rot. Formerly common, it is now a major offense.
HOOK TENDER	Boss of the rigging crew. Inevitably, the name is shortened to "hooker," which gives rise to hundreds of stories and jokes, most of them scatological.
LANDING	The place to which the logs are dragged for loading.
LOADER	Also sometimes called a "shovel." The machine at the landing that loads the log onto a truck.
LOGGING SHOW	A logging operation.
LOKIE	The old-time steam locomotive, usually a Mallet or a Shay, that could run anyplace a logger could lay a track. A logger could lay a track anywhere.
LONG BOOM	Essentially, a derrick equipped with a mechanical grapple used in loading.
LUMBERJACK	Old-time eastern and midwestern term for a logger. In the Northwest, it has acquired overtones of crudity and stupidity, so the term is not usually used. In the Northwest and Alaska, the term is, and proudly, "logger."
MAINLINE	The heavy cable which is wound up onto the drums of the yarder and which drags the logs to the landing.
"MAKE 'ER OUT!"	"Make out the check. I quit!."
MECHANICAL SIDE	A side on a logging show where most of the operations are mechanized.
MISERY WHIP	The old-time falling saw, up to twelve feet in length, and brutal taskmaster. Also called a "Swedish fiddle."
MONKEY BLANKET	A griddle cake.
NOSEBAG	A portable lunch bucket.
OLD GROWTH	An old, usually majestic but often decadent stand of trees over 150 years old that has not been logged although second-growth trees in that condition would be considered "old growth."
PEAVEY	A steel-spiked pole with a hinged tong which provided the leverage necessary to move large logs.
PECKER POLE	A small, slim tree.
PIKE POLE	A long, slim pole equipped with a twisted steel point, used in brailing.
PLUS TREE	An exceptional tree, selected as breeding stock because of its superior qualities.
PRE-COMMERCIAL THINNING	A first thinning on a tree stand. A straight expense because the wood removed is too small to have commercial value.
PUMMY	The local South-Central Oregon word for pumice, usually "pummy dust." An all-pervasive volcanic powder that is practically impossible to remove.

PUSH	A foreman. Also, on the log drive, the operation itself.
REARING CREW	A group of river-trained people, mostly loggers, who follow the drive and clean up the banks of hung-up logs.
RIGGING CREW	The group of loggers who handle, set up and maintain cable systems.
ROAD CHANGE	Moving to an area adjacent to that which has been cleaned of logs. Done by changing the tailhold.
SALE	A definite amount of timber put up for sale by bid. Also the site on which the timber is standing.
SCALE	The amount of board footage in a log.
SCALER	The person who determines the amount of footage in a log. Usually castigated as a blind, illegitimate robber by loggers, he or she is a highly skilled, completely ethical worker performing an essential service.
SEXY TREE	A vigorous tree with good growing characteristics or selected for breeding because of superior growing qualities and its ability to put out a good seed crop every year.
SHAKE BOARD	Also "shakebolt." A piece of cedar split from a tree or stump, two feet long and approximately two inches thick, which is re-split or cut into shakes.
SHAPE UP	A gathering of a crew, usually at the beginning of a shift, where assignments and recommendations are handed out.
SHAY	A steam locomotive adapted to logging and noted for agility and indestructibility.
SHOOTING	Blasting, as in "shooting" rock. Also called, locally, "shotting" in Alaska.
SIDE	A logging operation, but more specifically the place where it is going on. Thus, a logging show could have one or more sides.
SIDE-HILL SALMON	A deer, usually one reduced to venison and procured illegally.
SIDE ROD	Straw boss of a logging side.
SKIDDER	A machine, either rubber-tired or tracked, used to drag logs to the landing.
SILVICULTURE	The planting, usage and management of a forest. Thus, a forester practices silviculture the way a farmer practices agriculture.
SLASH	Debris left after a logging operation.
SLASH FIRE	A fire deliberately set to clean up logging debris.
SNOOSE	Logger's term for snuff.
SPAR TREE	A tall, centrally-located tree, which when topped, properly guyed and rigged with blocks is used as a derrick to yard logs to the landing.
SPIKE TABLE	A table of food where a logger can make up his own menu, usually for his nosebag.
SPRINGBOARD	A lightly flexible, iron-shod, strong board, which is inserted into a notch chopped into a tree and used as a precarious platform from which the tree is felled. A relic of hand-power days, it now has only a few practitioners.
SPOTTER	A person equipped with a walkie talkie, who directs the yarder operator on a grapple show.
STINKPOT	A diesel engine.

15

STRAWLINE	A small, light cable.
STUMPAGE	The amount a contractor pays the landowner for standing timber.
SWEDISH STEAM	Hand power.
TAILHOLD	A sturdy stump or tree which is used to support a block through which a cable runs back to the yarder.
TALKIE TOOTER	A belt-carried radio device which enables a chokerman to blow the yarder whistle in code and also talk to the operator.
TIMBER BEAST	A rough, crude logger.
TIMBER CRUISER	A forester or logger who estimates the amount of timber in a sale, usually by walking over it.
TIN SPAR	A telescoping, movable steel tower, which replaces the old-time spar tree.
TROUBLE SHOOTER	A mechanic who has the tools and the expertise necessary to fix almost anything on a logging show.
TURN	A load of logs, especially as it refers to a yarder or loader.
VIRGIN FOREST	A forest untouched by the hand of man.
WANIGAN	A combination bunkhouse and cookhouse, usually floating but also sometimes on wheels.
WHISTLE PUNK	The person who actuated the whistle on an old-time steam yarder by pulling on a long wire.
WALKIE TALKIE	A portable radio transmitter and receiver.
WIDOW MAKER	A loose limb, hanging precariously, just waiting for some unlucky logger to pass under it to fall.
YARDER	The machine that powers the mainline. The big machine on a landing.
YELLOW BELLY	A ponderosa pine, especially a really large one.

Judging from the side-positioned pistons, I would guess that this old logging locomotive, the famed "lokie" of old-time logging, is a Shay or maybe a British Columbian version thereof. Lovingly preserved at the Logging Museum in Duncan, B.C., it is a colorful relic of the province's equally-colorful past.

The red alder and the Douglas fir came up neck-and-neck in this harvested strip near Castle Rock, Washington. Operations within sight of a road or of a salmon spawning stream are supposed to be bordered with a "leave strip" to protect the road or stream. It usually blows down in the first high wind.

FOREWORD

For sheer diversity as well as natural beauty, few areas of the world can match the North American continent. In this magnificent stretch of real estate can be found representations of just about every type of climate and soil condition that this planet offers. It is not surprising that this area encompasses what can justifiably be called the world's outstanding tree-growing region.

Stretching in a vast crescent from the Gulf of Alaska to the coast of Southern California, this region, blessed by deep and fertile soils, plentiful moisture and a benevolent climate sustains a luxuriant growth of trees from the very edge of the continent, across the coastal mountain ranges to the lush plains and fertile hollows of the inner valleys, in some cases deep into the interior of the country. In this area, in a continuous cycle since the end of the latest Ice Age, approximately seventy generations of trees have taken root, grown to maturity, attained old age, and died, to be followed by succeeding generations. The character of these forests has often been altered by natural disaster, but always the principle of adaption which is such an integral law of nature has produced those forms of arboreal life best suited to survival in each region, and so keeps the cycle inexorably marching on.

It is this miracle of adaptation, birth, growth, death and rebirth that makes possible the vital industry which is the subject of this book.

It is no simple chance that this arboreal growth should foster an industry, for wood has been so intertwined with the progress of man that the two are practically inseparable. The earliest forms of human

The Chilkat River near Haines, Alaska, runs a milky gray from rock flour ground out by the glaciers which feed this stream. In spite of this, the stream supports a good population of trout and salmon with grit-filled but operative eyes. The preservationists insist that streams near a logging show should run without siltation, otherwise the trout will die!

life lived a very precarious existence: for untold millennia they barely survived, hunted by carnivores extremely well equipped for that purpose and escaping extinction only because of that convoluted mass of tissue called a brain which made it possible for them to alter their environment to their benefit and survival.

The use of fire was a gigantic step forward, but it was not until man first sharpened a piece of wood into the first crude spear that he ceased being the hunted and became the hunter, thus setting his feet firmly upon the path that would lead to his dominant place on the face of this planet. Wood first fed his fire, lifted him above the place of the animals, then became an integral part of the process that has resulted in the highly evolved lifestyle we enjoy today.

Wood, by its very utility, has always been part of our lifestyle; and because of the capability unique to itself, most likely always will be. Unlike other depletable natural resources, wood, coming as it does from a living entity, is infinitely renewable. Because its main component is carbon, the cycle upon which human life on this planet is based, it can be made into a bewildering complex of useful materials, even including organic food; and the supply, properly managed, is inexhaustible.

The first Europeans coming to this continent found here forests whose magnitude and variety made the forests of their native lands pale into insignificance. From the Eastern Coast to the Great Plains, the country was a solid blanket of forested wilderness, so that a long-lived squirrel could have traveled from the East Coast to the Mississippi without ever once touching the ground. The only breaks in the carpet of foliage were holes torn into it by natural disasters: fire, windstorm or a bug kill. These are perfectly normal and natural occurrences, Nature's way of clearcutting a woodland so that a new generation of trees would be born. It was a magnificent, gorgeous wilderness, but like all wildernesses, a harsh, hostile, and, by the standards of civilization, a largely unproductive land.

The wilderness is not a friendly place to anyone unfamiliar with its ways or unwilling to abide by its harsh laws. A person knowledgeable in its ways can survive or even thrive in it, but changes must be made in one's lifestyle in order to live in harmony with the environment. That can mean a drastic change in the ways to which modern man has become accustomed; a fact rediscovered annually by myriad nature enthusiasts who have been spending an idyllic summer in the woods subsisting on modern dehydrated foods. The first icy blast of winter sends them scurrying back to civilization where they can extol the benefits of the "wilderness way of life" while enjoying the comforts of central heating.

The pioneers who first ventured into the Pacific Northwest well knew the meaning of "wilderness," for they encountered here woodlands so thick that progress through them was measured in feet rather than miles. The forest consisted of tangled masses of trees so huge that the first covered wagons that ventured into this area were to penetrate it only after they had been dismantled and moved over, around, and even under, fallen giants which were more than a match for the

Near the headwaters of the Clearwater River in Idaho a sawyer patiently puts an edge on his chain so that his cut through the white pine will be a clean one.

puny axes and saws of the immigrants. As in a wilderness today, those fallen giants were everywhere. It is no wonder that the first settlements were usually along the rivers, the highways of those times. The large streams were generally open, but some smaller streams ran from one silt-filled pool to another, where fallen trees or busy beavers had effectively dammed the river. Only the roaring spring floods, relentlessly sweeping all obstacles before them under the pressure of millions of tons of cascading water, kept these waterways open for even a part of the year. It was to be years, in some areas many years, before the unceasing toil of the pioneers was to open enclaves of cleared land in the forest carpet and make possible the good life we enjoy today in the Pacific Northwest.

There is no doubt that this is a favored part of the United States: if nothing else the steady migration of people from other parts of the country would attest to that fact. But how many people would there be here if the land were still in its pristine state, covered with forests? Demographers who have made a study of these matters estimate that at the time Europeans began the colonization of the United States, this vast wilderness sustained a population of less than one million aborigines, and many of these were existing on the ragged edge of starvation. Much of it was covered by the kind of woodland extolled as desirable by many modern preservationists; a sobering thought indeed, but one that is not nearly enough indulged, especially when one considers that the population of Washington and Oregon alone now totals close to eight million people.

In the last few decades, concern over environmental

issues has become not only prevalent but a way of life with many activists. This is significant, for the more people that are aware of the ecological problems facing the country, and the more brains there are working on them, the better are our chances of obtaining their solutions. However, like the proverbial pinch of salt which adds zest to a meal, it can become too much of a good thing...try eating a stew laced with two pounds of that salt! And, unfortunately, that is increasingly becoming the problem.

A preservationist may be anyone from a well-educated, thoughtful, well-intentioned individual who sincerely believes that his efforts will result in a better environment to the rebellious drop-out who is happiest when he is demonstrating for a cause...any cause, as long as it will give him a chance to strike back at the system. Almost invariably, he or she is an urban dweller with very little understanding or sympathy for those whose lives are rooted in the soil or who produce the products that are taken very much for granted in our everyday life without too much thought of whence they originate. One of the reasons for this may be that the forest products industry, aware of the worth of its products and services, has largely taken it for granted that these facts are so obvious that they need not be explained to the general public. That is a mistake and one that must be rectified if the industry is to function efficiently.

The opponents of the industry, on the other hand, have waged a skillful propaganda war, using every means of modern communications to promulgate their theories as facts. Note the number of well-known media people who have been persuaded to climb onto the ecological band wagon, even though many of them have never been closer to a "wilderness" than a trip to the paved floor of the Yosemite Valley. A casual thought on the matter would seem to make their views justifiable.

An unspoiled wilderness, with cathedral-like groves of ancient trees is certainly more aesthetically pleasing than a clearcut. Clear streams, rest and recreation and the peace and quietude of an unspoiled sylvan grove are outwardly more appealing than jobs and the everyday goods those forests can provide. That is the feeling a casual thought provides. The situation is such, however, that a more than fleeting thought must be given to the usage and disposition of those forests. But first and foremost, some ground rules should be established.

The first of these ground rules, and the most important, is that human life and well-being are more important than any animal, fish or bird...even owls. If one cannot agree to that fact, then he may as well go back to living naked in a cave, freezing in the dark and let the animals, fish and owls become lords of the Earth. If, on the other hand, he believes that man is the dominant form of life on this planet and was destined to become the master of the world and make use of the things the earth provides so liberally, then he should act in a responsible manner so that the treasures Nature has so liberally provided be not squandered, but utilized to man's...and Nature's...best advantage, and in perpetuity.

It is a simple, unassailable fact of life that for man even to exist, he must eat; and whether, to that end, he plucks a fruit, digs up a tuber or kills an animal, that act involves taking some form of life. It is a fact of Nature as fixed and immutable as the laws governing the stars. The more sophisticated our civilization becomes, the more demanding it is upon Nature, for every one of the comforts we take so much for granted originates in the natural environment, and somewhere a trade-off of some kind must take place. The sophisticated French say, "You can't make an omelet without cracking a few eggs," while the more pragmatic Americans embody it in the saying "There ain't no free lunch." The meaning is the same: somewhere, somehow, a toll is exacted, and if we want to enjoy the bounty of Nature, we must be prepared to pay a commensurate price.

Does that mean that the environment should be ruthlessly sacrificed in order to maintain our way of life? Of course not! That would be sheer stupidity, for that would be killing the goose that lays the golden eggs. Even a forgiving Nature has its limits which, altogether too many times, especially in the not so distant past, have been exceeded so grossly that we are still paying a price for those excesses. The trick lies in blazing a fine line so that the good things of life the forest can and should provide for us can be balanced with a benevolent protection of the woodlands, so that they can still exist in a form where they can continue to fill their part in the ecological balance of the planet. To that end, thousands of intelligent men and women, both from the ranks of the environmentalists and the forest products industry, are bending every effort; and the results of their collaboration should result in a healthy environment that still meets the needs of a burgeoning population.

People imbued with a love of the outdoors can become fiercely protective when they feel the environment is threatened. In their zeal to maintain the forests in their pristine state they are likely to pass harsh judgment on anyone whose actions detract from the beauty of the forest or the clarity of its streams. In timber country, first on these preservationist's list of villains, and justifiably so, is the logger. I know, for I am an avid outdoorsman, and I held that view for many years.

My first good view of the Pacific Northwest dates back to the first week in January 1946 when, still in a wartime uniform, through a frosty windshield I beheld the Columbia River Gorge sheathed in the shimmer and glow of a silver thaw. Since the road that day was a narrow, twisting ribbon of glare ice winding along seemingly bottomless precipices, I could be excused if my feelings alternated between acute apprehension and sheer terror. But even under those circumstances, I could not help but marvel at the magnitude of the natural splendor displayed all around me, even if it was somewhat overwhelming. I really believe that my continuing love affair with the outdoors of the Pacific Northwest dates from that first terrified glance.

As a man who had spent his boyhood in the woods of Vermont, it was only natural that I should fall in love with the Pacific Northwest: Vermont on the grand scale. In the ensuing years, when I have joyfully climbed its mountains, penetrated its most remote forested vastnesses, and even achieved an appreciation of the sere beauty of its deserts, I have learned to love this, my adopted land; and it is only natural that I should view anyone who despoiled it with a certain amount of antipathy, hence my ingrained dislike for loggers.

Like most urban outdoorsmen, I have many carefully cherished opinions about loggers–all bad. Every outdoorsman, I thought, knew that these rough, profane, largely illiterate men ruined the woodlands with their noisy chainsaws, huge trucks and roads that desecrated the most remote fastnesses of the forest. They were looked down upon as a vaguely inferior species of sub-humans with no education, ambition or talent other than that of transforming beautiful forests into acres of ugly, blackened stumps. Their bosses, of course, were the legendary timber barons, men whose incredible wealth was matched only by their venality, who routinely bought whole legislatures and the right to pile up colossal riches by vandalizing the public woodlands. Only a few of us intrepid outdoorsmen stood between these depredators and a raped, ruined Pacific Northwest.

Of course, up to this time I had never met a live logger, and had absolutely no desire to ever associate with what I considered to be little better than human trash.

In May 1971, Potlatch Forests Inc. hired me to make a pictorial record of the last log drive down the North Fork of the Clearwater River in Idaho. The drive crew consisted of supervisory personnel, some office employees…and loggers, all picked for their intelligence, stamina and ability to work together under very tough conditions.

Loggers? I thought, with intelligence? This I had to see!

To my utter astonishment, I was unable to pick the logger from the supervisors. These were literate, sensitive, intelligent men, some of them deeply religious, who loved their wives and children and had hopes, aspirations and ambitions like any other men. Somehow these men just did not fit the preconceived idea I had formed before I got to know them, and in time I had to face up to the idea that if I were to be true to myself, I would have to make a radical change in my ideas regarding them. My prejudices against loggers began to erode rapidly, but the final touch came when I discovered that every logger on that drive was a dedicated outdoorsman and that their love of the forests was every bit as strong as mine. Along the cascading waters of the North Fork, I began reexamining my previously held opinion about loggers, and as a corollary, logging. The things I discovered in the next two years through extensive personal involvement with the men and women who plant, nurture, protect and harvest our most valuable natural resource form the backbone of this book. Mind you, this book was not written from

On Bob Gardner's mechanical side near Chewelah, a loader piles the small timber onto a truck for a load that will have many logs; but all parts of these logs will be usable for lumber or chips.

information garnered in the comfort of a well-stocked library. It is a site book, written from first-hand knowledge, because to get the real story of loggers and logging, you have to experience the work they do. It's easy to damn someone you don't know, especially if you're not man enough to keep up with this rugged breed, but if you can wade through waist-deep snow to fall a tree, or wallow in the mud to set chokers, get jaggers in your fingers or risk getting run over by a cantankerous skidder, then you can write with authority about these men and form a valid opinion about them and the work they do. For anyone else, it's just hearsay.

That was eighteen years ago, and in that time the changes in the industry and the ecological structures under which it must operate have been enormous. Those changes will be dealt with in this return to the timber country, but some other things will be familiar, old friends, because some values are so basic that they have stood the test of time, and will be as valid a hundred years from now as they are today. They are the basic foundations upon which the forest products industry is built, and it is only right and proper that they be defined.

First and foremost is the fact that our forests are a national resource of supreme value, because a properly managed forest, a thousand years from now, can, without depletion, still be producing wood and the things made from it in a completely renewable cycle. It is the only resource we have, other than sunlight or running water, which is completely renewable, and thus more valuable than all the petroleum, iron ore or natural gas ever found. A treasure of this magnitude deserves the best care it can possibly get; and the forest products companies, well aware that their survival is linked to that of the forests, are determined to give it just that.

The second fact is that the men and women who plant, grow and harvest this, our most valuable renewable crop, are performing a useful task and that fact should be recognized by a general public all too often ignorant of the work these people do, or of the tremendous impact that their labors have on our everyday lives. The time has long ago arrived that the major sins of which the logging industry was admittedly guilty in the past have been rectified, but that knowledge has largely been buried under the vilification heaped on an industry largely undeserving of it. It is not in the nature of loggers to be punching bags, especially when it is undeserved, and the time has come to fight back.

The third fact that must be admitted is that not everyone agrees on how our forests should best be preserved or utilized. Public opinion is a volatile thing, easily influenced in often erroneous ways, but it plays an often disproportionate role in the management of our forests. Rock stars and movie actors pontificate on matters of which they have only a superficial knowledge and are often believed by some of the people. That these matters should best be left to the trained personnel who have made a lifetime study of how to manage, protect and preserve our forests is a fact that is all too often ignored, and one that can lead to disastrous complications.

Another fact, and one that has assumed great importance in the last decade or so, is that a large part of the logging done in the United States and Canada is done on public lands, and more and more, the voice of the people is being heard as to how those public lands should be best utilized. It used to be that forestry was left in the hands of the foresters, but more and more, in this age of ecological awareness, the general public is getting involved in the management of what they rightly regard as their own forests. This is both good and bad. It is good because public awareness of how our most valuable natural resource should be utilized throws a glaring spotlight on forest practices, and so mandates that they shall be the best possible, but it is also bad because that easily manipulated public awareness can be bent to the side of restrictive and not always silviculturally sound regulations.

The interplay and friction caused by the views held by preservationists and the forest products industry necessarily will be a good part of this report on modern logging. I make no claims to be an expert on these matters, only an interested and trained observer who has a foot in both camps, for I am not only an avid outdoorsman who wants to see the forests preserved so that my grandchildren may enjoy them as much as I do, but also a thinking person who realizes that man does not live on beauty alone. After all, I live in a wood house, use copious quantities of paper, and the photographic film which I use to make a living started life as a hemlock growing on a lonely island in the wilds of Alaska. It probably would still be there if I and myriad others had not preferred to have that wood made into film rather than letting it eventually rot away in the vastnesses of a primitive forest, and of the two, I think the fate I chose for it is the more useful one.

It is my intention, in this book, to call a spade a spade and to let the chips fall where they may. I am beholden to no one, and this book is strictly a record of my own feelings. It is my intention to be as objective as humanly possible. I also realize that while objectivity is desirable, it is also sometimes very difficult to achieve, but it must nevertheless be sought. If, in my estimation, something is wrong, I intend to say so, just as fervently as I will laud something that my experience in this matter has shown is worthy of praise. This book is about modern logging and that includes its faults as well as its virtues: I honestly believe that the industry can stand this and even achieve merit with a factual report. The report card may not be all "A 's," but on the whole, I think it will show a passing grade...but I do intend to be a stiff marker, and if I do make mistakes I can always take consolation in the fact that the path of human discovery is bordered by all the mistakes that have been made along the way.

One of the surprises awaiting anyone investigating the forest products industry is the sheer staggering, size and complexity of this, America's second oldest industry. Roughly one person in ten in the United States and Canada is in an occupation directly or indirectly dependent upon our forests. Washington and Oregon together contain three out of every eight trees growing in the country today and supply material that will go into most of the nation's housing. All through the timber belt, entire towns and even counties have their economies built upon the bounty that comes from the surrounding forests, and of course the things they produce touch the life of every person. Wood products are so diversified that our civilization could hardly function without them...a thought that has obviously never occured to the lunatic fringe who advocate the total shut down of the logging industry.

The obvious uses of wood; lumber, plywood, particle board and paper are impressive enough. But it is when you consider some of the lesser known by-products: rayon, textiles, commercial solvents, film, even animal feed and the flavoring for the ice cream on your dinner table that's when the full implication of just how important wood is really strikes home.

Prophets of gloom who predict a wood famine for America are nothing new: they were forecasting that as early as the turn of the century. Per capita usage was approaching an all-time high and dire predictions were being made that "America is running out of wood. The forests will be all gone in twenty years." After seeing the seemingly interminable forests of Alaska and British Columbia, one is more apt to agree with the old-time logger who used to say "We ain't never gonna cut all this timber." Of course, that isn't so. America still has vast resources of timber already grown and even more growing, but it is not limitless. It will all be needed if America's and the world's insatiable need for wood and wood products is to be met, but the good news is that the demand can be met; and will be, as long as responsible forest managers are allowed to make wise use of the renewable resource growing at our doorsteps.

It has been my very enjoyable experience to revisit some of the places where logging operations were going on eighteen years ago when I first took pictures for my book on logging. Invariably, those sites are clothed in a mantle of growing green trees, some of them already of a size where a merchantable piece of lumber could be milled from them. Of course, that would not be done, unless extensive thinning were indicated by a too profuse growth but it does indicate how the world's demand for forest products will be met in the future. Those trees were planted and fertilized precisely like any other crop because that's exactly what they are: a crop, planted, nurtured, with the intention that it will some day be harvested. Much of the "old growth" that is the center of so much ecological concern today is growing in a forest where even a coursory examination would reveal the even larger stumps of trees that were harvested eighty or ninety years ago. "Old growth" is simply second, or seventieth growth that has achieved the majestic maturity of a forest in its middle and old age...and they are growing all over the Northwest.

This is not meant to foster a feeling of complacency. It must be remembered that if the number of second-growth trees attaining merchantable size is constantly growing, so is the demand for more and more timber. Now, more than ever, there is a need for intensive management, for even better methods of logging and for complete utilization of a tree. There are still logging practices condoned that consign a six-inch tree to the slash pile, ultimately to be burned. That log would be a prime log in the Black Forest of Germany and would be converted into beautiful, though by our standards, narrow lumber. Fortunately, this need is being recognized and more and more chippers are being towed into the woods to convert limbs and small trees into chips for paper or hog fuel that can power steam-driven generators and so reduce our dependency on imported oil. Biomass is the oil of the future, and we can grow all we'll ever need.

This is an idea whose time is long past due and, while it has been recognized for a long time, has lain in limbo for altogether too long. The primary source of practically all the energy in this world is the sun: running water is the result of solar activity. Petroleum, natural gas and coal, all originated from plant matter that is nothing but fossilized sunlight. And wood, our infinitely replacable resource is the result of sunlight activating a living organism which stores the heat of the sun in its cells in the form of carbon. Heat is energy and when stored as wood, it can be released and utilized.

Anyone who has ever experienced the cataclysmic heat of a forest fire doesn't have to be convinced that there is a tremendous amount of heat stored in wood. For that matter, the heat generated by even a medium-sized slash pile, if gathered and utilized, would more than suffice to heat the average home for several years, and the heat generated by the Yellowstone Fire could have furnished New York City with heat and light for over a decade. That heat is every bit as real as that

On ITT Rayonnier land on the Olympic Peninsula, a sign announces the date of harvest, emphasizing that timber is a crop, and that this land has alreagy produced a generation of trees.

generated by expensive and often imported oil and could be substitued for it with the proper technology. The best part of the process is that it is fed by wood, an infinitely renewable substance.

Why has this technology not been developed? True, the idea of heating a home with wood is centuries old, but it is usually small-scale, crude, inefficient and in the infantile stage of its development. What I am talking about is large-scale utilization of wood in technologically advanced power systems: systems that burn biomass to produce electricity or convert wood to gaseous or liquid fuels with a high thermal value. If the same amount of research had been given to the efficient utilization of wood as a fuel as has been given to oil, we would not be held in economic blackmail by foreign elements not always friendly to us, and with modern management, we'd never have to worry about depleting the supply. We even survived the wasteful methods of logging in vogue at the turn of the century!

The excesses of old-time logging have been very well recorded and tend to be remembered in vivid detail. Timber was everywhere and the highest grades were readily available at a stumpage rate of fifty cents per thousand board feet. Labor was cheap and plentiful, even in surplus, so that it was feassible to take only the best part of the tree. The rest was left in the woods to rot, which may have satisfied those who believe that the best possible fate for a tree was to decay in the woods and so feed another generation of trees but is hardly what we would consider good logging today. The demand was for clean Douglas fir or cedar: anything else was considered nothing more than a gigantic weed, something that only got in the way and was treated as such. Land was a commodity that was acquired cheaply, stripped of its trees, then surrendered for taxes. The philosophy of the day was "Cut and run," with no thought of taking care of the land or of regrowing another crop. This philosophy sometimes produced barren, eroded hillsides that even after fifty years show the effects of the rape they had endured and have not yet regenerated a new crop of desirable trees. This keeps alive an antipathy to the logging industry that persists long after the perpetrators of these atrocities have been laid in their graves.

Then again, there are instances of just how forgiving Nature can be. One of the best examples is in the range of hills west of Olympia, Washington. The Indians called them "Klahle," the Black Hills, from the dense growth of old-growth firs that blackened them. At the turn of the century, they were ruthlessly logged over, according to the wasteful logging methods of the times. Ravaged by one savage wildfire after another, they became "The Blackened Hills," a scene of such consummate ugliness that the citizens of Olympia preferred not to view sunsets because they would also be viewing one of the worst scenes of devastation in the state. Eroded, gullied by the heavy rainfall of the region, it was considered so ravaged that when some farsighted legislators proposed to buy this land for the state the bid price was fifty cents an acre. The owner felt so guilty to be taking advantage of the state that for every acre purchased he threw in an additional acre free.

That's how Capitol Forest, one of the most beautiful woodlands in the entire world came into existence at twenty-five cents an acre! The process of rehabilitation was not done overnight; but over the years, those burned, ravaged acres have become covered with a vigorously growing, intensively managed forest which every year plays host to thousands of appreciative visitors who hike its trails, fish its streams and relax in its campgrounds. There is an invigorating quality to Capitol Forest that seems to be the trademark of any young timberland: Oxygen-rich air from thousands of young trees, a profusion of bird and animal life and the distinctive peace of mind that any beautiful woodland fosters so liberally.

Capitol Forest with all its undeniable beauty, is also a productive, actively working woodland. It is planted, fertilized, thinned and harvested on a perpetual yield basis so that every year it returns to the state treasury a sum far in excess of its purchase price and, in the meantime, pays a tidy dividend in the form of recreation, watershed control and beauty.

While this is unquestionably an outstanding example, it is by no matter or means unique. The idea of treating timber as a renewable crop is not new: forestry has been practiced in Saxony since the fourteenth century and in China and Japan even before that. What is comparatively new to the United States is the idea that timber could be grown under controlled circumstances, that it could be planted, fertilized, cultivated and eventually harvested. Up until recent years, America has had a large enough reservoir of naturally growing timber that the idea of intentionally growing it was not considered necessary. All that has changed, and one of the greatest changes I have observed in the last eighteen years has been in the tremendous growth of the tree-farm idea.

The Weyerhaueser Company, which rightly bills itself as a tree-growing company, started its first tree farm at Montesano, Washington, in 1941. The idea was so successful that today most major forest products companies have their own tree farms and all pursue a vigorous program of replanting harvested lands. It is mandated on state and federal lands and becomes part of the contract when a timber sale is let. Up until the advent of replanting, regeneration was largely left to natural reseeding which, while this is undeniably Nature's way, does not always lead to a desirable growth. Cut-over land, left to itself, will often sprout a vigorous stand of red alder or vine maple, both of which are prolific seeders while the more desirable fir puts out a good seed crop only once every seven years. Fir needs sunshine to grow and there is precious little of that at the bottom of an alder thicket. With hand planting, a fir seedling that has already had a good start in a nursery is planted in a good location and given a better than even chance of survival, especially if the competing brush is eliminated or suppressed during the planting process.

The success of this method of regeneration is evidenced in the luxuriantly growing hillsides that would otherwise be brush patches with only an occasional struggling fir making it to maturity. While some places seem to naturally regenerate a good crop of fir (Lewis County in Washington State is a good example) most places benefit by the management that predicates what kind of arboreal crop will be grown.

While this is universally conceded to be a good thing within the industry, this practice has really raised the hackles of some environmentalists when it is applied to public lands. They point out that the forest that was harvested was almost certainly a mixed stand, and they object to the fact that it is being replanted to a pure stand of one variety, simply because it would make a more desirable stand of marketable timber. "Do what you want on your own land," they tell the timber companies, "But when you replant a forest which is the property of the people, it should be replanted to replicate the original forest as closely as possible, not to something that best suits your commercial interests."

The argument has merit, and the Forest Service caught between its duty to make the most desirable use of the land and the threat of a lawsuit from a group of fired-up preservationists, must draw on the patience of Job and the diplomatic skills of a Talleyrand to keep all parties happy. The companies who own their own land, not hindered by these strictures, replant their acres with the best possible trees, watch their trees grow at an astounding rate and count their blessings.

More and more often, those acres are replanted with the genetically selected, and nowadays even genetically engineered trees, that are the products of all that research that has been going on for the last twenty years in the tree-farm nurseries. Fast growing, straight, definitely a superior tree, they are the tree of the future, and they are being planted by the hundreds of thousands. Douglas-fir seedlings approximately eighteen inches long are usually two years old, and visitors to an experimental station might be forgiven if they were to assume that this is the age of the seedlings they are viewing. These trees however, are the offspring of "super trees" genetically selected to have the qualities desired for the timber of the future and are only three months old! I saw some of these seedlings planted eighteen years ago and have since had a chance to see them at their present stage of growth. A picture tells the story better than any words but I could only imagine what those trees would be like in another forty years. They are expected to be one hundred and fifty feet high, straight as a well-stretched string and almost completely free of knots and taper. Built-in genetic traits will have taken care of that.

This is believed to be the tree of the future: the answer to the ever greater demand for wood and wood products, and it is the result of intensive research and forest management. Some idea of the effectiveness of these controlled conditions toward influencing growth may be gained from the fact that the timberlands held and managed by commercial companies constitute only eleven percent of the country's commercial

Wildfire, often regarded as an outright scourge, has a place in the regeneration of a woodland, a fact that is being belatedly acknowledged and utilized. Still, a large, uncontrolled wildfire is a tragedy because of the many adverse effects it leaves behind.

acreage, yet produce thirty percent of all the timber harvested. In other words, a managed woodland outproduces a wild one almost three-to-one. Timber grown as a crop with all the skills that modern silviculture can command will always far outproduce that grown in unmanaged conditions. A legitimate corollary could be drawn between a wild timber crop and the maize the Pilgrims found here when they first landed–a little nubbin of inferior kernels, compared to today's well-filled ear of juicy hybrid corn. After all, timber is a crop, the end result of a living entity, and it can be benefited by the same basic rules that have been applied to a better ear of corn.

It may seem far-fetched, but very careful estimates by conservative foresters have established that if all the commercial woodlands in the United States and Canada were placed under intensive management, they could supply the softwood needs of the entire world and even keep pace with the increased demand as more and more forest lands come under intensive management. It is very unlikely that this will happen; there will always be natural growth and that is as it should be, but the undeniable fact is that more and better wood can be grown under controlled conditions than can be grown wild. As the general public comes to accept the concept that timber is a crop and should be grown under optimum conditions, the better are our chances of meeting the demands of the future.

Trees grown under the tree-farm system are just now reaching merchantable size, but eighteen years ago the system was still only a promising experiment. Another approach, however, was already in full swing with already visible success. Near Powell River, British Columbia, a tract of naturally seeded, second-growth Douglas fir had been twice thinned to bring them to a somewhat even-aged stand status. With additional space, moisture and sunlight, the grove had taken on an unprecedented growth and was rapidly attaining the maturity that precedes harvest. That grove has been clearcut now and produced high-grade logs with practically no waste; a sure indication that the management it had received was a step in the right direction. This time, regeneration was not left to the vagaries of a good or bad seed year: it was replanted with two-year-old seedlings and is already well on its way to producing a third crop of harvestable trees. The even-aged stand that will result from this management will reach the same size as the century-old grove in sixty years, a time saving whose implications are so obvious that even the most adamant opponent of forest management must give it sincere, even if grudging, consideration.

However, great as the improvement has been in forest practices in the last eighteen years, there is still room for improvement. Admittedly, those improvements started from a comparatively low base: because, at the turn of the century, it was easy to categorize forest management: there wasn't any! Even as late as the end of World War II, forest practices still reflected the wasteful, destructive methods inherited from an age when America's resources were so seemingly limitless that conservation had a very low priority, if it was considered at all. World War II brought us to a rude awakening. The Mesabi Range, which had easily provided the iron for the cannon of the Spanish-American and First World War, was largely depleted, and America was already depending on foreign supplies for many things that had previously been produced domestically. Public awareness of the finality of our resources may have had something to do with the first steps toward a policy of conservation, but it was greatly strengthened by the forest products industry's new-found awareness that sound silvicultural practices were good, solid business that ensured a long-range profit...and a continued existence.

The ecological awareness of the late 1950s and 1960s unquestionably also spurred the industry along the path it had already largely chosen to follow. The combination has resulted in the present-day policy of blending fair return from a woodland investment with that of preserving that woodland so that it will not only be productive a hundred years from now but in even better shape ecologically. The ecologists like to say that their efforts are responsible for the improvements in forest practices while the industry claims it was already headed that way, maybe just because it was good business. Whatever the reason, and there is probably a good dash of truth in both claims, the ultimate winner is the forests and the general public.

No matter how carefully the work is done, no matter how many euphemisms we use to describe the process, there is no denying that logging is essentially a destructive process even if it is the necessary first step in the creation of a new forest. Useful, yes. Necessary? Certainly! But it is still the application of brute force to an often beautiful woodland; and when it is completed, unless the operation was a cosmetic one, beauty is replaced with ugliness. Like many birth processes it can be quite messy, and from this phase of the operation comes much of the criticism that is leveled at the industry.

A timber tract may be diseased, ravaged by insects, falling down, but as long as it is even a partially standing forest, there are people who will criticize anyone who will cut it down. If a logger had invaded that forest and left it in the same condition as Nature has he would be dammed as the most rapacious of vandals; but as long as the condition is the result of natural causes it is somehow considered acceptable. The forest fire that ravaged Yellowstone National Park a few years ago leveled over one and a half million acres of standing timber. Granted that much of that timber was long past its prime and could only be improved by burning it. But now, just suppose that instead of that timber being burned, it had been harvested by the best available logging methods and the residue burned in controlled slash fires. The damage to the enviroment would have been minimal, a new forest would have quickly grown up and a considerable amount of wood would have been salvaged for the good of man. Naturally, this would never be done because those trees were in a national park, forever safe from the logger's chainsaw. But remember, we are supposing! Can you imagine the storm of protest that would have arisen from opponents of the industry? The cries of "Greed!" and "Abomination!"

Now, ask yourself honestly which of these two solutions to the problem of creating a new forest would have been the better ecologically and economically: Nature's way, or man's?

The simple truth is that the logger, in clearing off a mature forest so that a new one can take its place is simply doing a job that Nature would have done by itself with fire, wind or a bug kill. It is a fact that is not well known and certainly isn't proclaimed enough by the forest products industry. The fact is that wood that is harvested and put to the use of man has a longer, more useful life than that which is allowed to fall victim to the diseases of old age and eventually rot in the forest.

In an old chateau in France, I once leaned on a huge oak table, massive and black with age, but still as sturdy and strong as the day it was pegged together. I was establishing a tie with history, for that table had heard the voice of Charlemagne and witnessed the dissolution of the Carolingian Empire. Over one thousand years old! The rest of the oak tree from which it was fashioned has long since turned to dust but while that table exists, so does that old oak. Wood that is manufactured lives, while that which topples to the ground and rots is useful only in that it helps to regenerate a new generation of trees. That of course is very important, but Nature with her usual prodigality furnishes much more nutrient than is necessary for the sucessful regeneration of a new tree. Most foresters agree that only one or two percent of a tree's bulk is necessary to nourish a replacement properly. Far more than that is left in the harvest, which by today's standards is not as wasteful as nature.

The need of our civilization for the products of our forests is so apparent that it is almost universally recognized. Where people are not in agreement is in the method whereby those trees should be harvested and increasingly, the ecological conditions that must be met before that harvest can take place. Roads are a necessary part of logging and unfortunately are one of the most common causes of the siltation that can change a crystal clear stream in an area being logged into a muddy rivulet, at least for a while. It is one of the penalties that must be paid if we are to enjoy the bounty of the forests but it is only scant consolation to people who decry a muddy creek. Long after that stream has cleared up, the road will provide access to an area that would have otherwise remained inaccessible to the average person.

Unfortunately, the problem of aesthetics plays a disproportionately large part in the management of our forests. There is no denying that the average clearcut, raw looking, denuded, is a far cry from the beautiful woodland it replaces, so that in the popular mind the world "clearcut" has become a dirty word, synonymous with ugliness and destruction. Granted, it is ugly: so is the incision a surgeon makes to better or save a person's life in a surgical operation. Should that operation be foregone because some blood is shed or should we realize that a minor temporary hurt must be done so that an ultimate greater good can be realized? The fact is, that under certain circumstances, a clearcut where all the trees in a tract are removed, is the quickest, most ecologically sound way of regrowing a new forest. It will be ugly for three or four years, while the scars still show and the new growth establishes itself, and usually it will be in a gangly, more or less awkward stage for another ten years till a more mature growth is well under way.

For the next fifty to eighty years it will be beautiful and people glorying in its beauty probably will never realize that they are viewing the result of a clearcut. Travelers through the Coast Range of Oregon marvel at the beautiful "old-growth" Douglas fir covering the hillsides. Very few realize that they are looking at the result of a "clearcut" that happened over one hundred and sixty years ago in the form of a huge forest fire that swept from the Nestucca estuary to the Columbia River, denuding three million acres of western Oregon in the process, as attested by the journals of Hudson Bay trappers. The cause? Arson, we'd call it today; but the Indians who set it were only following the time-honored custom of setting a fire that cleared the dense, ancient forest where practically nothing big lived so that sunlight could generate the lush new growth that supported the deer population on which they subsisted. This one got away from them as so many of them did, but if it had not done the job, lightning eventually would have. The forest was only following its natural cycle of life and death. The sad part of it was that all that beautiful timber, in its fiery death, produced only ashes,

Jim Mason of Weyerhaeuser Company inspects a Japanese cedar, one of several ornamental and commercially valuable trees being tested by his company. This tree is very prized by Japanese cabinet makers, who make fine furniture from it.

Capitol Forest, one of the most beautiful woodlands in the world, was bought for twenty-five cents an acre because the land had been so abused by the logging practices of the day that it was considered worthless–a fine example of just how forgiving Nature can be.

eroded hillsides, polluted streams and the small plus of quite a few largely unwitnessed spectacular sunsets.

No one advocates burning over half a state simply to regenerate a crop, especially when it is not necessary. The fact that is not often enough stressed, even by the forest products industry, is that the logger in removing a mature stand of trees, is doing the same job Nature would eventually do with less damage to the ecology than a removal by natural causes would entail. And considerable good benefits man in the form of a useful necessity, timber. Near Tollgate in the Blue Mountains of Oregon there is a blow-down, the result of a violent windstorm, in a relatively young forest. If a logger had clearcut that tract and left behind the mess of torn-up earth and jumbled masses of criss-crossed fallen trees that Nature did, he'd never be allowed into the national forests again! Nature is a very poor logger even if her clearcuts are sometimes devastatingly efficient.

We long ago made our peace with the farmer who "clearcuts" a field of wheat. The big difference, of course, is that the farmer is working with a much smaller "tree," one which grows in one season, and so has not had time to attain a degree of affection in the eyes of the beholder. Also, most people do not yet look upon timber as a crop, which it most assuredly is, albeit a very slow-growing one. The matter therefore becomes one of education, and that, as any teacher will tell you, can be a slow and sometimes painful process. It is, however, one that must be undertaken if we are ever to realize the full potential and usage of the forests entrusted to our care.

In this age of heightened ecological awareness, more and more wooded areas of the national forests are being locked up into wilderness preserves that will always be kept in a natural state, so that future generations may some day possess a wilderness completely uncontrolled by man. The latter part of that statement is as it should be; very few people will argue against that principle, least of all outdoorsmen. The big argument seems to be over the amount of our wilderness that should be forever locked up, its treasures held in an inaccessible state forever, with no chance of their largess ever being used by man. Again, the principle of a pinch of salt being palatable applies, but some preservationists seem to have a taste for salt that borders on the ridiculous. Our forests are a treasure, a rich bank account which, if the interest is used wisely will last forever, but which has very little use for man if it is never drawn upon.

This conflict between those who hold divergent views on how our national forests should be used and managed was already well under way eighteen years ago, but it has intensified considerably in the intervening years. A maze of ecological restricitons has added to the already complex problems facing the logger and added considerably to his cost of operation. In the normal course of business, this is added to the cost of the product he produces so that lumber today is hardly the inexpensive commodity it was before the days of extensive regulation. The ultimate loser? The general public of course, most of whom don't realize that they are the ones who will ultimately pay...and dearly...to protect some obscure species of owl that would have easily adapted to changing conditions on its own.

Our national forests were long ago dedicated to multiple use, a principle that has stood the test of time, and should be continued. They should not be used strictly as a reservoir of timber to feed a wood-hungry world anymore than they should be reserved to the elitist few who have the means and the stamina to make them their own private playgrounds. Somewhere in between the views of the two opposing camps, a compromise must be reached that will meet the demands both of those who advocate using the bounty of the forests and those who believe that the best use of a forest should be to leave it alone. The road to that agreement may be a long and rocky one, and both sides will inevitably be forced to make some concessions, but the encouraging news is that men of goodwill from both camps have set their feet upon the road. The conflict is emotional, often bitter and isn't likely to be settled overnight. Only time and education will bring about a better understanding, each of the other's position, and in that very fact may lie the solution to the complex problems of managing our most valuable natural asset.

In the meantime, under the influence of the rains, the mists, and the warm sun, the tender shoots of green spring up, spread their needles toward the sun and keep intact the eternal cycle of growth.

The Pacific Northwest is still busily growing its trees...

Earl Roberge, ASMP
Walla Walla, Washington

CHAPTER I

BIG TREES, STILL BIG MEN

The first reports of the North American continent brought back to Europe were received with more than a little skepticism.

Those Vikings had been known to bend the truth here and there, not only once in a while, but as a matter of course, and no one was inclined to believe their tall tales, most of all about the tall trees they had found in the new lands. It was only after later, more reliable voyagers began backing up their claims with deck cargoes of remarkably long and straight timbers that claims about the forest resources of the new world were taken seriously. Incredible as these stories were, they were only a small part of an even more incredible tale. The colonists were only nibbling at the edges of one of the most prodigious stands of timber on the face of this planet, and it was still two and a half centuries before the astounding trees of the Pacific Northwest and California were to be discovered.

With the exception of the Great Plains and the desert areas of the contiguous United States, the whole country was one vast forest, broken only by an occasional clearing where a forest fire, windstorm, or bug kill had opened a hole in what was otherwise an unbroken carpet of arboreal green. It was a mixed stand, with deciduous trees freely mixed in with conifers in some areas, and pure stands of either species in others; but regardless of which species dominated, it was emphatically a forest domain. It is little wonder that logging was one of the first industries in the new country: the decision was not so much one of choice for the colonists as one forced upon them if they were to make a home in this wilderness.

The sheer magnitude of the forests seems to have overwhelmed and even terrified the first colonists, who were more accustomed to the more sedate, even park-like forests of the Old World. Here was a forbidding, untamed wilderness, teeming with game in some places, it is true, but also teeming with hostile Indians: a wily implacable foe who had long ago made their peace with the wilderness and were very much at home in its wild depths.

The forest was the enemy: dark, menacing and hiding a merciless foe. One of the things the colonists had in their favor, however, was the fact that while America may have been colonized by the misfits of Europe, no one knowing them would ever call them cowards. Since the forest was the foe, they attacked it with characteristic vigor. With axe and fire, with sweat and unremitting toil, they leveled the woods of the East Coast, hacked homes out of the wilderness, and in the process developed the strength and the stamina that

were to become the hallmarks of a proud new nation. It should be noted, even if only in passing, that the efforts of the colonists were dedicated more to destroying the forest at their doorsteps rather than using its resources, except for the rather minimal usages required to build homes and fences. The colonists were more land clearers than they were loggers. The logging industry came later, but the skills acquired as land clearers were close enough to those of the loggers that the transitional step was a very simple one.

In the two and a half centuries that passed before white men came in significant numbers to the Pacific Northwest, Americans had come to terms with the wilderness. While they still accorded it the respect that was its rightful due, they no longer feared it. By this time Maine was being logged for the second and third time, the great pine forests of Wisconsin and the Great Lakes region were largely replaced by farms, and the westward tide of colonization was already lapping at the shores of the Pacific.

The motivating force behind the westward march of the colonists was hunger for land and it drove them westward until they reached the Pacific Ocean. Many of them were Europeans of peasant stock to whom land ownership was the cachet of nobility, and in this wonderful new country any man could be nobility providing he was willing to forge his own coronet with the sweat of his brow. Here was a land of illimitable acres where a strong man could wrest an empire from the wilderness and proudly pass on that heritage to his children.

There was, however, a small problem. That empire was completely covered with the largest trees anyone had ever seen, and in its present stage was hardly the arable land that had impelled that westward march.

Those Northwest forests! Never had anyone seen such trees! Ten feet or more in diameter, over two hundred feet tall, thick as the hair on a dog, they stood in a solid phalanx that was seemingly impregnable. Anyone who could endure the rigors of getting to this region had already proved his toughness, but now he was put to an additional test: he was pitting his strength, and, more importantly, his intelligence, against a natural force of such colossal magnitude that any lesser man would have given up the struggle before it was even begun. The northwest pioneer, fortunately, was just about as tough a man as any region has ever produced, and it soon became evident that here was a man to match the trees. He would never agree that a static force, even one as massive as an old-growth Douglas fir, was more than a match for a determined

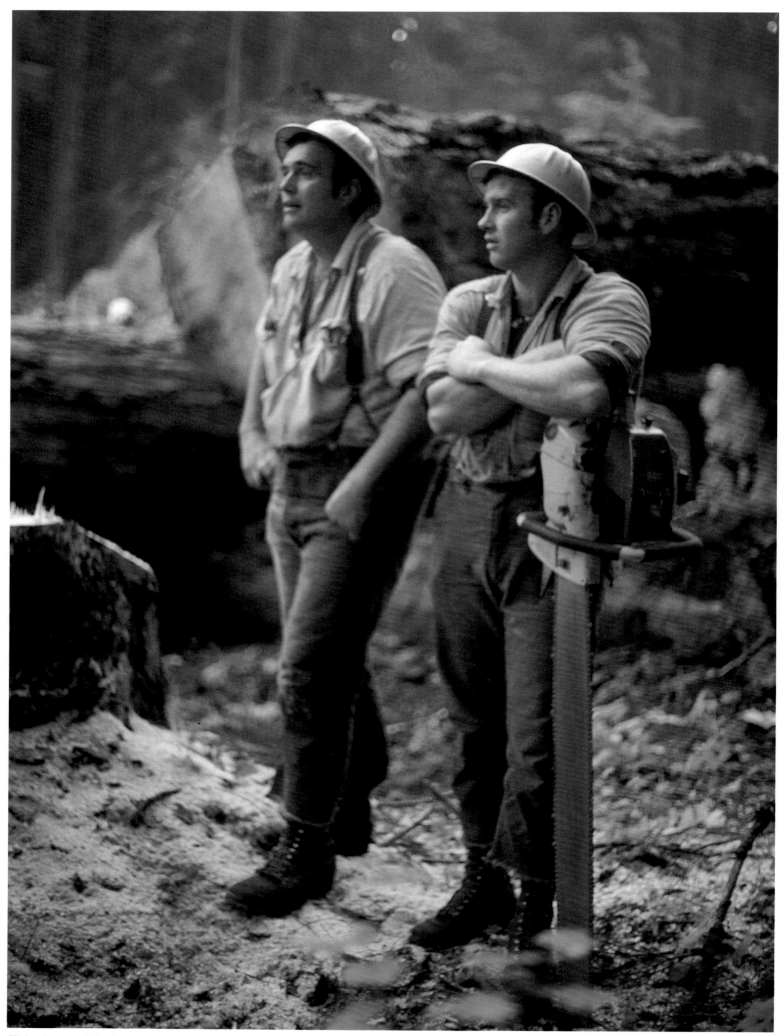

This picture of the Pollman brothers was made years ago, but it still illustrates the point that many loggers are big, big men. Whether or not they are physically big, they are all big in spirit. It goes with the territory.

man with an axe, a saw, a team of oxen, fire and an occasional charge of black powder. It was a classic case of David against Goliath, but little by little, holes were gnawed into the forest cover, and stump farms began to flourish where only a few years before there had been an unbroken stretch of evergreens. It was a brutal struggle, one where progress was measured in mere feet per year, and many a pioneer, after a lifetime of toil which made him old before his time, could still throw a stone from his front door and hit the encircling forest wall.

The usual method of clearing land in those days was the same one Nature uses so liberally: fire. One pioneer recalls that for the first forty years of his life, he was never away from the smell of wood smoke, but in the rain-soaked Pacific Northwest this was often a painfully slow process. With the advent of dynamite, the process speeded up a bit, but this was a method that often produced tragedies, and the splintered stumps still had to be laboriously pulled out of the ground by laboring bull teams. With the possible exception of the Redwood Country, no section of the United States yielded its grip on wilderness more grudgingly than did the Pacific Northwest, and the ground that had been so laboriously cleared had to be tended regularly lest Nature reclaim it for the forest cover that is its natural state.

Painfully slow as it was, inch by inch, the forest cover of the Northwest began to yield, and farms and a new way of life became established. It is no wonder that many of the early settlers, after battling the dense growth of the rain-soaked west side for a few years, exchanged the rainy forests of the Puget Sound region for the sunshiny eastern slopes of the Cascades where Nature smiled more often, and enough trees grew to provide fuel and fence rails for their broad acres.

The tougher, or maybe more stubborn pioneers remained, loathe to lose the progress that had been bought with so much labor. The forest, however, was demonstrating something that only in recent years has been admitted, however grudgingly.

What the Puget Sound-Cascades region does better than anything else is...grow trees!

The forests of the Northwest were, for most of the pioneers, a colossal nuisance, something to be eliminated if farms and homes were to be established. Some people, however, were quick to recognize that what was such a nuisance to some could be a veritable bonanza to others. Sailors saw in the arrow-straight timber superlative masts and spars, for sail still ruled much of the seas, especially in the lucrative China trade, and timber was an easily obtained, readily saleable cargo. It may come as a surprise to people who today decry the sale of our timber to foreign interests that this trade has been going on from the earliest days of white occupancy when it was first realized that those logs that

To a logger, a dull saw is like being married to a lazy wife. Neither is tolerated too long, especially when you can sharpen up a saw.

were so laboriously removed from the land and burned to get rid of them had a market value in other parts of the world.

Primitive sawmills soon proliferated on Puget Sound, especially after gold was discovered in California. The sloppily finished lumber these early mills provided rebuilt San Francisco not once, but several times, for that early city was fire-prone; and each time it was rebuilt, more and more Northwest lumber was involved in the process. Sailing ships could pull up to the docks of Portland, take on a full cargo into its holds, then tie on a monstrous deck-load and pray that the murderous Columbia River Bar would not sweep their decks clean as they headed for San Francisco and the small fortune which that deck-load represented. If they lost that, then the trip would show only a modest one hundred percent profit rather than the fantastic profits that would be realized from that awkward load piled onto the deck.

To show what a major part lumber played in the economics of the Northwest, one only has to remember that the lumber ports of Puget Sound prospered over those on the Columbia even if they were farther from the major Californian markets. They didn't have to face that deadly bar, and their product was competitively priced. That it was a profitable business is testified by the stately homes that can still be viewed at Port Townsend, which were largely built with profits of the lumber trade. Portland did not fare too badly, either, as the beautiful homes of the lumber barons still dotting the West Side hills will amply testify.

It soon dawned on the settlers of the timber region that there was more money in lumber than there was in vegetables; and with typical Yankee shrewdness, they began to use the same energy they had applied to clearing their land to marketing the trees that had so lately been nothing but an ubiquitous nuisance. The logging methods of the Great Lakes region were adapted to the larger timber of the Northwest, and soon a new method of harvesting trees, one indigenous to the Northwest, evolved.

The westward migration had swept along in its wake thousands of New Englanders, Swedes, Finns, Canadians, Norwegians and Scotsmen who had worked the pine stands of the Lake States and Minnesota until those vast stands were largely depleted. In the Pacific Northwest these men found trees to match their strength and stamina. They brought their logging methods to the region, quickly realized that they did not fit the new environment and changed them to suit. They labored with the local settlers, married their daughters, and from this melding emerged that local folk-hero, the Pacific Northwest logger.

His grandsons and great-grandsons are still logging the Pacific Northwest today and are the worthy inheritors of Paul Bunyan's ample shirt. These are the men with a generous dash of timber sap in their veins, the men who plant, protect, harvest and have an undiminished love for the crop that forms the backbone of the Northwest's economy and have provided the most colorful pages of the region's history.

The great Seattle fire of 1889 and the 1906 San Francisco earthquake and fire gave the industry a tremendous impetus, especially since by this time the quality of Northwest lumber had improved to the point that it was the standard by which all others were measured and was exported to all parts of the world. By 1910, logging and lumbering were firmly established as the Northwest's leading industry, and the logger was its uncrowned, unwashed and unenvied king.

The stereotype that emerged in those ancient days was so firmly imprinted onto the American mind that it persists to this day, even though it is largely no longer valid. The popular concept is that of a man with a big shirt and a small hat, a person of limited intelligence and unlimited animal instincts, most of which are regularly indulged. He is cast as a coarse, brutish type with no feelings, no emotions, a swaggering two-fisted braggart who lives only to feed, fight, fornicate and cut down trees. Unfortunately, the turn-of-the-century logger sometimes lived up to this image and his memory perpetuates the stereotype. This was the legendary timber beast who terrorized the timber town on payday, or any day, and he is the source of the many legends built around this bigger-than-life image.

The lode of colorful stories was much too rich to be long ignored and much has been written about the old-time logger and his way of life. Unfortunately, many of those stories tend to perpetuate a character who has long since ceased to exist but whose shadow is so long that it reaches down to the present day. The turn-of-the-century logger was an often -illiterate iron man who for a dollar a day felled the forests of the coastal Northwest, slept in a vermin-infested bunkhouse nauseous with the stench of unwashed bodies...and was a broken down old man at forty. He could be fired on any pretext, or no pretext at all, was completely unconcerned over his illiteracy and made no provision at all for the inevitable day when he would be too worn out to keep up with the rest of the crew and would be callously discarded as one would a broken, worn out tool. Labor was in surplus, but being fired presented no big problem: there was usually another lumber camp down the skid-road, and even a camp inspector could always pick up another job, if just long enough to finance a glorious, hell-roaring weekend in town. It was a roisterous, raucous way of life, but to thousands of iron-muscled young bucks to whom old age was a nebulous neverland that they might never reach, it seemed like a natural enough way to spend one's life, and the tales that have grown up around this time probably do much to perpetuate the image of the logger that persist to this day. It was a brutally hard, but to many a romantic way of life; and the reputation that the logger gained in those days as a bigger-than-life figure is one that is still with us.

A host of legends have sprung up about the skills of the old-time loggers, and certainly, viewing the stumps of the trees they cut, they must have had a solid basis in fact, but compared to the skills a present-day logger must command, they were very elementary. Many a fine, successful logger signed his name with an "X," and didn't feel the slightest bit handicapped over that fact. After all, most of the men in his crew could neither read nor write, so why should he be any different?

The technology that the modern logger uses

routinely would have absolutely stunned the old-timer. In his day, balanced on a springboard eight feet from the ground, an undercut was laboriously cut into a massive tree with double-bitted axes, then two young giants patiently pulling a twelve-foot ribbon of oiled, sharpened steel, the famed "misery whip," would cut through that tree. It would be sectioned into movable lengths, then ponderously moving bull teams would slowly haul a massive log to the nearby mill. For the old-time logger, the height of technology had been reached when huge steam-driven yarders spooling miles of thick steel cable replaced the bull teams and small but powerful locomotives moved logs out of the woods over some of the most ingeniously located railbeds ever conceived by the mind of man. It was a colorful era, and they moved a lot of wood, but by present day standards it was slow, wasteful and downright primitive.

The modern logger must be versed in the same basic skills, but he must also be able to use an array of machinery that would have been completely incomprehensible to his old-time counterpart. He not only must know how to use this machinery but also how to maintain it and coax the best performance from it. The electronic equipment the modern logger so casually takes for granted would have seemed miraculous to the old-timer, as would the amount of wood daily moving out of the woods. The safety regulations would have puzzled him, but the ecological strictures of modern logging would have been the biggest puzzle of all and the one that would have convinced him that modern man would never be allowed to be a good logger.

According to the views held by the old-time logger, that is perfectly correct. Modern logging cannot exist and prosper using the rules of a century ago, and it has no desire to do so. The modern logger will grouse about the restrictions under which he must labor, but he would not want to return to the "freedom" of his ancient counterpart if he also would be forced to accept the conditions under which his grandfather worked. Safety is part and parcel of a modern logger's way of life and gives him hope that he will ply his trade for many years to come. His modern chainsaw enables him to fall in twenty minutes or less a tree over which his grandfather would have sweated for several hours. The modern logger's bulldozer can in a few hours move earth and rocks that would have engaged the combined efforts of a whole crew for a week at the turn of the century. A modern skidder, combining as it does the strength of several elephants with the agility of a mountain goat, would have caused an old bullwhacker to shake his head in wonderment, and the equipment on a modern landing simply would not have been believed at all. Only the present logger's classic, high, steel-spiked caulk boots would have been familiar. There is, however, another intangible thing that is a strong cord of continuity between the old-time logger and his present-day counterpart: it still takes a lot of man to fill a logger's boots and do the job well.

What kind of a man is a logger? What does it take to be one of this fabulous breed?

Eighteen years ago, when I had lived and worked with these men for several years, I had gained some

One reason safety classes are well attended by loggers is that they may be getting patched up by one of their buddies the very next day. No one wants to be worked upon by some bungler, hence, peer pressure is applied to become an excellent first aid man.

insight into what motivated them, and the passage of time has only reinforced those first observations. The big difference between today's logger and that of twenty years ago is that the present logger must necessarily be better educated, if only because the industry has become so mechanized, so replete with computers and electronic devices that an illiterate simply cannot function in the higher echelons of logging. This is one thing, in a sea of changes, that has changed only for the better. The illiterate could still get a job...maybe. He could still set chokers, function as a hook-tender or even fall a tree; but that would just about be it, and there is a lot more to modern logging than those very basic skills. The other basic things it takes to make a man a good logger have not generally changed because a logger is the combination of many qualities, some physical, others mental, and those qualifications have not basically changed over the years.

The old-time pioneer evolved into a logger quite naturally, not only because circumstances forced him into it but also because the same requirements that made him a pioneer also qualified him to become a logger. Toughness was a basic requirement for a pioneer and that was a quality that was needed, and in spades, for his new occupation. His is an environment that requires unusual physical strength and stamina. He must be able to work well in any kind of weather as a member of a closely integrated team, for each logger is his brother's keeper. Part and parcel of his job is his consideration not only for his own safety, but also for that of his fellow workers. Knowing that all on his team think likewise and will be watching out for him fosters a feeling of camaraderie that is always so evident in an elite group proud of their own merits and dependent upon each other not only for their well-being but for life itself.

This is probably the reason why so many lifelong friendships have blossomed among men working on the same crew. It is a liking based on respect for men who all recognize that each man on that team is a person to whom you daily entrust your life, and if there is a better foundation for friendship than that one, I have yet to discover it. It is not a new situation; it is as old as the history of mankind itself for from prehistoric times, when man first learned to hunt animals larger and stronger than himself by forming a hunting group, the bond between members of that band has been as strong as a blood bond. Indeed, it actually became a blood bond, and the logger, working as a part of a closely integrated group, considers each man as his brother and watches out for his safety accordingly. Under these circumstances, it is no wonder that a logger would be highly selective of his company and critical of anyone who doesn't hold up his end of the bargain. Thus, the widest breach of trust a logger can commit is to do something that will endanger the well-being of his partner. Logging is a dangerous game, and no one wants to make slim odds even slimmer by sharing them with an incompetent.

The evaluation of the logger as a person is unquestionably colored by each person's attitude towards the work he does. One may see him as a man who rapes the environment and spends his life creating ugliness: another may see him as a useful, skilled workman who does his job with dignity and speeds the advent of a new, healthy forest. The adversary to the forest products industry thinks of him as a roistering, drunken brute, while his admirers will see him as a solid, God-fearing citizen who pays his bills and feeds his family with the honestly earned proceeds of his labors. One sees a savage, the other a quiet husband and father. It all depends on your point of view.

Actually, a logger can be any or all of these, a very simple person or a man of unequaled complexity. Aside from the formidable physical requirements of his job, he could be almost anyone. In education, he may be barely literate, if he doesn't mind doing the more menial jobs, or a person who has the right to string several very impressive letters behind his name. If he should have that right it would not be indulged because no one could care less about that than his teammates: they would be much more impressed if he showed he knew his job and did it with thoroughness and dedication. He is a very human person, with all the strengths and frailties of a normal man, and that is why he can be a hero to one person and a villain to another. He can be a very stolid, unemotional man, or one who savors the beauty of a forest dawn with a depth of emotion bordering on ecstasy. A man can be a clod or a poet without detracting from his ability as a logger.

Loggers come in all sizes from small to extra large and in all dispositions, from downright amiable to that of a grizzly bear with hemorrhoids. His color, which may be white, black, brown or red, is not too important since it usually is smeared with oil, dirt and sweat. He may be the strong, silent type or one who seemingly was vaccinated with a phonograph needle. He may speak with a New England twang, a Southern drawl, the sing-song of Norway, a Scottish burr, or even some completely unintelligible growl; but each and every man has one common, unifying trait.

The logger is one of the proudest men alive! That is a claim that is made by many industries and professions. Construction men and oil roughnecks claim it. The 82nd Airborne Division, marching in superb soldierly formation after their demolition of the enemy in the Iraqi War certainly had it. Many men and women will tell you that their trade or profession demands the most of a person and so merits the adulation in which it is held. The highly trained and elitist astronauts probably have as good a claim as anyone, but loggers would yield to them, if at all, only very grudgingly, paying them a very high compliment by saying that there may be the makings of some pretty good loggers in that group.

Pride is something that is endemic to the whole logging craft. It is compounded not only from the formidable physical requirements of the work, about which the logger is seemingly very matter of fact but actually very proud, but from many other things, any one of which would be the high point of anyone else's month. He sees many sunrises, because his work days often begin in the dark of night. Seasons mean little to him because he must work in the numbing cold of winter, the chill rains of spring and the sweltering heat of summer with equanimity. Each day he fights clinging brush, poison oak, brambles and devil's club and accepts the frustrations of bad timber, temperamental machinery and rough terrain as part of the job. He must every day make decisions involving machinery worth a half million dollars or more and trees that were old when Columbus landed. He lives with danger, in perpetual dread of rolling logs or the deadly widow-maker, striking silently and with deadly accuracy. Routinely, he puts his life into the hands of his buddies and accepts the awesome responsibility that comes with the same obligation towards them. He is faced with spiritual turmoil when he turns vistas of sublime beauty into scenes of horrible ugliness knowing that it will be years before the beauty returns. But the worst knowledge of all is that some day he will be either disabled or too old to take it anymore, at which time something in him will die, because he is a logger, and logging is his life.

Why, you may ask, does he do it? Why does he put up with a way of life that many would consider torture?

He does it because he has of his own free will chosen this way of life. He is an outdoorsman who would rather be outdoors doing what he knows is a useful and honorable work than anywhere else, and if there are hardships to his job, there also are compensations; and to the logger, the good is more overriding than the bad.

His job and the open air of the woods foster a monumental independence that is both the strength and the weakness of the logger. His "workshop" seems to breed a freedom of thought that is downright disconcerting to people accustomed to more subtlety and much less honesty in their daily dealings. A logger's work leaves little room for the polite euphemisms and downright evasions that are such a common part of the usual business routine, so that a logger will speak his mind, maybe in strongly biologically tinted language, but it will be direct and to the point, and you can believe what he is telling you. Non-loggers are apt to consider this directness a bit crude, but that is because they have probably never before encountered this kind of honesty, and it is only natural to be a little wary of the unfamiliar.

Loggers generally divide people into two groups: those who are good enough to be loggers, and those who wish they were. It is a natural way of life in the timber belt for a boy to get his first taste of the logger's way of life during his high school vacation, and many of them naturally gravitate towards the woods as soon as they have completed their formal education. An increasing number of them, a change that is very apparent in the time span separating my first book on logging and this one, are returning as university trained foresters who effectively wed the logger's practical knowledge with college theory and so become the leaders of the industry. The practice of logging has become so much more complex in the last two decades that anyone desiring to have a significant impact on the industry must have the correct tools, and more and more, these are the products of a high education. The day when a logger was a man with a strong back and a weak mind, if it ever existed at all especially in the higher echelons of logging, has long since passed.

The small-town youngsters who from early childhood have had a close association with machinery, from the time-honored jalopy to the souped-up hot rod, feel right at home on a modern landing, where machines do practically all the work and man is only a guiding intelligence with thousands of horsepower at his fingertips. However, before he can qualify for the logger's "college," he must attend grade school; and on his first day, he is only in kindergarten. He is told to show up bright and early wearing calks, the logger's classic, high, steel-spiked boots; a hard hat; tough, snag-proof jeans and a hickory shirt and introduced to that instrument of torture known as a choker. This is a short length of steel cable equipped with a knob and fitting bell which he must learn to loop around the end of a log in such a way that when the yarder pulls upon it, it will roll free of obstructions and ride all the way to the landing without hanging up. Right from the very first day, safety is emphasized. He must learn to poke that choker under logs as well, and if that should entail wallowing in the mud to do the job, that is considered a useful part of his training, as well as a reminder that, on this show, he is low man on the totem pole. He also develops a marked agility, especially when logs start to roll, and discovers firsthand why he is wearing spiked boots: if his only avenue of escape is over downed logs, it is good to be wearing something that will give him a solid footing.

As he progresses, he may even be trusted with explosives and taught how to use a "Talkie-Tooter," a radio device that blows the yarder whistle in code, enabling all crew members to know what is going on. He may graduate to other jobs, but almost any logger will remember his days as a choker-setter as the toughest he ever put in. If he lasts three days, he may become a logger; if he lasts a week, he almost certainly will make it. By that time the weakling will have either quit or been culled out.

The usual practice is to team up the novice with a patient, experienced man. He teaches the novice the elements of survival, then the fine points of the game. Natural selection usually dictates who will be in charge of a crew, a marked difference from the old days, when a man's fistic ability had much to do with his position. If he could whip the man in charge, and competently do the work, the job was his, a practice known as "running a man off" and which persisted down to the time of the unions. Of course, if his bid for advancement failed, that man usually found it expedient to find employment elsewhere, or he would soon find out how often it was necessary to do the dirtiest jobs and just how rough a choker setter's life could be.

On a small operation, the work force is largely interchangeable because the average logger has worked at all phases of the operation. This was especially true eighteen years ago. Today, some of the expensive equipment at work in the woods requires specialized training, so that today's logger may be a specialist, competent in most phases of the operation but especially skilled in one, and that is where he will spend the greater part of his time. The usual ingenuity and skill with machinery which seems to be the hallmark of the logger is nowhere more evident than in the field repairs that can be effected in the woods. Barring a major breakdown, the average logger can fix almost anything with a jack, a cutting torch and a bit of haywire.

The logger's day begins before dawn, with a hearty breakfast and several cups of coffee. By dawn the crummy will have delivered him to the work site which may be anywhere from next door to seventy miles way from home. The first break is usually around eleven-thirty, when the contents of his nosebag are thoroughly investigated around a pyramidal warming fire. Conversation is quite animated, in direct contrast to meals in the old-time logging camp which were usually grimly silent events dedicated to bolting enormous amounts of food in the least possible time. Fallers usually quit around one-thirty, with the rest of the crew knocking off around three o'clock, although loaders will sometimes work till four to get in one more load. During the summer fire season, one or more members of the crew may stay a few hours more at the job site to make sure that no smoldering fires erupt. The average logger is home by five o'clock, dead tired and ready to hit the sack. Tomorrow is another day, and dawn comes early.

A streak of fatalism seems to run throughout the craft. The logger knows he is engaged in a dangerous occupation and that the chances that he will be killed or seriously injured in his precarious calling are very high. This is accepted as part of the price one must pay to be a logger, but it also may account for the high degree of attention that is given to safety courses and those involving first aid. Every logger has seen accidents

Putting on the nosebag in the Cabinet Range of Montana. This lunch break is dedicated to ingesting enough food to fuel the human machine for another few hours. A fat logger is a rarity because the job requires a remarkable degree of agility, and those extra pounds slow one down.

A logger routinely works with equipment scaled to the size of the logs he will be moving, which means that a lot of it is pretty massive. It takes a lot of man to do this job.

and is acutely aware that he may be the next victim, but human nature seems to have provided an escape route to what would otherwise be a very depressing situation. Every logger believes that accidents will happen to the other guy, never to himself. Nevertheless, he studies his first aid assiduously and makes sure his buddy does likewise. If an accident should inadvertently happen to himself, he doesn't want to be worked on by some bungler, hence the popularity of first aid courses that are provided by the industry and insurance companies.

Insurance for loggers is more prevalent now than it was twenty years ago, probably a reflection of the soaring cost of medical treatment. Still, the highly independent logger still likes to take care of his own. All over the timber belt, well-attended logging shows funnel funds into the coffers of associations set up to take care of injured loggers and their dependents. They are usually no-frills organizations with a minimum of paperwork and a maximum of effective help. Within hours of a disabling injury or death, some logger representative will show up with cash in hand ready to do whatever is necessary to alleviate a situation that he knows very well could be afflicting him tomorrow.

Loggers have been accused of being a cocky, swaggering lot, and that is one thing that has not changed any over the years. It is a feeling that comes naturally to men in good physical condition who meet the demands of a very demanding craft and are conscious of their worth. The half-wild timber beast is now outnumbered by good family men who keep their lawns mowed and are regular, if unwilling, attendants at PTA meetings; but enough of the wild breed exist to give the whole industry a certain reputation for a love of fighting, not all of which is undeserved. The modern logger, however, is more apt to direct his zest for conflict into the struggle with preservationists. It provides an outlet for his high spirits and can even lead to some positive results for him and his industry.

Living as he usually does in a comparatively small town, the average logger is apt to be bewildered by the lack of knowledge urban dwellers have about his way of life or effect it would have on the general population if that way of life were to be seriously curtailed. He knows he's doing a useful, necessary job, he's doing it with dignity and a high level of competence, and he has a hard time understanding the antipathy in which he is held by many people. As a result, he has a tendency to draw back into his own environment where his work will be understood and appreciated. Unfortunately, no problem is ever solved by ignoring it, so little by little, the loggers, especially the better educated ones, are beginning to fight back because they realize that if some of the more radical environmentalists were to have their way, a whole way of life would cease to exist; and this, they are adamantly determined, will not come to pass!

The big change in logging, a change that has accelerated markedly in the last two decades, came with the unions and a decent living wage. For the first time, a worker can toil all day in the woods, come home at night in a new pickup to a decent home, send his kids to good schools, pay his bills and feel that he is a solid member in good standing in his community. One of the big changes in the industry in the last two decades has been the increased sophistication of the equipment used in logging. With this sophistication has come an added sense of responsibility and appreciation for the men who run this equipment, and that is reflected in the wages they are paid. No longer is a logger an underpaid wage slave with an uncertain future. He is more apt to be a valued employee, who every week brings home a paycheck that would shame many an executive with a fancy office with his name on the door.

Today's logger is a far cry from the old-time lumberman who leveled the forests of the Northwest with no thought whatsoever of restoring them. The modern logger realizes that timber, although it is renewable, is not inexhaustible, so his efforts are slanted toward regeneration so that his grandchildren may someday log this same land. One of the more common charges leveled against the industry, and one of the most easily refuted, is that the industry is short-sighted, creating long-term problems for short-term gains. Any industry that is planning and implementing plans that will not come to fruition till the year 2060 can hardly be called shortsighted.

Most people unfamiliar with loggers judge them by their work-stained clothes and think they are unskilled, underpaid laborers, a statement which most loggers will agree is at least half true. No logger is paid as much as he thinks he should be, and given the formidable demands of his craft, he probably has a valid reason for this belief, but if the industry were to pay those wages it would be bankrupt in six months. Loggers are smart enough to realize that closed down, bankrupt logging outfits don't pay any wages at all so they go along with their present wages and complain about it all the way to the bank.

The diversified character of the logger is evinced in many surprising ways. On the Olympic Peninsula, a road swings in a detour around the grave of a pioneer woman whose very name has been forgotten. In her lifetime, she helped open up this country, but that was a long time ago and a hurrying world would find her burial place of little significance. Yet, every year, white stakes surrounding the grave are painted, and fresh flowers are kept beside a simple cross. It is a popular resting spot for loggers, by legend that tough, unsentimental, unfeeling breed more at home in a roaring saloon. They care for this historic grave and perpetuate the memory of someone who would otherwise be forgotten. And if you were to ask one of those loggers why they do this, he'd probably grumble from embarrassment and reply that he didn't exactly know why except that it was something that needed doing.

That's the way of the logger.

The annual Deming Logging Show for Busted Up Loggers is always well attended, partly because the proceeds go to loggers injured on the job, but mostly because it is a rousing good time where old friends meet at least once a year.

In the Blue Mountains of Washington, a knot bumper trims excess limbs off the log to make a smooth, easily loaded piece of timber.

Stan Leach of French Gulch, California, proudly answers to the name of gyppo, although the modern shows he owns could very well be considered a contract logging operation. Like many gyppos, he is proud of the name.

CHAPTER II

GYPPO

One of the changes that has taken place in the last eighteen years, not only in the logging industry but all over the country, is the proliferation of euphemisms, presumably to add dignity to certain jobs. Thus a janitor is now a "custodial engineer," a bus driver is a "transportation expediter" and a housewife is a "household administrator." The logging industry has not completely escaped this verbal mayhem, for, believe it or not, a gyppo is now a "contract logger."

A rose by any other name would smell as sweet and a gyppo by any other name would still be a gyppo. He has always been a contract logger; he just was never called that, but this is one trend I am going to buck. Too many of my friends are gyppos; and if I started calling them contract loggers, some of them would think I'm putting on airs. There is no denying that the new appellation does have a nice ring to it, and in time it may be adopted by the rank and file, especially as it applies to the new breed of contract logger; but the term eighteen years ago was "gyppo" and everyone in the industry knew what it meant. It still means the same thing, but with a few added flourishes brought on by the passage of time that may, just possibly, make the new name a worthy one that will be universally accepted. But please bear with me if I use the term "gyppo" instead of "contract logger." It's shorter and more expressive.

No one knows for certain how the word originated. The usual story is that it started after World War I in the wake of the agitation brought on by the International Workers of the World, the Wobblies, as they were better known. The IWW thought that the piecework that had been introduced by some logging companies was really a device to "gyp" or cheat the workers rather than a way whereby an industrious worker could be rewarded according to his production. At first, the word had overtones of larceny; a suggestion that anyone doing business with that small independent company would emerge from that experience a little wiser, somewhat sadder and considerably poorer.

Over the years the word has lost all its pejorative implications and become a generic term for a highly colorful but usually perfectly honest businessman, one involved in logging by contract. Far from being denigrated by the word, it is worn like a badge of honor by a host of men who constitute one of the more colorful branches of the logging industry.

Simply put, a gyppo is a logger who contracts to do work for another company, usually the owner or lease-holder of the land on which the logging takes place. The gyppo, for a fixed or negotiable price, furnishes the equipment and manpower to log the area and to restore it to a predetermined condition after the logs have been removed. To say that he is an important segment of the logging community simply denigrates the word: he is not "important," he is "essential." In Washington State for instance, he logs 92 percent of all the timber produced in that state. Without the gyppo, logging as we know it simply would cease to exist.

The history of logging in the Pacific Northwest and that of the gyppo are so closely intertwined that to tell about one is to relate the story of the other. When the first pioneer with enough cash in hand hired another to do a little logging for him, he started the gyppo system. The lumber that built the burgeoning cities of California and the Pacific Northwest was almost entirely provided by small, independent companies whose available cash was usually tied up in sawmill machinery, leaving precious little surplus for the expense of setting up their own logging camps: that came later, after they had generated some surplus capital. Instead, they contracted the work out to a logger who, on the basis of the contract, begged or borrowed enough capital to buy the minimum equipment he needed to fulfill that contract and more than likely never paid his workers the full amount due them for their labors until he himself collected from the original contractor. The whole deal operated on borrowed money and handshake agreements and set the unwritten but well-understood ground rules by which the whole industry would operate for the next hundred years.

The logger who took that contract, if by some lucky chance he survived and made a few dollars on the deal, was now a gyppo, or if you will, a contract logger. His present-day successor has not changed that much, except that with the passage of time some of those original ground rules have necessarily been changed to meet changing conditions.

A gyppo outfit may be very small, as small as one man with the very basic minimum of equipment needed to cut down a few merchantable trees and get them out of the woods. It also may be a somewhat larger operation with several pieces of equipment and employees, or even a good-sized enterprise with millions of dollars worth of machinery and hundreds of employees. They are all gyppos and wear that name proudly. There is absolutely nothing derogatory about the name unless it is used with the wrong inflection in which case the user had better be smiling, because these rugged men who call themselves gyppos are not only fiercely proud of that name but also apt to be very handy with their fists.

Land clearing in the Puget Sound area usually involves cutting and stacking alder, which is not all bad. Alder makes good firewood and in sufficient size and quantity is a merchantable hardwood

A gyppo outfit in Eastern Washington, in this case, operates with all new equipment on a highly-mechanized side. This gyppo has been in the business for twenty years and through hard work and good business sense has prospered. His equipment wasn't this good when he started!

As independent and individualistic as he is, the gyppo makes the perfect whipping boy for the many evils of the logging industry and, in truth, he is responsible for his share of those abuses and even a bit more. By nature the gyppo is tough-minded and independent: traits that are essential if he is to survive in this savagely competitive business. Many gyppos go into the business with a lack of managerial and business skills, few of them have sufficient capital, and even fewer can count on a labor force willing to assume the insecurity of working for an outfit that has to scratch from week to week to make payroll. It is only natural for some gyppos afflicted with even one of these conditions to cut a few corners to save a few dollars, especially since most beginning gyppos are saddled with a crushing combination of all three of these evils. The corners they are apt to cut usually involve some environmental regulation that the gyppo considers non-essential to logging, and that's where he gets into the environmentalists' doghouse and becomes, in their eyes, the embodiment of all that is evil in the logging industry. Fortunately, this is a minority. Gyppos constitute a vast majority of the companies doing logging, and by peer pressure and good example help to shape up their errant brothers, partly because they are all part of the same brotherhood but also because of the realization that it takes only one bad apple to spoil the whole barrel.

It is a sheer miracle that some occasionally learn the necessary business skills and prosper mightily...and this includes some of the present giants of the industry. They are acquiring sawmills and their own land holdings, cease to be gyppos and become instead employers of their former colleagues.

This, however, is a comparatively recent business trend. Eighteen years ago the majority of gyppos were wedded to what was usually a way of life, the small independent logger, usually up to his ears in debt, who worked on contract from job to job and survived only because of the ingenuity, stubbornness and hard work that are the hallmarks of the gyppo. And certainly, these qualities, inherited from his pioneer ancestors, have not been diluted over the years, for the gyppo up to this day is one of the most resourceful businessmen in existence. In the course of one working day, this Machiavelli of the forests must cajole, bully, outwit or evade his banker, his itinerant-minded workers, his wife, assorted creditors, the Forest Service, militant environmentalists and his contractor. It is a striking tribute to his ingenuity that he keeps them all, if not happy, at least sufficiently mollified to allow him to function. A man of lesser stuff would be driven stark, staring mad; and it is no coincidence that few gyppos belong to the Temperance League.

The rodeo cowboy dreams of having his own ranch, some day, preferably before some Brahma bull cripples him. His logger counterpart dreams that some day before a log rolls onto him he will have enough money to buy or lease the minimal equipment it takes for him to become a gyppo. To that end, he is even willing to forego the usual weekend party and saves his money to make his dream come true. Sometimes long-term friends will pool their resources to start an outfit,

although more times than not this leads to broken dreams and strained friendships unless it can be clearly understood beforehand who will be in charge. A logging show cannot function with several bosses and no one hates to give up his independence more than a logger, which is both a logger's main strength and his most vulnerable weakness. The ideal pattern, one not too often achieved, is of one man fulfilling his dream, trading the backbreaking eight-hour day of the employed logger for the sixteen-hour day of the gyppo...and considering himself lucky.

"Just think," one will say, "anytime I want to go fishing I can toss my things into the company pickup and head for my favorite fishing hole. Of course, I never go fishing: too dammed busy making this haywire outfit work!"

The fierce independence that is so much a part of the logger's make-up is the spur that drives him toward the goal of becoming his own boss; but as soon as he has achieved that end, he runs into the problem that propelled him into the ranks of the gyppo. To make his outfit work, he must employ loggers, most of whom are as independent as he is and thus have a strong streak of the nomad in them. The smart gyppo fights this condition by paying wages that are as good as those prevailing in the area but mostly by giving his men a freedom of action they would never have if working for a large company bound by a formal set of rules. Naturally, the basic rules of logging apply: work safely, watch out for your partner and get the logs out. One of the conditions that prevails in a small outfit actually is a magnet to the superior man: in a small outfit, a man is expected to be able to do every job on the show, so one cannot complain of monotony and this appeals to a man proud of his versatility. A smart gyppo hand picks his crew, and if he has a reputation for fair dealing and treating his men well, usually puts together a group whose efforts mesh into a smooth-working, extremely efficient operation that every day turns out a greater output of logs than other, less efficient crews of much greater size. There is a lot of pride in the logger's make-up, and the pride of belonging to a really topnotch outfit is often the cement that holds such a crew together as a practically permanent unit.

It is usually quite easy to spot such an outfit; there is no wasted motion, no lost time. Everything meshes together and whenever there is a pause long enough for conversation, there is usually banter and laughter that says that these people are not only a smoothly working organization but also good personal friends whose friendly relationships will go back with them to their homes when the day's work is done.

Simply as a matter of economics, the usual route into the gyppo ranks is a partnership, much as this often strains friendships. Logging, even on a small scale, required an outlay of capital that stretches the resources of the average logger to the breaking point. By pooling capital, not only is this problem partially alleviated, but part of the manpower problem is solved. More than likely, the gyppo will be operating on Forest Service land and the ecological restrictions in force on such a sale regarding road building, harvest and reforestation are so stringent that anyone taking that contract should be prepared to meet some absolutely staggering expenses.

This is probably the reason why fewer "gyppo" logging outfits are being formed and more "contract loggers." Years ago a gyppo could go into business much more easily, and with a much smaller outlay of capital, than he can today. Companies that are being formed today are aware of the formidable problems ahead of them and have a tendency to be formed by men with business as well as logging experience. They are better financed, have more lawyers, accountants and computers at their command and probably fit the mold of the contract logger much more than they do the gyppo. A handshake contract with these newer outfits would be a rarity; more common would be a multi-paged written contract with particular attention given to plugging loopholes. The old-time gyppo as often as not operated on a handshake that sealed an unbreakable bargain which usually was scrupulously honored. That is one change that has taken place in the last eighteen years and, while it may be progress, in my book it is not an improvement. The modern contract logger may be every bit as dependable as the gyppo, but he is nowhere near as colorful.

There is no doubt that he was a colorful character as a vast body of folklore about him will testify. Most of the stories are humorous and many of them have to do with how he went from rags to riches, or started out

wealthy and lost his whole fortune gyppo logging, usually because of some circumstance he brought about through his own bullheadedness. One of the most often repeated stories may even have some basis in truth, simply because it is so widespread and related so often. In this story a gyppo, through years of hard work has become quite wealthy but that has never changed his lifestyle too much, so he customarily wore the kind of clothes he wore on the job even to social occasions. He is taken for some down and outer at a swanky hotel and refused services by a haughty maitre d'hotel. Of course, he buys the hotel and gives the maitre his choice of either starting on his new job of cleaning toilets or drawing his time.

Now, that story just may be true, but it runs counter to one overriding passion that seems to control most gyppos. Even a wealthy gyppo would hardly invest in a hotel when he could buy more logging equipment with the same amount of money. The average gyppo is enamored of logging equipment, preferably shiny new and expensive... a possible reaction to the days when anything he could afford was battered and cheap. The temptation to pass up a few new towers or skidders might be strong, but no hotel could give him the feeling of accomplishment that he would get from a batch of shiny new equipment. He would be much more apt to demolish the offending establishment, pay his fine and damages, and go back to his first love–getting out the

The lady is a logger! Betty Walker runs a highly successful logging operation in the Blue Mountains of Washington. She may be nice, but she is also the boss...and you'd better believe it!

Bill Hermann is a contract logger working on the Olympic Peninsula. The old-time logging arch is at the entrance to his home near Port Angeles. No, he doesn't use it in his work, preferring the most modern equipment

This gyppo near Castle Rock, Washington, is lucky that his show is on comparatively flat land, enabling him to yard in his logs with relatively inexpensive skidders rather than the more expensive high-lead equipment.

logs.

The casual treatment of wealth is no affectation but based on a very pragmatic assessment of facts. Knowing the vast swings of fate to which his business is prone, the gyppo knows that he may be wealthy one year and broke the next, so wealth does not materially change his life-style unless it has become solidly established. For that matter, a financial setback does not particularly deter him except to teach him what not to do the second time around. No one begrudges good fortune to a gyppo or attaches stigma to bad: the breaks of this game are such that today's boss may be tomorrow's chokerman, a fact that is recognized and acknowledged throughout the whole fraternity.

Just as the small businessman is the backbone of our national economy, so the gyppo is the mainstay of the logging industry. Although it is perfectly possible for a small gyppo outfit to grow to be an industrial giant, it is still the kind of establishment where the lowest chokerman calls the boss by his first name and feels free to express his opinion on any subject, including how the business should be run. Of course, he is also privileged to draw his time anytime he so desires, a right readily granted and used. The old-time logger was independent as a hog on ice, untrammeled, untamed, a free soul with few material ties. His modern counterpart is more apt to be a family man who has been considerably tamed down in the last hundred years, but there is still enough of the wild blood around to give the whole industry a decided flair. Maybe it's something imprinted in a logger's genes...and the ones most deeply imprinted seem to have a tendency to become gyppos.

There is one unspoken rule that is nevertheless well-known and accepted by all. The boss gyppo is unquestionably the Head Man. He gives orders that he rightfully expects will be obeyed as long as the man to whom that order was given is a part of the crew. But if he is to keep the respect of his men and that is absolutely essential in this organization of rugged individualists, he never issues an order for work that he would not himself take on. As a result, it is not at all unusual, especially with a small crew, to find the boss doing the dirtiest or most dangerous jobs on the operation with the possible exception of setting chokers. He grouses about this, of course, usually in very colorful, biologically- oriented language, but he is only fulfilling a long, old, logger's tradition. His crew would wonder about him if he didn't complain.

One of the changes I've noticed over the years is the relative education of the present gyppo. Eighteen years ago it was not unusual to run into a working gyppo with a minimal education, at least as far as formal education was concerned. He would be wise in the ways of the woods and may even have acquired a good working knowledge of the business, but his English would still be a bit on the primitive side, and the diamond that he might be was still definitely in the rough. To a great extent, that has changed. Anyone in the contract logging business today, of necessity, seems to have either at least a high school education, or considerable self-acquired, practical knowledge about his complex trade. This is probably a reflection of the very high stakes for which the contract logger is playing today. The old time gyppo, of necessity, often had a much more humble beginning.

It was not unusual to find a gyppo who was relatively unschooled in formal learning but wise in the ways of the woods and of his complicated trade. He may candidly tell you that, after a rough beginning, he has finally made a better-than-comfortable life for himself at gyppo logging, is now a pillar of society, a member of the school board, sits as an equal on the board of directors of the local bank and, in general, is a man of substance in his community. He will also cheerfully admit to having "gone broke," maybe several times, but each time the innate stubbornness of the logger prevails. He picks up the pieces of his shattered life, profits from the mistakes he has made and gives it another try. Apparently the system works, for some of them become excellent businessmen with a respectable net worth, as long as they can keep away from equipment salesmen.

It was my pleasure to renew an acquaintance I had made eighteen years ago with a then young, lean, just-starting-out gyppo. He had started cat-logging with a venerable old tractor that he had bought on time, and when I met him, he was just completing his first job. Eighteen years later, he is now middle-aged, the flat belly has yielded to a generous paunch that bespeaks some very good eating over the years, and he is the owner of three active logging sides and several million dollars worth of logging equipment, a fair part of which is paid for. He is now, in every respect, a contract logger, but you don't have to scratch very deeply to uncover the gyppo. He now has an accountant who, when he first went over the gyppo's books, discovered that on at least three separate occasions, he had been bankrupt. The way the gyppo kept books, or maybe didn't keep books in those days, was such that he was unaware that he was more in debt than usual and eventually worked his way out of it. There may be more than a little worth in the oldtime system!

Some woodsmen will tell you that the new ecological regulations have doomed the gyppo. He may be a threatened species; but then, he always has been and doomed he certainly is not, especially if he has anything to say about it. In fact, some recent developments actually may be working in his favor. One of the biggest of these is that many of the large companies who previously maintained large and expensive logging camps have decided that the contract logger can do the job more economically and are now contracting all of their work with gyppos. Camp Grisdale, on the Olympic Peninsula, is no longer in existence. The camp's owner, Simpson Timber Company, now contracts all of its logs from gyppos. Headquarters, in Idaho, formerly the home of over four hundred loggers and their families, is practically deserted now that contract loggers provide the logs for the Potlatch mills at Lewiston and Coeur D'Alene. Does that mean that those loggers are out of work? Some may be, but most are either working for gyppos or have taken the plunge and are in business for themselves. Right now, they worry far more over the ecological restrictions that make their work so difficult rather than over the lack of work. "People," they figure, "have always needed wood, and that's what we provide."

The gyppo has quite a few things going for him: knowledge, drive, ambition, and the willingness to put in many, many very hard hours. He knows that more and more large organizations are turning to the gyppo, and this for a simple economic reason. Once a contract is let, that is a fixed expense that can be fed into the maw of the omnivorous computer, thus eliminating possibilities and replacing them with a definite factor. Another thing working in the favor of the small operator is that some jobs are best handled by a small outfit with an overhead to match. This is usually a thinning or a cosmetic operation that a large outfit, geared to a high output of logs per day simply could not handle economically. The small gyppo takes this in stride and when weather or an equipment failure shuts him down he finally gets to go fishing, with as clear a conscience as a gyppo can muster.

Although by nature the gyppo is a loner, he has learned, by bitter experience if nothing else, that no man is an island. He is a good enough businessman to realize the strength that can be realized by association with his fellow gyppos and so loggers' associations specifically aimed at helping him are active throughout the timber belt. While these are universally called "contract loggers' associations," they are organizations founded by and for the betterment of the gyppo. They provide low-cost insurance, a source of capital from people who understand the logging game and a strong right arm when the gyppo or his way of life is threatened. An area-wide radio communications network is sponsored by the associations, so that all the members are tied together into a network that can disseminate valuable information in a matter of minutes. It must have been highly difficult, especially at first, for these highly individualistic men to each surrender a bit of their independence for a common good, but the fact that the contract logger associations are flourishing would seem to prove that their worth is being realized and what is even more important, utilized.

Most of the small gyppo operations are headed by young men who are full of enthusiasm and in love with logging. They may be from logging families, trying out their wings under the more or less approving eyes of their fathers. For these young men, logging is far more than just a job: it is a way of life. They realize they are taking a big gamble, for most of them grew up in families where the grim specter of failure was such a constant presence that it had ceased to be terrifying. They are willing to take the chance because they feel that they can always swing the odds their way with a little luck, lots of sweat and the judicious use of haywire. The gyppo is by nature a born gambler and he has a tendency to marry a girl equally willing to take a chance on making the operation either a rousing success or a crashing failure. To a gyppo, there are only two places in the race of life, first, or last, and he plays the game with equal enthusiasm when he is headed in either direction. That may be the reason why I have so many friends in the ranks of the gyppos, because, ever since the age of thirteen, I have lived my life like a cavalry charge, and in the gyppo I see a kindred spirit.

Two people in particular stand out in my memory from the many gyppos I met eighteen years ago. One was a young man who had been a working logger with his father for several years, so he had a good general knowledge of logging as well as a burning ambition to be his own boss. He gambled his life savings on a battered old tractor with a good winch and a noble ruin of a shovel that had definitely seen better days. With much welding and many borrowed parts, he made the ambulating scrap iron workable and took a small contract. The job almost paid for the welding rods he had used. Encouraged, he took another small contract, worked twelve hours a day and made a few thousand dollars. From this foundation, he wangled enough capital to buy an old but sturdy log truck while still keeping his original equipment in usable condition.

Another contract, and this time serendipity definitely was a factor. He bought a sale that gave him all the down timber in an easily accessible site with a high recreational potential. The job was strictly a cosmetic logging operation, with very few live trees slated for falling, and too small to merit the attention of the larger gyppo operations. The area was crisscrossed with large, old blowdown timber that had lain there for years and at first sight looked like an economic as well as an ecological disaster. But this gyppo had done his homework. He had personally cruised that site and he was gambling that the long-lived fir windfalls were sound. And he was right.

Some of the most beautiful yellow fir ever cut in that area came out of that sale. In an area that had been cruised at seven hundred and fifty thousand board feet, much too small to merit the attention of even a medium sized gyppo, over four million board feet of perfectly sound logs were salvaged. Because this was a cosmetic logging operation, each log was carefully winched out of the woods with great care being taken to minimize contact with standing trees. Another reason may have been that that venerable old winch, which was possibly at least as old as its owner, was working at or near capacity at all times, and so care was an operational necessity as well as part of the contract. It was the natural habitat of the small gyppo and everyone rejoiced at his good fortune. Every so often a lucky break will result in a bonanza, but everyone knew that he could just as easily have lost his whole outfit had any one of several variable circumstances turned out differently. That is logging, especially gyppo logging.

Another young gyppo, in partnership with his father, had been in the game long enough to have a million dollars' worth of equipment, several fat contracts and headaches scaled to size. This young college graduate, with a degree in forestry, knew that his chances of some day being a millionaire were quite good. He also knew that one serious miscalculation on his part could thrust him into bankruptcy. Although he employed two full-size crews and could justifiably delegate authority, this man was up at the crack of dawn, highballed all day, and returned at night tired but happy to his pretty wife, new baby son, and forty-thousand-dollar home. It was wonderful to touch bases with this man again. He is now the sole owner of the business, runs five sides, still highballs all day, but is already delegating considerable authority to his teenage son who, as soon as his college forestry course is

Ed Lewis Jr. seated, with his father Ed Lewis Sr., is a fourth-generation gyppo logging Pacific Lumber Land near Scotia, California. Note new shoot sprouting from the ever-living redwood stump. Ed Lewis III is in school today, but he's on his way to making it the fifth generation in logging.

completed, wants nothing more that to follow in his father's footsteps. After all, he has a very good example. His mother is still pretty, he has a younger brother and an extremely pretty sister and the house is now worth at least a quarter of a million dollars. And, oh yes: his retired father, proudly, still calls himself a gyppo.

Another gyppo told me of his beginnings while I was relaxing in his beautiful home and sipping an excellent scotch. This man has a formal education of high school...only. Right out of high school he took a job clearing a small section of land with the understanding that, in addition to his wages, the wood he cleared was his as long as he removed it from the property. A good part of the wood was second-growth cedar, which this enterprising young man, working some very long, hard, summer days converted into fence posts and sold at a sufficient profit to buy a second-hand pickup. With the word-of-mouth advertising that came from his neatly done first operation he quickly got a succession of jobs but soon realized that clearing stumps with a pickup supplying the pulling power, even with an intricate system of pulleys, was a losing proposition. So his next acquisition was a broken-down tractor which, with much tender loving care and application of the things he had learned by watching mechanics, he made reasonable operative. The next acquisition was a second-hand skidder, and with this addition to his equipment, he felt he was ready to make the most important and, as he proudly tells me, the smartest move of his life. He married his childhood sweetheart, thereby acquiring not only a good bookkeeper but also a tireless booster and source of encouragement.

Today, that man and his wife run a good-sized, thriving logging business that every year does millions of dollars of business. He is a director of the local bank, sits on the school board and is a respected man of substance in his community. He is an enthusiastic supporter of higher education: all of his children are college graduates, but it is doubtful that any one of them are as well educated as their father. His formal education may have taken second place to his driving ambition to become a success in his demanding profession, but his practical education has been an ongoing thing and is progressing faster today than ever. He has to do this if he is to keep up with the advances that are being made every day and with which, if he is to be competitive, he must be familiar. This man leads a busy, productive, useful life, and he proudly calls himself a gyppo.

These three have made a success in a game where failure comes as often as success, but the reasons they have succeeded are so basic that they can be the financial underpinnings of a man, or of a country. They use their brains as well as their brawn, they do a useful work, and they keep faith with themselves and their fellow men. The formula is scarcely new, but the fact that it still produces success proves that it has stood the test of time.

What is the future of the gyppo? Ask a dozen different people and you may get as many different answers. The gyppo has been consigned to the dustbin of the industry by numerous "experts" none of whom

A living legend in the logging industry, "Hap" Johnson has done it all. Logger, gyppo, high climber, and very popular performer at logging shows, there are few aspects of this craft that he has not mastered.

could see how a small businessman faced with the ecological problems of the day can possibly survive. The day is gone, they say, when a man can go into business with old, practically worn-out equipment and make a profit. In this respect the gyppo is very much like the bumblebee, which any aeronautical engineer will tell you is so constructed that he cannot possibly fly. The bumblebee, cheerfully unaware that he has been consigned to oblivion, happily zooms off to his rendezvous with a queen and confounds the experts. If he isn't flying, he certainly is putting on a pretty good imitation!

The gyppo is very much in the same class. He knows that in spite of all the regulation, even if more stringent and strangling ones are imposed, man's need for wood will continue and, while the realization of that need may be belated, it will some day be realized...and someone will have to be there to provide the wood. He is also getting smarter by the day and realizing that in a modern world, a loner is very vulnerable. For that reason, he supports his professional associations and at last is fighting back at his adversaries who would not only deprive him of his way of life but also deprive the country of an industry which it may only belatedly realize is essential to its economic and social well-being.

One of the most frequent charges leveled against the Forest Service is that they are too friendly to loggers, especially gyppos. This is generally not true, but it is easy to see why an outside observer would think so. The Forest Service is increasingly caught between a rock and a hard place, especially in light of

55

increasingly complex ecological regulations. By law, it must make the best use of the land entrusted to its crew and, in many places, that means removing a mature forest so that a new one may be propagated. To some environmentalists, that is not acceptable and the Forest Service can be subjected to some really frightful pressures by these well-financed and media-smart organizations. Under these circumstances, a regional forester would usually look upon a conscientious, competent gyppo who would do a neat job of logging and replant the site efficiently as a gift from Heaven. Many foresters have been loggers, or from long association with them understand the part the logger plays in perpetuating a healthy forest environment and so are far more sympathetic to a logger than someone whose approach to forest management is founded purely on aesthetics. Many small jobs are not subject to the bidding regulations and can be awarded to the contractor who, in the regional forester's opinion, would do the best job. A gyppo who has demonstrated over the years that he is that kind of an operator can be kept quite busy doing small jobs that would bankrupt a contractor geared to a large production, especially if he has demonstrated an awareness of the ecological problems involved and has shown a willingness to work within those parameters.

Simply as a matter of good business if for nothing else, most of them do. There are exceptions, and these are the bad apples in the barrel that give the whole industry a black eye. A bad job of logging is much more apt to be conspicuous than a good one and will be remembered long after a neat job of forest restoration will have been forgotten. In the Blue Mountains of Washington, there is a glaring example of bad logging which even after twenty years is still a blot on the landscape and an embarrassment to the local loggers even though they had nothing to do with this atrocity. A gyppo high graded the sale, with no consideration at all for potential erosion, then skipped without doing the required restoration work. The area is still scarred with gullies and piles of discarded timber which only after twenty years are partially hidden by new growth. Enough remains to give logging in this area a bad name and this was done by a gyppo. They are not all good operators and this one was one of the worst.

It would be unfair to rate all gyppos by this standard just as it would be to paint them all as paragons of efficiency and virtue. They are men, with all the faults, virtues and failings of men. There is one thing, however, about which there is not a single thread of doubt. They are as colorful, useful, hard-working representatives of the system of free enterprise as America has ever bred.

No wonder that they call themselves "Gyppo" with so much pride!

Loggers will claim that all scalers have long thumbs and are blind, illegitimate robbers. Not so! They are actually reliable, ethical workers who take great pride in accuracy of their estimates.

Given a welding torch and a bit of haywire, a gyppo can fix practically any piece of equipment on a landing and this skill is called upon regularly for much of his equipment has been long and well used.

CHAPTER III

THE LAST LOG DRIVE

The fabled cattle drives of the Old West that moved vast herds of Texas-bred cattle to the railheads in Kansas are rightfully the stuff of which legends are woven. The drama, set on a canvas of vast distances and etched in the acrid alkali dust of the Great Plains, is so compelling that it has been the subject of numberless epics and has firmly established the cattle drive as the ultimate piece of Americana. The cattle drives, we are told, were the most formidable tests of man against nature and made greater demands on human endurance and stamina than any other endeavor ever conceived by the mind of man.

Tell that story to a veteran of another kind of drive and he will either laugh himself into a hysterical state or regard you with the condescending pity usually reserved for not-so-bright children or the village idiot. To this veteran, the cowboy had a safe, easy, comfortable time sitting on a horse probably smarter than he was, who did all the work, handling comparatively docile animals that could be turned with a shout, the crack of a whip or, in extreme cases, a well-aimed rifle shot. He may have occasionally have been briefly uncomfortable, but very seldom in real danger unless he brought that onto himself with his own stupidity.

Of course, it is only human nature to belittle the accomplishments of someone else, especially if one has no first-hand knowledge of what those accomplishments entail. Still, anyone who has survived a white-water log drive may be forgiven if he adopts a somewhat patronizing attitude toward what he would consider a lesser breed of man; that being anyone who has never taken part in that activity. The action in a white-water drive, the danger inherent when mindless tons of hurtling logs had somehow to be directed to a predetermined destination, the milieu in which the action took place, the toughness and stamina that was required, all were so awesomely dramatic that, by comparison, the fabled cattle drives of the Old West seemed downright tame.

It may come as a surprise to some Americans who look upon the log drive as an uniquely American event to find out that the idea came from the Old Country. For countless millennia, man has known that the easiest way to move large, bulky masses has been to float them in water and let the current of the stream supply the motive power, with only an occasional directional nudge applied to get the load to its destination. The short, swift rivers of Scandinavia were often used to move logs in this way and when emigrants from those countries came to the new World they brought their forest skills with them.

The forests of America, however, are on a vastly larger scale than the comparatively smaller timber that is the norm in Europe and so a new type of log drive gradually evolved. The rivers of the East Coast are relatively sedate; and, although the logs were much larger than the European timber, still the action was not too different than that of the Old Country. It was only on a much larger scale.

As the forests of the East Coast and Middle West were gradually cut over, the center of logging shifted to the West Coast and a completely new type of operation, adapted to the much larger timber encountered there, evolved.

Those western forests! Loggers from the East gazed in unbelieving awe at trees ten-feet thick, breast high, and a hundred and fifty feet to the first limb. Falling one of these monsters was an accomplishment in itself, but that was only half the job: getting it to the mill was as big or sometimes even bigger undertaking, and it is no wonder that sawmills were almost invariably built next to water to take advantage of the transportation that water afforded.

A log weighing twenty tons is quite a stable platform when floating in water, especially to an agile young daredevil wearing steel-spiked boots, so in no time at all it became standard practice for a logger to ride one of these floating monsters to the mill, occasionally giving it a guiding nudge to make sure it grounded reasonably close to its destination.

As the timber close to the mill was cut over, logging shifted to the regions upstream and the basic pattern of the log-drive evolved. Logging was carried out during all the winter months, and the logs were piled in huge decks along the river banks. The rising waters of the spring run-off floated the piles down to the mill, where a log-boom directed them into the mill pond. Simple as that! Since most of them made it, the method was used for years and as long as logs were cheap and plentiful, with a fair degree of success.

Two factors combined to gradually eliminate the log-drives. For one, with the gradual colonization that was bringing houses to the edge of the rivers, the danger inherent in the log drive began to land in people's backyards. Logs coming down the rivers in huge bunches would occasionally jam up and in a matter of minutes the log dam could be causing a flood, costing the lumber companies millions of dollars in compensatory damages. Then, too, improved transportation methods were making the transfer of logs to the mill by railroad or truck, if not as economical, with considerably more certainty and with far less

This jet boat can operate in eight inches of water and is powerful enough to move all but the most solidly embedded logs. This is the riverman's workhorse.

Waist deep in the icy waters of the North Fork of the Clearwater River, these rivermen are moving this big cedar into the current with pike poles. It's all part of the last log drive in the United States, which took place in May 1971.

Executing the classic maneuver of "getting the Hell out of there!" When a log jam breaks and the only way out is across the water, you'd better have a log or two handy unless you've learned to walk on water. Very few people have.

chance of crippling lawsuits.

Little by little, logdrives were becoming a bit of nostalgia, something that was part of America's colorful past, until by 1971, there was only one major drive left in the contiguous United States: that of the Potlatch Forest Industries down the North Fork of the Clearwater River in one of the wildest portions of Idaho's Panhandle.

Potlatch Forest Industries, Inc. is an industrial giant with large stands of timber in the wild North Fork area. It also maintained a large logging camp at Headquarters, Idaho, where several hundred loggers and their families lived the year around and, all through the winter, piled up a huge deck of logs along the river bank. The North Fork of the Clearwater, draining one of the outstanding timber producing areas of the United States, is a natural route of transportation, especially for logs. A swift, turbulent stream with many rapids, it has practically no habitation down its length, thereby eliminating the chances of flood-caused lawsuits. It has been used since 1928 to move 1,774,000,000 board feet of logs to the mill at Lewiston. This was to be drive #40.

A purist might say that this should be considered drive #41. The first log drive down the Clearwater was in 1840, when the Reverend Henry Spalding, the famed early missionary to the Nez Perce, organized a party of three white men and thirty-two Indians to cut timber above the mission for a school he was building at Lapwai. Forming it into a raft, they floated it down to the mission site where, after some considerable difficulty, it arrived more or less intact. Log drive #40 would be following in the steps of a long tradition.

In one very important respect, this drive down the river was to be very different from any other: this was to be the last one. Two miles above the confluence of the North Fork and the main stream a concrete monster had been growing for several years. Dworshak Dam, now almost completed, sat massively above the river channel ready to impound the waters of the North Fork into an eighty-five-mile-long lake. For the time being, the waters poured through a forty-foot wide tunnel in the base of the dam, but only temporarily: next year the tunnel would be permanently sealed and the log drive would become only a memory.

Theoretically, once the logs stockpiled at Camp X, twenty miles from Headquarters, were consigned to the not-so-tender mercies of the river, they should have floated sedately to the mill at Lewiston, arriving there in about eighteen hours. Like so many other supposedly fool-proof theories, it did not always work out that way.

Mid-April of 1971 saw the usual cold-deck at Camp X stretching along the western bank of the river for almost half a mile. Mostly of western cedar but also with considerable quantities of Douglas fir and the precious Idaho white pine which is the specialty of this camp, it represented the labors of several hundred men working through the heart of a brutal winter and an investment of several million dollars. Of course, this was an old story to the logging veterans who for years had watched the swirling waters sweep away the results of so much hard work, and usually the logs dutifully wound up in the mill-pond where they belonged, but everyone knew that it was possible for things to go wrong, as it had a few years before. Then, a log boom under fantastic pressure from the logs piled up against it by exceptionally high water had snapped...and fifty million board feet of logs had headed for the Pacific Ocean as fast as a racing river could take them.

That is called a "Snake River Log Drive" and to say that it is undesirable is the understatement of the year. Because of stringent ecological regulations, those logs must be retrieved, often at a cost several times greater than the value of the timber. It is understandable that when the time comes to consign the year's harvest to the river, it is done with considerable anxiety and only after every possible precaution has been taken to ensure that the whole operation will proceed smoothly.

The cold-deck had been constructed by experts so that once one end of it was tripped into the river, the whole deck would gradually unravel until all the logs were water-borne. To ensure that reluctant logs do not stop the whole operation, there is a massive power shovel, nicknamed "The Monster," on hand to give a rugged push as needed.

On a bright spring morning, the river was considered to be at the proper level and right on schedule, "The Monster" started the deck unraveling into the river. With a deep-throated rumble that could be heard for miles, the far end of the deck tumbled into the raging waters of the North Fork, to be instantly sucked away into the swirling waters. Thirty-two-foot logs tumbled into the river like straws to be instantly snatched away by the noisy waters and the surface of the river was carpeted with floating logs. The deck was unraveling well now, with the "Monster" waddling along the shore as fast as its laboring diesels could take it. An occasional shove was all that was necessary: the log-stackers had done their job well, so that in less than two hours, fifty million board feet of timber had been consigned to the river.

Just as the vast majority of people are law-abiding and probably could exist quite well without a mass of regulations if everyone simply followed the basic rules, so it is with those logs. Most of them float down to the mill, are dutifully guided into the mill pond and begin a new career as finished lumber. It is the mavericks who make regulations necessary with people and it is the logs that somehow refuse to obey the rules that make the rearing crew a necessity and, in so doing, provide the most picturesque aspect of the log drive.

No sooner had the last log disappeared around the bend than the rearing crew began to assemble. Very simply, the rearing crew was to follow in the wake of the log drive and retrieve any stray pieces of timber that had somehow escaped the raging waters of the North Fork and beached themselves. The job of the rearing crew was to heave those logs back into the river and send them on their way to Lewiston.

This may sound like a relatively simple procedure, but actually it was an operation that would require the full-time efforts of thirty-five of the toughest men in Idaho for the next three weeks. Some logs, driven by a seemingly perverse set of currents, would imbed themselves for half their length into a sandbar or rock crevice and then collect anywhere from a dozen to several hundred others into a jam, sometimes large enough to raise the level of the river ten feet or more.

This ungainly looking contraption actually is a floating cookhouse-bunkhouse. It's called a "wanigan" and is the lineal descendant of similar structures used by Germanic tribes at the time of Caesar's Gallic Wars.

This was not exactly a pleasant development, since ecological as well as company rules dictated that this or any other similar dam be broken down as soon as humanly possible.

The rearing crew was made up of men from wildly diverse backgrounds. There were engineers, telephone linemen, accountants, trappers and realtors, but the backbone of the drive was composed of a group of men who wore their spiked boots with the ease of long association: loggers. All were veterans of previous drives and had been hand picked from a long list of applicants, for this was a particularly historical drive and seemingly everyone wanted the honor of being included on its roster.

All the scheming, conniving and pleading might just as well have been skipped. The drive boss, Charlie McCollister, a tall, soft-spoken, silvery-haired veteran of twenty drives was in charge and knew from experience who was good enough to rate a berth on this drive. The men he selected were picked for intelligence, strength, stamina and, above all, the ability to work with other people as a smoothly functioning team. When Charlie would call his men together by the dawn's early light to hand out the day's assignments, it was always with a feeling of unalloyed pride: he was bossing a crew that was the cream of an already select group.

This feeling was not at all one-sided. Each man knew that he was a member of an elite group and also knew that from those to whom much had been given, much also was expected. Charlie, they knew, would give praise when it was deserved, but would instantly replace any man who did not pull not only his own weight, but also quite a bit more. In this crew, where superiority was the norm, if you wanted to be still part of the gang that would celebrate the successful conclusion of the drive in Lewiston, you had to be better than good: you had to be outstanding. Anything less was simply not acceptable and would not be tolerated.

There was a very simple reason for these rigorous standards. These men, working as a team downstream from a jam that could break at any moment, loosing mindlessly cascading logs that could in seconds reduce a man to an unrecognizable mass of mangled flesh, just simply had to be the best in the business if they were to get through the drive alive. Previous drives had shown that when men are working up to their waists in water just barely above freezing, wrestling with a log that outweighs them ten to one, it takes a very special kind of man to survive and still get the job done.

Charlie had found thirty-five of them and was determined to make this last drive the best one on record. To make a good omelet, it helps considerably if you start with good eggs; and when it came to picking, Charles was in a class by himself.

For the duration of the drive, "home" for these men would be the wanigan, an articulated canvas-sided combination cook-house and bunk-house floating on large, inflated rubber pontoons that had previously done Army service as support for pontoon bridges strong enough to support heavy tanks. The origin of this type of structure is hidden in the mists of history; but Caesar, in his Commentaries on the Gallic Wars, mentions that some Germanic tribes had floating log structures similar to this, whose basic means of defense was to cut the hawser tying the wanigan to the river bank and to float out of reach of their enemies. The Venetians lived on similar floating platforms before they learned how to drive piling and build their golden city, so the wanigan could justifiably boast of an ancient and illustrious ancestry. On the North Fork it served as a readily movable camp that catered to most of the needs of the rearing crew. It was generally kept ahead of the rearing crew on the theorem that a man always worked better if he were headed toward a good meal and a warm bed. With a total length of over a hundred feet, the wanigan was a structure that seemingly would not have the ghost of a chance of surviving a trip through even the smaller riffles of the North Fork. Built in three sections, it had a couple of outboard motors operating in wells near the midsection which theoretically supplied the motive and steering power to get the wanigan moving into the current of the river. From thereon, steering was done by a few sweating men with an intimate knowledge of the river's vagaries and a deep, abiding faith in the power of prayer. Strangely enough, the wanigan easily negotiated the most murderous rapids of the North fork without even spilling a drop of the cook's nonchalantly sipped coffee.

The most important man on this drive was Charlie McCollister, no question about that! When the boss gave an order, it was carried out instantly as a fitting tribute to the respect due a man who was bossing the toughest outfit in Idaho and had proved by past achievement that he had every right to do so. The second most important man had a somewhat more tenuous claim to respect, but one that he wielded with an iron hand. In his domain, the cook-house, Harvey Spears was unquestionably the king and woe to the man who ever questioned his authority or tracked mud into his kitchen! Harvey had been the cook on several previous drives and the fact that he was cook to this elitist crew said much for his ability. Blessed with a ribald sense of humor, a definite culinary ability and an inordinate love of his own food, Harvey was a very popular member of the drive, yet this backwoods chef-de-cuisine ruled his domain with the iron hand of a feudal lord. His cook-house, located in the center of the wanigan between the two end sections that served as bunkhouses, was always a place where you could find a good cup of coffee and some fresh-baked doughnuts, providing that you wiped the mud off your feet before entering.

Harvey's day began at 3 a.m., when he began preparations for an absolutely monstrous crew breakfast. Sausages by the hundreds, eggs by the dozens, mountains of flapjacks and oceans of coffee all were consumed in the grim silence of men totally committed to absorbing a good part of the 9000 calories per day each man routinely consumed. The logging camp custom of silence during meals, broken only by the demands for more food, was rigidly observed: conversation could come later, but eating was serious business and could not be done in earnest if one were talking.

This tremendous caloric intake was a necessity on

the log drive. If a log could be dislodged no other way, then the men would wade into the ice-cold river, attack it with peaveys and often bodily lift it by brute force to send it on its way down the river. Even though the wool pants and heavy woollen shirts that were practically a uniform on the drive offered a degree of protection, the loss of body heat caused by immersion in ice-cold water for a good part of the day would have inevitably led to severe hypothermia were it not for the tremendous caloric value supplied by large amounts of food. Besides, eating is fun and was one of the few diversions available deep in the wilds of Idaho.

Every man wore the obligatory logger's steel-spiked boots and a safety work-vest that would ensure flotation in the not unlikely event that he might be swept away by the swift current. In that event, he was supposed to relax and wait. The system which provided that each man was his brother's keeper guaranteed that in a few seconds a jet boat would roar up to him and he'd be fished out of the river in short order and not much wetter than he ordinarily would be in the normal course of the day's work.

The work-horse of the drive was the jet boat; a flat-bottomed aluminum boat driven by a jet of water propelled by powerful pumps. Tremendously powerful (they were each rated at 440 horsepower) and with its four-inch draft superbly adapted to the rock-studded waters of the North Fork, this was the river-cowboy's steed. With its twin 220 horsepower engines, it had sufficient power to negotiate the wildest rapids of the river and, with its pulling power, could usually untangle all but the most stubborn of jams. Jams basically fell into two categories. A wing jam was caused by a log hanging up on the bank and extending into the river. It usually could be attacked from its down-river face and almost always by locating the key log. A thick polypropylene rope equipped with a choker and also with a quick release device that could be operated from the boat was looped around the offending log. The pulling power of the boat often was able to start the jam on its way. If it did not, the jam was unraveled the hard way: log by log, until the jam started moving. Then, the classic maneuver, known as "getting the Hell out of there," was executed by the whole crew and as quickly as possible...and when there are a few tons of logs bearing down onto one, that is apt to be very, very quickly.

It sometimes happened that the quickest avenue of escape was by jumping from one floating log to another, and often the lumberjack was treated to an impromptu ride down a raging wilderness river. While an agile young man wearing sure-footed, spiked boots and riding a stable five-foot cedar log could hardly be blamed if he were enjoying the ride, this was in strict contravention of the rules and if it happened too often was apt to bring a quiet warning from Charles, along with a few tips on how to improve the ride. On this push, every man was needed every minute of the working day and joy-riding down the river, however enjoyable, was not considered part of the work curriculum.

A center jam, usually much larger and more dangerous, happened whenever a log hung up cross-wise, usually against a rock in the river. In no time at all, hundreds of logs could pile up and a jam of monumental proportions could build in minutes. The usual method of attack was to locate the key log, try to jerk it loose with the jet boat and, failing that, saw a cut into the offending log. At the first crackling sound or any sign of breakage, the man wielding the saw would beat a hasty retreat, often with a mass of cascading logs hot on his heels. This definitely was no job for sissies!

The riverman's basic tool was the peavey, a stout steel-spiked pole with a short hinged hook hanging from its side. With the leverage provided by this tool, a 200-pound riverman was able, at least in theory, to move a 4000 pound log. With the teamwork that was the hallmark of this crew, that was seldom necessary, because if a man were faced with a problem that anywhere near taxed his capacity, one of his teammates was always there to lend a helping hand. This was taken for granted, both in the giving and the receiving, and the ability of each man to mesh his efforts with those of his mates as a member of a superbly well-drilled team was one of the criteria required for his initial selection.

The other basic tool of the riverman was the pike-pole, a long, slender, javelin-like wooden rod with a twisted steel point. Hurled full force into a log, it provided a convenient handle by which a log floating in an eddy could be guided into the current where a quick twist released it. Other tools were chainsaws and occasionally, high explosives. Ecological considerations made the use of explosives much less frequent than on previous drives, when many a recalcitrant jam was cleared by the explosion of a few cases of strategically placed dynamite. On this drive, the dynamite was piled casually next to the cookhouse, where it made a good seat for the men who gathered to chat after dinner. On drive #40, there was no dynamite exploded, although the temptation to announce the successful conclusion of the drive to the people of Lewiston was almost overwhelming.

The work day was roughly from 7 a.m. to 6 p.m. with time out for lunch and several "orange breaks," when each man consumed two or three oranges. The idea was that the citrus fruit, being high in vitamin C, would ward off the colds to which these men were excessively exposed. Whether it was the oranges or the exuberant good health enjoyed by every man on the drive, the fact is that not one man came down with as much as a case of the sniffles.

The wildest ride of the whole day would begin when Charlie's calm voice would announce, over the radio which tied all the crew boats into one communications network, "O.K. boys, let's wrap'er up." Tools were hurriedly stored and the three powerful boats would start off in a sheet of spray. "The Run for the Wanigan" was unquestionably the social event of the day and the boat jockey who didn't at least once in a while win that race was liable to be bumped, accidentally of course, into the river.

When the boats arrived in camp, the bull-cook already had a good drying fire going and the washing stand set up with plenty of hot water and stacks of warm towels. Wet, work-stained clothes were exchanged for

When a really big one is stranded way up there on the river bank, the usual, but not the easiest way, is to attack it bodily with peaveys and return it to the river through brute strength.

An accumulation of brush and trash called "beaver bait" must be cleared away before this log can be returned to the river which will carry it to the mill pond at Lewiston.

more casual and dry attire and the evening meal, freed from the exigencies of the coming workday, was more leisurely enjoyed. Harvey always outdid himself for the evening meal and, since he had "carte Blanche" as far as groceries were considered, the meals were often of a type that not many kings could enjoy, or even afford.

In the lingering twilight of spring there was often an hour or so of light before the men turned in for the night. Portable shoe-lasts were provided for those who wished to tune up the steel spikes of their boots: a life-saving precaution on the slippery logs of the drive. Those who were not involved in the impromptu poker games that inevitably started chatted and showed off snapshots of their loved ones. By common consent, "lights out" was at eight o'clock. A day's hard work not only made sleep easy, but essential. Dawn would not be long in coming and there were still logs to be wrestled into the Clearwater.

Once the North Fork had been cleared of logs and the wanigan dismantled and trucked around Dworshak Dam to be reassembled on the mainstream of the Clearwater, the pace picked up considerably. The mainstream is wider and not as susceptible to jams as the North Fork, so that now sunburn and tourists became the main impediments to work. Since the stream is close to the road, at every place where a work-party was in progress, there were apt to be a dozen tourists, cameras at the ready, seeking to record this piece of Americana while it was still possible. Harvey was driven to policing his kitchen with drawn cleaver so persistent were the interlopers.

It was with mixed emotions that on a bright May morning the last log was driven into the pond and the crew gathered on the floating logs for a group picture. The final chapter had been written in an American saga and, somehow, things would never again be the same. The drive had taken nineteen days, not a record, but very respectable time and it had been accomplished with a perfect safety record. Charlie was both sad and proud and the farewells that were said were so awkward that instinctively one knew that many a man was hiding deeply felt emotions behind a gruff exterior. They had each shared an exciting adventure and the spirit of camaraderie that is so evident in any logging endeavor had been, if possible, even stronger than usual.

The logs now ride sedately from Camp X to Lewiston on a truck. Progress it certainly is, but somehow, to me it never will have the drama, the excitement, of the log drive. And I must admit that I have a very personal reason for my prejudice. On the very first day of the log drive, when a sudden burst of rain made all but one of the photographers who had gathered to record this event dive for cover, I stayed with the crew, got soaking wet, got some of my best pictures and apparently earned the respect of these rugged men. Little by little, I was allowed to take at first a small part and later an

Harvey Spears, an unmitigated tyrant in his kitchen, was also a darned good cook who could keep thirty-five of the hungriest men in Idaho fed to satisfaction. That pile of meat is only part of what he will cook for dinner.

almost full-fledged part in the activities of the crew. No one ever had a better chance than I did to record this bit of Americana at first hand, and I became quite adept at grabbing my camera for a quick shot before spearing an errant log with my pike pole.

In a week there was a bunk for me in the wanigan, a place at the table and a seat in boat #2. When the drive was over and the crew broke up, every man signed the work-vest which was given to each man–a souvenir of the drive–and one of my proudest recollections is that my name, as a member of the crew, is burned into a peavey that rests today in the Potlatch museum as a memento of the last log drive.

The last log drive is a memory, but is it completely dead? Not as long as any one of the men who took part in it is still alive to talk about it! Dworshak Reservoir is now a scenic lake, impounded behind the concrete monolith that blocks the North Fork. Stretching well back into the wilderness area of the North Fork, it is one of my favorite kayak camping spots, for the crystal clear water not only teems with land-locked salmon, but it also affords some of the best swimming in the Pacific Northwest. When, in the comparative comfort of my two-man Klepper foldboat, I glide over its placid surface, I cannot help but remember the days when I first became acquainted with this aquatic paradise. It was a lot wilder then, and untamed, but then, so was I.

Paddling twenty or thirty miles a day in comparative comfort, stopping whenever I feel like if for a cooling swim, is a far cry from those days when, with blistered hands, I hurled a pike-pole into an errant log, yet this is the same country. It is true that it is considerably changed now, the roar of the rapids is stilled and at night the muted obligato that lulls one to sleep is the gentle lapping of wind-driven waves on a shelving beach rather than the wild roaring of white-foamed rapids. But when I curl up for my well-deserved night's sleep, my head is pillowed on a time-worn work-vest on which the names of the last log drive crew are still faintly legible. And when I dream, it is only natural that it should be of those stirring days when I took part in a vivid piece of Americana, the last log drive in America...and my dreams are sweet.

There is one thing, though, that can never be replaced. I sure miss Harvey's cooking!

After a day spent up to your waist in ice cold water, a wash-up with warm water is an appreciated luxury. We take warm water for granted, obtained simply by turning a tap. Here it is provided the hard way, heated over a wood fire. Thank God for wood!

The Chilkat River outside of Haines, Alaska, is only one of the many scenic attractions that make Alaska a land of wonders.

Ketchikan Pulp Mill at Ward Cove eight miles north of Ketchikan not only makes high-grade dissolving pulp but also cuts dimensional lumber for export, one of the few bright spots in our balance of trade with the countries of the Pacific Rim.

CHAPTER IV

LOGGING, ALASKA STYLE

A great part of the pleasure I have experienced in revisiting the places I first saw eighteen years ago has come from once again viewing some of the most beautiful scenery on the face of this planet, and high on that list is that section of Alaska known as "Southeast." If ever a land were blessed with superb ocean scenery, beautiful mountains and lakes and absolutely magnificent timber, this is the place, for from the water's edge to the snow line on the Coast Range a dense mantle of hemlock, spruce and cedar cloaks the slopes in seemingly endless waves of verdure. It is a land alive with the thunder of waterfalls draining eternal glaciers and pierced everywhere by inlets and bays that make Southeast a place consisting mainly of islands...and those islands are covered with some of the finest timber on Earth.

The warm waters of the Japanese Current and the moist air it engenders are the reason for the comparatively mild climate of Southeast, while an annual precipitation of over eighty inches accounts in part for the lush forestation of the land: growing conditions for hemlock, spruce and cedar are excellent and these trees make up the bulk of the coastal forests. The forests even farther inland are mostly of poplar, white spruce and the birch that always seem to thrive on the taiga; and while some of these resources are beginning to be tapped, the problems endemic to getting them to a mill are so monstrous that this vast reserve, at this time, is getting only marginal usage. The fact that it is there is well known, and if ever the demand for it warrants the effort, it can actively become a part of the riches that typify Alaska.

Where timber can be had there are usually loggers, and Alaska is no exception. The Russians, under the reign, for it can be correctly described in no other term, of the imperious Alexander Baranof, used this region as a base for their fur-gathering expeditions, reaching as far south as California, and cut only as much timber as their local needs indicated. When Secretary of State William Seward bought Alaska in 1867, it was largely on the basis of the fishing and wealth of timber that had been reported to him; and at $7,200,000, which boils down to about two cents an acre, he got a fantastic bargain! Alaska contains reserves of over one hundred and fifty billion board feet of commercially valuable timber. Several times that much is not presently marketable but undoubtedly will be as the need for it escalates if it is not all locked up in still another wilderness preserve.

Since hemlock and spruce are excellent fiber producers, it is only natural that pulp mills would locate close to the source of supply; but in this frontier wilderness the large mill at Sitka, unexpectedly bursting into view around the bend of a forest road, is one of the most surprising sights in this land of many surprises. In 1959, Japanese interests built this large, modern plant to take advantage of the enormous hemlock and spruce stands of the region. That mill wasn't the first: six years earlier the Ketchikan Pulp Company, becoming the largest employer in Southeast, constructed an even larger sixty million dollar plant at Ward Cove, eight miles north of Ketchikan, thereby helping to make Ketchikan the fourth largest city in Alaska. Both plants make one of the most difficult-to-manufacture products that modern technology has produced: the snow white, high-quality, dissolving pulp from which rayon, cellophane, photographic film and myriad other products, even pharmaceuticals and food, are made.

Logging presents problems no matter where it is undertaken, but in no place are those problems more complex than in Alaska. Many of these are related to the sheer, staggering size of the land; the Aleuts were quite correct in giving the name "Alaska," which means "Great Land" in their language, to this vast, jutting promontory. Alaskans justifiably boast about the size of their state: a popular Alaskan definition of "claustrophobia" is, "What an Alaskan feels when he is deep in the heart of Texas." Stretching hundreds of miles is a wilderness broken only by an occasional logging camp or the wake of a fishing boat plying one of the innumerable inlets. It is a vast, bountiful land but also a cruel one which grudgingly yields its riches only to the strong and the industrious and ruthlessly weeds out the weak and incompetent by relegating them to a lesser clime. For men and women willing to combat the wilderness and wrest from it the treasures it has held since the Ice Age, it is made to order; and it is this type of people that one is most apt to meet here.

Alaska is the last stronghold of that vanishing American institution, the logging camp. Unlike loggers in the "Lower Forty-Eight" as they call the contiguous United States, some of the northern loggers don't go home after their day's work, for Alaska is far from being urbanized. There has been a change or two in the last eighteen years. Thorne Bay, a logging camp when I first visited, is now an incorporated city with established homes where loggers come back to home-cooked meals and a romp with the kids when they are through with their day's work. This is the exception, and Louisiana-Pacific alone still has three camps on Prince of Wales Island that follow the usual pattern. Southeast's vast spaces contain only a few small cities and towns, and logging is usually done miles away from even these small centers. Add to this the fact that there are very few roads in Alaska and you have a situation where the logging camp is the most logical solution.

Inevitably, this style of logging has its impact on the timber operator; even a small gyppo must make a considerable investment to build and maintain a camp on a year-round basis if he is to operate an effective logging show, for a logging camp is in essence a small town where the operator is charged with all civic functions and responsibilities. It is one of the most formidable obstacles in the way of anyone wishing to start a new operation in Alaska and, unfortunately, no one seems to have found a viable alternative.

The typical logging camp is built around the cookhouse, by popular consensus the most important building in the camp. The first meal is breakfast, usually served around 6 a.m. or even sooner if conditions in the woods merit an early start; and no one, but no one, misses breakfast unless he wants to go hungry for the rest of the day. Conditions may vary from camp to camp. The tables may be quite small, seating a maximum of four, or be the more usual long table seating eight hungry men. Logging camp custom is that conversation at mealtime be kept to a minimum, usually due to demands for more food; the conversation can come later when it will not interfere with what is considered serious business in the logging fraternity. The cook has also established a well-stocked "spike table" where each man can build his own nosebag according to his individual taste. Some of the creations the loggers achieve would shame Dagwood Bumstead, that legendary prince of creative sandwich fantasies. These are stowed into the logger's lunchbucket and carried to the working site for his midday meal. The evening meal is usually a more elaborate affair, eaten with more leisure, since there is nothing ahead to occupy the evening other than the logger's individual plans.

The bunkhouse is a far cry from the old-time, vermin-infested shack where loggers slept in tiered bunks and privacy was as scarce as good manners. Nowadays, the logger can have his own spotlessly clean private room if he insists, although most men prefer to room with a buddy, simply as a matter of companionship. The rooms are not ornate, but they have a good bed, a desk for writing, good lighting supplied by the camp's generators and space where personal belongings can be safely stored. Strict tradition ordains that a man's private property is sacred; the quickest way for a logger to be blackballed throughout all of Alaska is to be caught with stolen property, and since this tradition is a double-edged sword and could possibly be abused, it generally is one rule that each logger meticulously observes. A good foot locker, securely padlocked, also removes temptation and keeps everyone honest. Sanitary and bathing facilities are usually down the hall and shared.

Among the first questions a logger will ask about a camp is, "How's the grub?" Almost always, the answer is "Great!" With so many camps offering good and often superlative food, the show that skimps in this regard will soon find itself without loggers. Camp operators are aware of this so it is not at all unusual for the cook to be the highest paid employee, simply because no one has a greater influence on morale. Premium wages go to the cook who is not only capable of turning out the usual staples in fantastic quantities but also can come up with pastries considerably better than those mother used to make. Nowadays, the camp cook is liable to be "Mother." The traditional camp cook, more and more is apt to be a female, who brings not only that traditional touch to good food but also the ameliorating effect women usually have on a group of lonely men.

Although Thorne Bay was probably the largest logging camp before it became an incorporated city, there are others almost as large. The usual camp, however, is much smaller, often an isolated outpost where a few men spend months at a time removed from the population centers. These men are up at dawn, spend a hard logger's day in the particularly rough brush of Alaska and are in bed by dark, or much sooner. In these latitudes in high summer "dark" can come quite late and be followed by an early dawn so that sleep becomes a very precious commodity. Most of the men in a logging camp, nowadays, are family men who look forward to the weekend as a chance to get reacquainted with their wives and children. There is always the maverick fringe who believe that to be a good Alaskan logger they must relive the lives of the Washington and Oregon loggers at the turn of the century and what those loggers did to Aberdeen and Hoquiam is legendary! When those old-time loggers visited town after payday, it was to let off steam and, in this respect, this minority of Alaskan loggers is only following an old, and to him, hallowed tradition. Fortunately, this is a minority, conspicuous mostly by comparison with their more sedate brethren who are enjoying an outdoor barbecue with the wife and kids while these mavericks try to recreate the past.

Most of the legends about Alaskan loggers were born at the turn of the century, although the genre was alive and well as little as forty years ago. Because of the logging camp set up, a much larger than usual proportion of the men were single or living away from home. Weekends, the bush pilots did a land-office business flying capacity loads of lonely loggers to Ketchikan, Wrangell, Juneau, Petersburg, even Anchorage; any place, in fact, where they could get a drink not made with muskeg water and find a few amiable women.

There was a universal, well understood rule in effect eighteen years ago, and that rule has stood the test of time; it is still very much the rule. Raise all the hell you want or can take on the weekend, but show up for work Monday morning on schedule, sober and ready to do your job, or you'll be unceremoniously handed your time and a one-way ticket to wherever you were hired. Logging in Alaska, as everywhere else, is exceptionally dangerous, and entrusting one's life to someone whose reflexes are impaired by a massive hangover is a poor bet and one few men are willing to take. That means that Friday night, all day Saturday, and Saturday night into the wee small hours of Sunday are the time to howl, for those so inclined, and the howling is sometimes legendary! Every camp has its

Gildersleeve's float camp is large enough to have its own school, meeting hall and even a church. When the timber in this area is completely harvested, the camp will be towed by a powerful tug to the next location.

stories about a particularly wild Saturday night, some of which must be true, for such fantasies would be hard to invent. These Alaska loggers, the last of their kind, seem to have inherited the mantle of the wild and wooly timberbeasts who terrorized Aberdeen and Hoquiam on payday and added to their repertoire of hell-raising a few local tricks inherited from the Klondike Goldrushers. There's a lot of liquor in Alaska and they can't drink it all up on one weekend, but they can try. And if they don't succeed, at least they have the distilleries working overtime.

Unfortunately, this is the popular view, especially in the eyes of the urban dweller who has never had any contact with a real, live Alaskan logger outside of the pages of popular fiction. It is true that there are enough of these fringe characters still on the loose to perpetuate the fiction, but the truth is that this is a very small, conspicuous minority loath to accept the fact that the day–or night–for those shenanigans has passed, and they are an endangered species. Given the choice, any responsible operator would much rather hire a responsible family man who will show up for work Monday morning wonderfully refreshed from a quiet week end with his family, rather than some timber tramp who has demonstrated over the weekend that he is unstable and, as such, a poor bet to be part of an elite crew.

As for other pastimes, remember that Alaska is pioneer country, and traditionally this has been peopled with strong men and women who like them that way. A good part of it is still a rollicking, roaring, raw wilderness that is practically irresistible to a man with a lust for life

and whose blood sings in his veins: that's one aspect of Alaska that has changed very little, if at all. Many of the strong, handsome outdoor families that are so common up here resulted from some timber beast coming to town to do a little howling and there found a girl who not only could match him howl for howl but was also adept at taming him into a more-or-less docile house pet. There are magnificent women in Alaska: they have to be to keep up with the men.

The howling is a bit more muted nowadays than it used to be, mostly from a dearth of customers. Ketchikan has turned Creek street, the old redlight district, into a trendy office and shop complex which, with a museum of what used to be the town's leading brothel, still has a bit of the flavor of the old days, when Dolly, the town's leading madam, financed many a businessman after having relieved him of his payroll and his frustrations. Creek Street was noted throughout the district as the only stream where both the fish and the fisherman went upstream to spawn, but today it caters to the curiosity of the hordes of tourists pouring off the cruise ships like a swarm of lemmings. Other establishments in town seek to profit from the town's lurid past. A very civilized restaurant with superb seafood and service, Annabelle's, has as part of the decor of its quite impressive dining room a large portrait. If it is anywhere near an accurate representation, it is little wonder that the fishermen and loggers were so eager to go up the creek.

This popular stereotype is more than offset by the hundreds of family men who head home on the weekends for some home cooking and a little hunting and fishing with the wife and kids. There is even a camp, admittedly unusual, where grace is said before meals and a very successful timber operation is carried on supposedly without the aid of profanity. That proves it can be done, although connoisseurs of the art have always maintained it is necessary as chain saws. There are even those who maintain that the Alaskan logger's isolation fosters a certain inventiveness in his profanity which gives it a unique distinction. That may be so. I have heard tirades from hook tenders in Alaska that are as good–or bad–as anyone's, especially when the logs hang up.

Tough conditions breed tough men, and since Alaska's loggers work under some of the toughest conditions in the industry, they can justifiably claim to be the toughest loggers alive. Logging in Alaska is something that almost all loggers want to do, at least once, just to see if they can hack it. If they do, it becomes a bragging point for the rest of their lives.

First, consider the climate. Southeast is not too different from the Olympic Peninsula or Vancouver Island, but there are subtle differences that give it the edge in the misery index. Those other regions are no strangers to rain, but not the kind of rain that you get in Alaska. When it rains here, it does so for weeks on end, and the humidity stays at one hundred percent so that one is never quite dry. Cold, clammy clothes and the discomfort they engender become a way of life. In the summer, the "no-see-ums" are a living torment, and the fabled Alaskan mosquito comes into her own, rising in sibilantly singing hordes from the nearby muskegs so that every breath draws in a swarm of buzzing, stinging insects. The brush of Alaska is exceptionally thick and tough...just one more irritant to an already almost intolerable situation. In spite of all this, the timber gets cut, quite a tribute to the men who make logging one of Alaska's larger industries and proof positive that the Alaskan logger is indeed one very tough man.

A geographical feature that dictates Southeast's logging methods is the accessibility to water, as it was in the Puget Sound's early lumber years. The densest growths are usually within five miles of water and under two thousand feet in elevation. Since the Southeast is threaded with inlets, most of the timber is within the reach of water transportation, the most feasible method of getting it to the mill. For this reason, the first and most common method of logging was by A-frame. In this method, a couple of large logs joined at the top in an "A" formation were mounted on a raft large enough to support both the logs and a yarder powered by a large donkey engine. The far end of a line running perhaps a thousand yards ashore was threaded through a heavy block mounted on a tall spar tree with chokers attached to the butt rigging. The timber was cut so that it could be yarded directly into the water where the logs were assembled into large rafts towed by patient, powerful tugs, sometimes hundreds of miles, to the holding pens at the mill. It was a simple, and in its day, efficient way of logging; but it depended on finding a suitable site with the right deflection and timber. Ecological restrictions have since outlawed A-frame logging; but in several camps, there is an old retired A-frame looming against the sky, a picturesque

reminder of what used to be.

Another peculiarity of Alaskan logging, and one which has much influenced the logging methods, is the muskeg. The heaviest timber is on the islands and on the hills and ridges of the Coast range where the generous precipitation has a chance to drain off, while the poorest stands are on the coastal flats where the heavy clay soils hold the water, seemingly indefinitely. Since the air has a high moisture content, evaporation is very poor, and the collected water forms a shallow swamp, effectively inhibiting timber growth. The resulting open, grass-covered flat spots, often mistaken for a clearcut by the uninitiated, are surrounded by scrubby timber gradually fading into a heavier growth on the ridges. Muskegs can occur any place where water can accumulate, even mountain tops, and are a favorite haunt for fauna, from mosquitoes to moose. They are the source of the weak, tea-colored muskeg water so prevalent in Southeast, which looks as though it would not support a single self-respecting fish. Actually, muskeg water, which gets its color from leached vegetable matter, teems with fish and has vigorous devotees who claim it is loaded with vitamins and excellent for drinking especially if laced with generous quantities of whisky. Since the muskeg inhibits skidder-type logging, it sharply restricts the area that can be efficiently logged. A large part of Alaska's forest reserves, which in theory are available for logging, are actually not presently utilized, since they are of such poor quality. Anyone flying over Prince of Wales Island, the third largest island in the United States and a heavy timber producer, is struck by this fact. He is probably also impressed by the large number of dead cedars that stud the island. This is due to the fact that the island is at the northern edge of the cedar's range–there are practically none north of Petersburg–so the attrition rate in this area is very high. Cedar is not used in pulp production, but the better trees have a good market for siding; and the ubiquitous shake-bolt cutters, many of whom enthusiastically uphold the larcenous traditions of their craft, take care of whatever sound timber is left. If ever the need for this marginal timber should escalate, Alaska's forest reserves would at least triple; but, barring some technological advance that would make logging near a muskeg practical, so would the production costs.

Islands are so popular with Alaskan loggers because they offer beautiful timber with the added advantage of convenient water transportation. Some of the islands that were first cut over forty years ago are ready for another round of harvest, although regulations dictate a hundred-year regeneration cycle. The timber cut on Prince of Wales Island is regulated in this way, in what is intended to be a perpetual cycle of harvesting. Most Alaskan logging utilizes the high-lead system with a spar tree or a mobile metal spar. This versatile system is quite capable of handling any timber likely to be encountered including the occasional ten-foot Sitka spruce. It has a couple of major disadvantages: it requires a large amount of timber and a road must be built to it. In any timber operation road building looms high on the expense sheet, but in Alaska the cost of

Naukati Camp on Prince of Wales Island has a female camp cook who keeps her "Boys" very much in line, and also pampers them with that special touch to cooking that only a woman can bring. This is the flunky, who helps her do it.

road building is magnified by ecological regulations that specify that a road built anywhere near a muskeg must be ballasted with at least four feet of gravel or crushed rock.

Most of the gravel in Southeast seems to be in the bottom of streams used by salmon as spawning beds, and so is patently unavailable. The other alternative is to make one's own gravel...the hard way. A convenient ledge is drilled, loaded with high explosives, and shot. The rock resulting from this blast is run through a portable crusher; loaded into dump trucks and used as the basic material that is extending a network of quite respectable and certainly sturdy roads spreading to all parts of Prince of Wales Island. These "borrow pits" as they are called, are spotted all over the island; and most of them are busy. A long-range advantage of what is a high first cost is the fact that these roads are integrated into the island's highway system and will still be there when the regrowth is ready for yet another harvest.

There was another method of logging being tried out when I first visited Kake Island. A beautiful patch of spruce and hemlock had been by-passed because it was on an ecologically sensitive slope that would not stand up to the usual high-lead method. An innovative logger, Pat Soderberg, had imported a huge, onion-shaped, helium-filled balloon and with the help of this improbable skyhook was wafting those premium logs off the hillside with no damage to the sensitive slope. Pat's balloon must have run out of gas, because no one seemed to know anything about any balloon logging going on. That's a shame. It certainly made good pictures!

Among the most common of the frustrations Alaskans must face is the fact that large parts of Alaska are virtually inaccessible except by air. The airplane is the lifeline of Alaska, and that contributes vigorously to the high cost of living in this state. A six-year-old Alaskan child may have never ridden in, or even seen, a taxi but since infancy has been riding in bush planes that seemingly land anywhere in this sprawling state. The old De Havilland Beaver and the rattling Grumman Goose, old planes that will land on the proverbial heavy dew, bring prices today several times what they did brand new, and they are never junked, just rebuilt over and over again. They are beautifully adapted to a state laced with water and fit well into the requirements of a people who care nothing for show but place a high premium on performance. Float planes are everywhere in Alaska where there is water, and the skill of the bush pilot is one Alaskan story that is only occasionally exaggerated. One thing that hadn't changed a bit in eighteen years is the fleet of antiquated float planes that serve Ketchikan. They still rattle and shake as though they were coming apart, and they still are the most superbly adapted plane for this type of country that the mind of man has ever devised. A native Alaskan boards one of these planes with aplomb, secure in the knowledge that the old Grumman will get him to his destination intact, even if the plane is a decade or two older than he is. Out-of-state visitors are not quite that confident, and many a plane takes off only after the passenger has liberally fortified himself at the nearest bar. There is an air service in Ketchikan that has cornered eight of the last De Havilland Beavers in existence and refuses to speculate what they will do when those planes finally get beyond the repairing skill of even the innovative Alaskan mechanic. A Southeast without the Beavers, Otters, and Gooses that are so much part of the landscape is unimaginable. There are still old time bush pilots who fly "by the seat of their pants" although their number is diminishing, replaced by young whipper-snappers who depend on instruments to tell them where they are. The satellites have made all the difference in the world in Alaskan bush flights, especially in the interior; and most planes now are equipped with electronic navigational devices that can pinpoint a pilot's position to within ten feet on the Earth's surface. It was not always so. I well remember a flight with a bush pilot from Thorne Bay to Petersburg. Within two minutes of takeoff, we were enveloped in cotton-wool clouds which were so thick that the only way I could tell which way was down was to check the direction gravity was taking me. The pilot didn't seem to be even slightly worried, although his navigational instruments seemed to consist only of a compass and a wristwatch chronograph. After what seemed to be hours of flying by dead reckoning, my pilot said, "This should be it," and let down through the clouds, there, directly underneath us, was Petersburg. I tried hard to make believe that I had expected it all along, but I'm not quite that good an actor.

Later, I was told that my pilot was either a whiz at dead reckoning, extremely lucky, or there was some other means of navigation aboard that I never noticed. Personally, I lean toward that first assumption. The

You have to be tough to log in Alaska. The weather can stay like this for days on end, but the logging goes on anyway. Loggers will tell you "If you can't take the heat, stay out of the kitchen," "If you can't take the rain get out of the Southeast." This is at Mud Bay on Prince of Wales Island.

usual bush pilot in Southeast to this day flies by ground contact. He is aided by an uncanny directional sense, very necessary in this land where compass deviations can be really wild, an occasional homing signal from a radio source of known location, a good map and an amazing memory for landmarks in a vast land. The fact that they make thousands of flights every year with only an occasional mishap is as high a testimonial to their skill as anyone could require.

There are still a few of these mavericks operating in the brush, and they are still there because they perform a vital function. Imagine the frustrations of a logger who has broken a part that he cannot repair and must depend on the services of a bush pilot to make contact with Air Alaska on which the part would be air-freighted from Seattle. Without that pilot, what would normally be a three-hour breakdown can easily become a three-day layoff during which time his costs keep mounting, but his production nosedives. For this reason, the Alaskan logger keeps his equipment as simple and as rugged as he can buy, steering away from the more sophisticated machines until they have proved that they can withstand hard usage with a minimum of upkeep. Today's sophisticated, computer-oriented machinery is establishing a beachhead and, as familiarity with it adds a bit more confidence, will undoubtedly achieve more widespread usage. For the time being, the Alaskan logger seems to go by the credo of "Keep it simple, keep it rugged, and if it ain't broke, don't fix it." Alaskan loggers have always favored efficient machinery of massive design that can absorb the pounding of the rough Alaskan terrain and which,

if it ever does break down, can be repaired by an ingenious mechanic with a good hoist, a welding outfit and the indispensable haywire. Field repairs are routine, usually undertaken by a traveling mechanic who is in constant radio contact and whose well-equipped repair truck can usually handle anything but a major breakdown. The larger camps have machine shops that can handle almost any trouble. At the northern tip of Prince of Wales Island, one logger solved his repair problems with typical ingenuity by converting a surplus World War II LST (Landing Ship, Tank) into a floating camp complete with bunkhouse, cookhouse, recreational room and a thoroughly equipped machine shop. This self-sufficient "wanigan" had the added advantage of mobility; it could be moved with comparative ease to the next logging site, but that, of course, is also true of any other floating shop.

Because transportation by water is so much a part of the Alaskan scene, it was only natural that the floating camp would evolve. With a few notable exceptions, they are usually small because everything–bunkhouse, cookhouse, recreation center, repair shop–has to be floated on a raft of huge logs. For many years the Blacky Neilly camp was a standout, for one interesting variation. Mrs. Neilly had a floating garden; and that patch of vivid green, easily spotted from the air, became a landmark for bush pilots who would casually drop in for a cup of coffee and some sprightly conversation. Some idea of the amount of work this garden entailed can be gathered from the fact that every spadeful of earth had to be carried to its floating bed. Those who have gloried in her tasty salads, fresh from the garden, will tell you that no matter how much work it was, it was worth the effort, especially since most of the effort was Blacky's.

Not all floating camps are small. The Gildersleeve camp is large enough to not only serve as home for over eighty loggers and their families but also to have it own gymnasium, recreational center and even church. Kids growing up in this camp learn to wear life preservers anytime they are outdoors and to play, often tethered with a long nylon line, in a front yard consisting mostly of salt water. A large camp, such as this one, has an air of permanence about it, even if, when the timber has been cut near the site where it is temporarily moored, it will be towed by a large tug to another location with equally superb scenery.

One of the things that has changed in the last eighteen years is the communications between Alaska and the Lower Forty Eight. Years ago, telephone communications were by radio, and anyone who happened to chance upon the frequency being used was in effect listening in to a big party line. One of the stories going the rounds at Thorne Bay those many years ago was the conversation overheard between a Seattle woman and her husband who had been three months in an Alaskan camp. Unless he came home that weekend, she told him, she was going to a party; and, with half of Southeast listening in, she detailed just what sort of a biologically interesting gathering it

promised to be. It's not nearly as much fun nowadays with satellite transmission giving you a clear but totally private conversation.

Working in Alaska may have its problems, but it also has its advantages, so that many loggers prefer it to any other place. High on the list of attractions is the unsurpassed hunting and fishing the state affords, a very potent lure for dedicated outdoorsmen, and these are legion in the ranks of the loggers. Another lure is the high wages usually paid as a premium for working in admittedly rough surroundings. A logger who saves his money, stays in camp and minds his business can come home with a nice little grubstake...often the legendary nest egg it takes to graduate from the ranks of the hired logger to that of small-time gyppo, but that would have to be in the Lower Forty Eight. Becoming a gyppo in Alaska takes dollars commensurate to the size of the state, as well as to the problems that must be overcome to be your own boss and have a crack at the legendary pot of gold at the end of the rainbow. Staying in camp isn't all that bad, if you can stand the loneliness. It offers a congenial atmosphere, people with like interests, the best food in Alaska and a sort of forced savings plan, since there is no place to "Blow 'er in" as yesterday's timber beasts describe it.

Alaska is a land of surprises, not the least of which are the two large plants making dissolving viscose pulp from the high-grade hemlock and spruce that are

This Grumman Goose is probably older than most of the people boarding it and, in spite of its venerable age is superbly attuned to the needs of Alaskans.

The heavy clay soil of Alaska holds water almost indefinitely, so shallow swamps accumulate even on mountain tops. They are the favorite haunt of Alaskan fauna, from mosquitoes to moose.

endemic here. The larger plant at Ward Cove, some eight miles north of Ketchikan, uses timber cut in southern Southeast on a one hundred year regeneration cycle, although the timber in this part of Alaska regenerates much faster than that. The hundred year figure was chosen as an average for the whole Tongass National Forest, the largest in the United States, which covers practically all of Southeast, and which has, within its vast stretches all kinds of reproduction rates from very slow to very fast. In theory, only one percent of the commercial forest is cut each year, so that the yield would be perpetual. In actual practice, it doesn't quite work out that way. In the national forest, only one percent is cut each year: that's the law. On the privately held native lands, there is no such requirement, with the result that more than one percent can be, and usually is, cut.

When the Alaskan native Settlement Claims Act was finally passed after long and skillful negotiations on the part of the native tribes, 23,000 acres of land, most of it in forests but some also rich in minerals, was awarded to each native village. Some of them consisted of as few as four people at the time the act was passed but swiftly swelled to the required minimum of twenty-five. The natives were not allowed to sell this land but otherwise were given a relatively free hand as to the disposition of the timber wealth it contained. As a result, large clearcuts are visible on native lands where

the timber has been cut to realize some immediate cash, so that much more than one percent of the native timberlands is cut in one year. All of the sawmill-grade logs from native lands are sold as unprocessed logs in the Japanese, Korean and Taiwanese markets.

On Annette Island, a native owned and operated state-of-the-art sawmill is leased to Louisiana Pacific and processes logs cut by that company on Forest Service lands. The mill residue is chipped and transported to the Ward Cove pulp mill by barge. As private landowners, the natives have an advantage over other Alaskan loggers: no one operating on national forest lands can export a log cut in Alaska, not even to the rest of the United States, unless it is a species not needed locally.

The ecological restrictions that have clamped such a stranglehold on logging in the Lower Forty Eight have also had their effect in Alaska, although this region has been spared the spotted-owl controversy. Instead, the Alaskan equivalent is salmon. Any stream that has a viable salmon run is supposed to be unaffected by logging. That means that the water may not be silted or warmed by removal of tree cover. To that effect, a "leave strip" is left along the banks of a salmon bearing stream. It is...and it promptly blows down. Windthrow is definitely a problem in Southeast, as the citizens of Ketchikan will attest. In 1968 a hurricane packing 125 MPH winds practically denuded the mountain behind

A black bear caught out in a muskeg, and desperately trying to get away from that oversized mosquito buzzing overhead. He made it!

the town, although someone not familiar with that fact would have a hard time seeing that for himself. Regrowth around here is so rapid that the whole slope is once again clothed in the green of new trees.

That same rapid regrowth is evidenced on the big island where Ketchikan Pulp gets most of its raw material. Revisiting areas where logging was in progress eighteen years ago is a problem in frustration, because these areas simply do not look like areas that have been comparatively recently logged. All regrowth is by natural seeding, and it is so thick that areas under management are routinely thinned by removing eighty percent of the tree cover. There is little chance that the pulp mills will run out of raw material, even though huge log rafts carrying as much as 2,000,000 board feet leave the Thorne Bay sorting area with monotonous regularity. It is good that they do. The huge mill every year turns 220,000,000 board feet of spruce and hemlock into snow-white dissolving pulp, which, because of its purity ,commands a premium price on the world market.

Inevitably, there have been changes in the logging industry in Alaska in the last eighteen years. Some, such as closer observance of sensible ecological rules are definitely good, but these improvements are often more than balanced by new rules and regulations that are seemingly spawned by legislators who have no idea of the chaos those regulations will produce when implemented. The ecological bandwagon on which everyone was climbing in the late seventies and early eighties has become a juggernaut that leaves a trail of destruction in its wake, and its effects are felt even here on America's last frontier. For example, the Tongass National Forest, the largest in the United States with an area of 16,9000,000 acres if it were administered according to the original mandate governing the uses of the national forests, would be more than adequate to supply the lumber needs not only of Alaska but also of a good part of the whole United States. Instead, one-third of the commercial timber volume on the Tongass is locked up in wilderness preserves that very few people will ever get to even see, let alone use. Another third is dedicated to uses other than logging; and the final third, the only part that might possibly pay its own way, is theoretically open to logging. To top everything off, because of the hundred-year rotation plan, only about one-tenth of one percent of the Tongass will ever be harvested in any given year. It's like giving a man a thousand dollars then telling him he can spend only a dollar a year. Apparently the idea that those mountains, muskegs and marginal timber would have been ideal for a wilderness preserve in exchange for some of the good timber is an idea whose time has not yet come.

The Alaskan's reputation for toughness has been well earned, and the present breed of loggers are every bit as tough as the pioneers who first founded this industry in the forty-ninth state. They are each surrendering a bit of their cherished independence to present a unified front to the more restrictive regulations, secure in the knowledge that if they can convey some idea of the problems that confront them, reason and good sense will prevail and they can once more go back to the job they love best of all–doing their logging, Alaskan style.

CHAPTER V

NO TIME FOR TEA, B.C.

There is a clause written into the union contracts of British Columbia loggers that may seem very odd to Americans: breaks must be given for morning and afternoon tea. Gracious British traditions remain very strong in the Canadian portion of the Pacific Northwest and the tea break is an old and time honoured ritual, much like the American mid-morning pause for coffee; but tea-time...for loggers?

Lest the popular American concept of the rugged Canadian logger be irrevocably shattered, it is only fair to report that this right is seldom implemented: the loggers are much too busy getting on with the job.

Like California in the United States, British Columbia is a province that can boast of having it all: strong men, absolutely smashing girls, scenery beyond compare, and some of the greatest stands of timber on this or any other continent. The forests have been a source of wonder ever since the first white man gazed in awe upon them and are so vast that, especially with intensive management, they will be supplying the timber needs of the province and a good part of the country for untold generations.

Geography does not recognize national boundaries and so it is no wonder that the topography of British Columbia is an extension of the coastal range of mountains extending northward from California clear up to Alaska. The climate, moderated by the warm Japanese Current, is moist and mild; conditions which almost always foster forestation. British Columbia, especially along the coast, can boast of as much a degree of forest cover as exists on the North American continent.

When the famous British explorer and navigator, Captain James Cook, cut spars for his ship on Vancouver Island in 1778, he made a discovery that was to affect British shipbuilding for over a hundred years; at least as long as sail still ruled the seas. Up to that time, New England white pine had been the preferred material for masts and spars. The better trees in the British colonies routinely bore the King's broad arrow as a sign that they had been selected for service in His Majesty's navy. The spars Captain Cook cut on Vancouver Island were of arrow-straight Douglas fir and much stronger than the previously favoured pine, which was getting to be in short supply anyway due to a bit of armed insurrection then rampant in New England.

Captain Cook may have been the first European to log in British Columbia, but he was centuries behind the natives who had long ago discovered that the straight-grained, easily worked cedar of Vancouver Island and the mainland was ideal material for beautifully crafted dugout canoes and totem poles. Using crude stone and shell tools, they crafted masterpieces of woodworking art and thus rank as the first users of the region's quality timber.

In choosing this area as their homeland, the tribes were showing very good taste. Even today, this glorious island and equally beautiful mainland evince a beauty that qualify them for a very high rating on any knowledgeable person's list of the most beautiful spots on Earth. From the mainland, Vancouver Island appears as a string of verdant hills floating on an azure sea, the result of a cataclysmic upheaval that raised mountains and submerged valleys, leaving the peaks as islands. It is a gorgeous land of mystery and promise, a mystery that is being solved, and a promise that is being fulfilled.

Even to this day, there are places on Vancouver Island that have never felt the footsteps of a white man, or even of Indians. When I was exploring the island eighteen years ago, there were places on the island's western tip where apparently no one went; there were no roads into the area, and no amount of money or cajoling would tempt the Indians to take me into those vastnesses...and I was smart enough not to attempt it on my own. The reason? "That's Sasquatch Country," an Indian who feared neither God nor the Devil told me. "No one ever goes in there." Obviously, this man's lack of fear of the supernatural did not extend to the elusive Bigfoot, whose existence is not even slightly questioned by the people living close to this area.

The area may not be settled or even explored, but in this day of satellite photos, there are shrewd men in Vancouver and Victoria who have a pretty good idea of what is in there. The island's full potential for commerce, recreation and industry is now being recognized, so that it is fairly bursting at the seams with development. A beautiful little grove of trees just outside of Nanaimo that eighteen years ago was one of my favored camping spots is now well within the city limits and has become a huge shopping mall. Largely because it is such a beguiling place, with probably the best climate in the whole of Canada, it seems that everyone yearns for a home on Vancouver Island, with the result that subdivisions spring up overnight and paved parking lots cover land that only yesterday was growing trees. In spite of this explosion, the land is so superbly adapted to tree growth, that practically every inch of Vancouver Island that isn't paved or under active cultivation is covered with the forestation that, ever since the province's inception, has been its chief source of wealth and has patently shaped its destiny.

Vancouver Island's mild, if somewhat moist climate,

Cathedral Grove on the Port Alberni highway is one of the top tourist attractions on Vancouver Island. An old, decadent grove, it nevertheless has an air of majesty that makes repeated visits imperative.

On the Upper Columbia, at Bush River, a pair of boom boats herd salvaged cedar from the backwaters of Mica Dam. So impervious to rot is this aromatic wood that even years after it is cut, it is still usable.

encourages a dense forestation that very quickly attracted the canny businessmen who provided the lumber that built picturesque Victoria and busy, bustling Vancouver. While the soil is not quite as rich as the bottomlands of Washington and Oregon, it is entirely adequate to grow the trees that have made lumbering the prime industry of this region. The southern part of the island was pretty well logged off by the turn of the century, and the rough and ready practices of the day had left their mark, even though a benign climate and forgiving soil have once more clothed the land in a carpet of living green. Mature second growth was being cut in this area eighteen years ago. Now the best silvicultural practices are being observed so that the time cycle for the next crop will be appreciably reduced; and the land is being treated with the respect it deserves.

The earth's upheavals and depressions that wracked Vancouver Island produced peaks and valleys. When the melting glaciers of the latest Ice Age raised the sea level they formed the fjord-like inlets that lace the west coast of the entire island with ribbons of water. As in most places where water is present and timber grows, those were the first places to be logged, since water transportation was the only feasible way to get the logs to the mill. The mills were therefore built close to water to take advantage of this comparatively easy transportation. The wisdom of this practice is obvious; but one mill, at Port Alberni, denied a waterfront site, chose to defy tradition and build its mill inland. That mill closed soon after it opened because it "ran out of timber." Within sight, there were stands of virgin

timber that would have been ample to meet the mill's needs if it could have been transported to the work site. Without water transportation, it stood untouched because it was out of the range of the slow-moving bull teams that supplied transportation other than water. It is no wonder that the mills and the towns that grew up around them were almost always adjacent to water.

Port Alberni is such a town. It grew up around a mill opened in 1861 by London-based interests and prospered with trade to Peru and Australia. Today, as it was eighteen years ago, it still has its economic roots in the forests around it, with busy sawmills and pulp plants still exporting forest products to the nation and the Pacific Rim. It exploits its strategic and highly scenic location at the head of a long inlet by catering to an ever increasing flood of tourists, but lumber and logging are still the solid underpinnings of its prosperity.

Relics of the early-day mills line Alberni Inlet, mute testimonials to the labours of the men who founded the great industry which subsists on this verdant land. What stories those gaunt, burnt skeletons could tell! How many cities have they helped build? How many lives were influenced by the events that took place here? Now, they stand by Alberni Inlet as charred monuments to a by-gone age, their timbered foundations slowly succumbing to the eternal tides and haunted by the shades of men who laboured to hew an empire from the forests. It doesn't take much imagination to people these ruins with ghosts, especially on nights when wild winter storms whistle mournfully through the pilings and in their wild banshee-like wail echo the whine of the bandsaw and the rumble of the headrig.

Logging on Vancouver Island saw its glory days with the advent of the steam logging railroad. Freed from the constraint of logging only those stands adjacent to water transportation, the rich stands a few miles inland were tapped and soon levelled. Most of the present-day logging roads follow an old railroad grade, and travellers on those roads are often confronted with trestles, where some impossible problem had been routinely solved with the materials at hand and typical logger ingenuity. While the railroads usually followed the easiest grade, taking advantage of every grudging advantage the terrain offered, they often ran into problems that required some imaginative and highly unorthodox engineering. Some of those sturdy old trestles still stand and probably, even today, would still support the monstrous loads of the age of steam.

The railroad loggers understandably first worked the stands of easiest access, bypassing the more rugged areas of the island's mountainous spine. This area of steep mountains and deep lakes supports some of the finest timber on the island and, with modern methods of transportation, is finally accessible. This is the area presently being logged, and every year logging roads penetrate deeper into what had been an impenetrable wilderness. Even veteran loggers, surfeit with scenery, are moved by the region's beauty and treat it with respect, so that its beauty will be as quickly restored as the best available silvicultural practices available will permit.

In spite of the damp climate, forest fires are not unknown on Vancouver Island and are even more common on the drier adjacent mainland. Nevertheless, because of the generally damp climate, the debris of logging rots so quickly that fire danger is much less than it is in the drier forests to the south. Natural regrowth is rapid and probably would be entirely adequate but is always supplemented by replanting that immediately follows a harvest. Areas that were under harvest when I visited them eighteen years ago now have tree cover so dense that they are in present need of a thinning, even though regulations say that this is at least seven years in the future. Those new forests show every sign of being very superior new growth, with high productivity and little or no waste. They have been grown under the best possible silvicultural care and are a wonderful example of what can be achieved through intensive forestry. There is no question but that Vancouver Island will yield more and better wood in the future than it did when its output was restricted to old growth. For the time being, however, the old growth is bearing the brunt of the harvest. The second growth that followed the first cuttings of a hundred years ago in the southern portion of the island has been largely used up, and the demand is greater than available supplies of suitable second growth can supply. Mills in the southern portion of Vancouver Island are often dependent on old growth trucked in from the central part of the island.

The island's southern part was the first to be logged, around the turn of the century, and so had the heaviest concentration of superior second-growth timber. Most of this has already been harvested, but every year a certain amount of second growth comes of age and is utilized. Supplemented by shipments of trucked-in old growth from the central part of the island, it is sufficient to keep the mills of Duncan and Ladysmith operating. The locally cut logs are rafted by way of the Nanaimo Lakes to the mills at Ladysmith and Nanaimo. The Franklin River district, a bit farther north, is ready for a second harvest. The general trend of logging is toward the northern part of the island, but I still wonder if they will ever get Indian loggers to go into the Northwestern corner that they still tell me is off limits as "Sasquatch Country."

Not far from Parksville, on the island's east coast, stands a majestic if somewhat decadent grove of old Douglas firs. Traversed by the Port Alberni highway, this grove was originally owned by MacMillan Bloedel Ltd., Canada's largest lumber firm, who very wisely deeded it to provincial authorities as an easily accessible, highly aesthetic example of an old-growth forest. It is a majestic, awe-inspiring grove and deservedly is one of the major tourist attractions of southern Vancouver Island, every year playing host to thousands of appreciative visitors, many of whom are paying the grove a repeat visit. However, a forester, or a person with a discerning eye would see that this wonderland is actually a dying forest. The trees have reached and exceeded their peak so that every year there is actually less wood in Cathedral Grove because the rate of attrition from bugs, fungus or the accumulated diseases of old age far exceed the rate of growth. The average visitor doesn't know that: all he sees is a majestic old forest which serves its purpose much better as an aesthetic attraction rather than as the source of inferior lumber. Even a decadent forest has about it an air of majesty that readily triggers a feeling of reverence in most people. It is only natural to speak in hushed tones in Cathedral Grove.

Could there be some atavistic memory in people that makes them regard ancient groves as temples? After all, for thousands of years the people of Europe worshipped in groves. Can it be that some vestiges of these memories are still imprinted in our genes and trigger a feeling of reverence when we approach a grove of ancient trees? The Druidic influence is still very strong in people of English, German and Gaelic ancestry; and to this day millions of naturists see in a tree the representation of a god. Could this be the reason why people instinctively try to preserve some grove of ancient trees? Are we subconsciously fighting against the desecration of a church? Whatever the reason, there is no doubt that large groves of ancient trees have a very profound effect upon people, which is the reason that Cathedral Grove is such a tourist and local attraction.

The grove is highly impressive, either as a scenic attraction or from a lumberman's viewpoint. In spite of the fact that the grove is way past its prime, there is still a tremendous board footage in those old trees, even if the amount of waste would be equally impressive. Its value in beauty far exceeds its value as lumber, for most of those beautiful big trees are also growing beautiful big conks, so that the estimate of cull logs now runs as high as eighty percent. The general public, not generally knowledgeable in the logger's trade, would be shocked if Cathedral Grove were ever to be logged and even more shocked when they saw the proportion of seemingly beautiful big logs that would be left behind simply because there would not be enough sound wood in them to make it worthwhile to move them out of the woods. The public reaction would undoubtedly be one of condemnation for the logger who would seemingly be wasting a valuable resource. Very few would stop to think that a logger works on such a slim margin, especially in a show with this much waste, that he would not leave any log in the woods that would pay its way out.

Cathedral Grove is doing its very best job simply by being a majestic though decadent old forest; a place where the Druids could still perform some of their gentler rites. That gentle singing sound may, after all, be the pipes of Pan calling to some woodland nymph; if it could happen anywhere, it would most apt to be here, in Cathedral Grove.

The east coast highway was quite a bit narrower eighteen years ago and deadheaded at Kelsey Bay. Now it is mostly freeway and paved as far as Port Hardy. The place names Victoria, Duncan, Ladysmith, Nanaimo, Courtenay, Qualicunm and Campbell River echo the island's British heritage with a strong streak of Indian thrown in. A really venturesome person with a good car, or preferably a four-wheel drive, can drive over much of this island that, on a map, doesn't have a road, for there is a network of surprisingly good logging roads reaching even to the edge of Sasquatch Country...and it is only a matter of time till even that remote vastness is penetrated, though not by Indians. A word of warning: British Columbia log truckers all believe that their huge rigs have only two speeds: fast and faster. Since the roads are not provincial roads, loads carried by log trucks may be monstrous. Huge made-in-British-Columbia trucks with eighteen-foot bunks are common and, even when loaded to capacity, are driven with an élan not often seen this side of Le Mans.

Provincial regulations regarding logging roads are very strict and rigidly enforced. As in Alaska, the cost of constructing the road to a logging site will be by far the greatest expense involved, but it does have a positive side. The roads must be deeply ballasted with rock, even if that rock must be obtained by blasting a ledge and crushing the debris. The mainline roads resulting from these strict requirements are wide, well graded and drained and are easily integrated into the province's road system once the logging in that area is completed. Even if they are abandoned, the stoney core is still there and, if it acquired a crop of new seedlings, is easily reopened by ramming a bulldozer down its centre. This is very much appreciated if you should happen to be, for instance, on your way to a forest fire.

Among Vancouver Island's unique features are its stands of candelabra cedar, a tree which grows quite extensively on the coastal areas. This strange-looking tree is distinguished by the vertical branches into which the tree forks at about two-thirds its total height. Many of these trees appear dead, or at least very sick, as they lift seemingly lifeless fingers toward the sky; but this gnarled plant yields some of the prettiest wood obtainable anywhere. It is very much in demand by Japanese cabinet makers who fashion exquisite furniture from it and who will pay almost any price for prime wood. In the days before power saws, many cedars were felled from springboards to avoid the excessive bell of the tree. These ten-foot-high stumps are often as sound today as when they were cut and are much sought after by entrepreneurs with modern power tools, who are often rewarded with perfectly sound and marvelously grained wood. There is some candelabra cedar on the Olympic Peninsula, but Vancouver Island seems to be its favoured range.

Summer is the best season on Vancouver Island, and it is during this time that logging activity reaches its peak. To take advantage of this good weather, a unique method has been devised to stretch the work day: mobile light towers, each with its own diesel powered generator, are strategically located around a logged area and the yarding operation goes on around the clock. The lighting is teamed up with a grapple loader and a voluble spotter using a walkie-talkie. The spotter gives explicit directions to the grapple operator, who cannot see the log he is picking up yet often manages to do so with uncanny ease. This method of yarding is not restricted to night time; it is often used routinely during the day and, with a good team of spotter and operator who have achieved a good rapport, often can equal the production of the more common team using chokers.

Canada, and especially British Columbia with it's long history of involvement in the forest products industry, has become largely self-sufficient in producing the tools used in the trade. The trade mark of Canadian equipment is that it is usually simple, easy to repair and incredibly rugged. This is simply a reflection of the terrain in which it will be used and reflects the rugged independence of the Canadian logger who wants to be beholden to no one. While he gets along very well with his American brethren and will gladly exchange information about better logging methods with them, he also likes to be in a position to be offering the advice and not just simply taking it. This feeling is well illustrated by the flood of sound, well-made Canadian equipment that is dominant not only in British Columbia logging but has also established a strong beachhead in the American industry. Skidders, towers, loaders, chain saws, delimbers, all made in Canada and of top quality, attest to the fact that when it comes to either logging or producing the tools whereby it is done, the Canadian loggers and engineers take second place to no one.

For many years, with its advantage in transportation, Vancouver Island was the leading logging area of British Columbia; but the mainland, with its tremendous reserves of outstanding timber, has lately come into its own. The province contains 584,600 square kilometres, an area greater than Washington, Oregon and California combined and, with the exception of a few dry spots in the interior, is completely covered with trees. While not all of this is commercial timber, enough of it is to make British Columbia potentially the largest producer on the West Coast, as it once was. The coast from Vancouver to Prince Rupert, as anyone who has ever sailed up the Inside Passage will attest, is covered with a solid belt of fine timber and it extends inland for hundreds of kilometres. Douglas fir predominates on the drier areas, while the wet northern coast supports a mixed stand of hemlock and cedar. Then a mixed stand of spruce, pine and balsam fir takes over to be succeeded by the primarily lodgepole pine and spruce stands of the central interior. There are a number of transitional zones where different species grow in joyous abandon, often in greatly mixed stands, for the province's diversity is such that almost any species of softwood will find a favorable micro-climate and proliferate there. All of the important forest areas, except the extreme inaccessible northern portions, have been placed under a sustained-yield management whereby no more timber will be cut than will be replaced by growth. Still, the province is so vast, its forest reserves so large, that in the untapped forests that constitute this reserve, millions of trees grow to maturity only to die, unused by man. At Powell River, the world's largest newsprint plant daily devours a mountain of pulpwood, while nearby, an island of solid limestone is quarried to feed the pulp mills. The resources of this sprawling land have hardly been tapped, but some innovative ideas are already surfacing aimed at utilizing those resources to their full potential. Eighteen years ago, a beautiful grove of naturally seeded Douglas firs near Powell River had been thinned to an even-aged stand. Those mature trees have since been harvested, but in a unique manner. Only the largest trees that had attained their full potential were taken, and the rest of the thinned stand allowed to grow for yet another few years. Growth has been so rapid that it is difficult to realize that this park-like stand of trees already has had better than half of its total growth removed. The experiment is slanted toward finding out whether the added expense of multiple harvests is justified by the additional growth and superb quality of the remaining stand. Thinning and fertilizing are standard procedure in Canadian forests, but there are also some very progressive minds at work to better an already good product. The experiments could very well have a positive result not only for Canadian silviculture, but also that of the whole world.

Another experiment was also underway near Nanaimo in 1973 where an already-established grove of second-growth firs had been thinned to an even-aged stand. Growth was so spectacular that within ten years of the last thinning, when commercial-size wood was removed, the stand had regained all the wood removed in the thinning and was burgeoning at an unprecedented rate. The thinning produced an open, park-like stand much frequented by horsemen and hikers, but there was never any doubt as to the final disposition of that park-like stand. Signs posted around it forewarned people that this was a crop which would be harvested in 1982, and there were certainly people who, seeing a loss of beauty, bemoaned that fact. The new planting on this land of superior, fast-growing trees is quickly regaining that beauty and promises to surpass the appeal of the original grove, but its owners are taking no chances. Signs around that property tell visitors they are welcome, and to enjoy the stand, but that in the

The Logging Museum at Duncan features a steam railroad tour of the premises on antique cars pulled by a genuine lokie. Here it whistles for a crossing, something it probably never did when every ounce of steam was needed to pull a load of logs.

year 2042: it will be harvested to be supplanted by a new forest. This is an idea that has proven its worth. Signs posted next to a beautiful stand of trees reminding the onlooker that he is viewing a crop at least prepares the general public for the harvest. No one would expect a standing field of corn or wheat, no matter how beautiful, to be exempt from harvest; but trees seem to be different. Part of the shock is alleviated by the announcement that the tract will be replanted and the example of the present new forest in all its beauty may even convince the thinking person that a managed forest with predictable beauty is better than one left to Nature's often brutal selection through survival of the fittest...only.

The forest wealth of British Columbia is one of the motivating forces that is causing the province's spectacular economic growth. Only a few years ago, Prince George, in the interior, was a small town of five thousand inhabitants, a jumping-off place for Dawson Creek and the Alcan Highway. In 1964, a six-hundred-tonnes-per-day sulphate mill costing sixty-five million dollars was proposed, followed in 1965 by an eighty-five million dollar sulphate pulp and kraft paper mill. The plentiful spruce and lodgepole pine of the area finally had a good market and the boom began. Ancillary industries using the products of the mills or supplying raw materials to them sprang up, so that when I visited the city in 1973, it was a modern, bustling community of forty thousand inhabitants in which it was difficult to find parking space. The parking must be even harder to find today, for now Prince George and the adjacent area has a population of over a hundred thousand...and

Along Alberni Inlet, the ghosts of mills that supplied lumber to rebuild San Francisco and Tokyo slowly succumb to the ravages of a tireless tide. Not many of theses are left, and it's a shame. They make such good photos!

it is growing! It is still dependent upon the forest wealth around it, even if log trucks now routinely travel a hundred and fifty kilometres or more to feed the hungry mills with high-grade lodgepole pine and spruce.

Another example is the town of Mackenzie, before 1965 a stretch of moose pasture and today a thriving town of fifty-five hundred. In that year, the British Columbia Forest Products Co. Ltd. put in pulp mills and began to energetically develop the region. Mackenzie was so well adapted to this industry that today the investment tops two hundred million and a thriving little metropolis booms along on land that only a few years ago was raising only spruce trees and mosquitoes.

British Columbia's vast resources, coupled with her geographical location puts her in an enviable position to service the burgeoning markets of the Pacific Rim and Alaska. Indeed, British Columbia forest products sell very well in the United States because they are of high quality and offered at a very competitive price. World trade is nothing new to these hard-driving businessmen; much of the lumber that rebuilt San Francisco after the 1906 earthquake and fire and Tokyo after the 1923 tremblor was British Columbian fir, much of it donated by generous Canadians, but mostly purchased by grateful Japanese. The latter experience evidently set a precedent, for Japan today is a major market, one that demands the best but is also willing to pay a commensurate price.

The fortunes of the export business have varied considerably, depending largely upon the position of the United States lumber industry. With the advent of the free trade agreement between Canada and the United States, British Columbia lumber was one of the first items to flow into the large market to the south, sometimes to the considerable discomfiture of an already beleaguered American industry; and the flow continues, so that a prosperous future can safely be predicted. British Columbia has the trees, the men who can harvest them, and a solid economy based upon a renewable resource–wood. As in the United States, there is considerable anxiety over how changes in political or environmental policies may affect the industry; but generally the optimism and hard work that have built this region prevail. A land this blessed can only prosper.

A glance at the map of British Columbia will note vast empty spaces in the upper two thirds of the province. This is where the vast potential of this magnificent land is located and in this region the greatest development of the province will take place. It is a largely roadless area; but when the roads finally do come, it is safe to say that they will be logging roads that will have penetrated this wilderness to tap its forest riches. They will have been so well built that when they are integrated into the provincial road system, it will be largely a matter of paving an already well built roadway. There is a modern highway between Prince Rupert on the coast and Prince George in the interior; and this route is already serving as an artery of progress, as manifested by the many small towns that have sprung up along it. The area is rich in timber; and in each one of these centres, the basic industry is lumbering. Tourism is only the frosting on the cake.

On the province's east side, the road from the south to Prince George serves the interior and connects at Dawson Creek with the Alcan Highway. This scenic road, now paved after a fashion, traverses over sixteen hundred kilometres of enthralling scenery and really gives one some idea of how vast the fibre resources of British Columbia are. There are only a few settlements to vary its panorama of rivers, lakes and mountains. Mile after interminable mile of woodlands, often, especially in its northern reaches, they are of stubby lodgepole pine and stunted spruce. In its southern reaches, there are quite respectable stands of poplar. One of the many surprises this intriguing highway presents is the unexpected sight of a modern pulp plant, belching steam miles from the nearest town and seemingly unaware that it is an outpost of industry set in the middle of a wilderness. Those scrubby stands would be scorned further south, but they represent fibre, and there are myriad of square kilometres of it available; that lonely mill is a harbinger of the future, for some day this otherwise useless reservoir of wood must perforce by tapped. The key to utilization is transportation, very expensive in this area; and that probably is the reason why that mill was built here. It is more profitable to transport a finished product than the raw material from which it is made.

For the most part, the inland forests of British Columbia, at least those not adjacent to a settled area, follow their age-old cycle. They sprout and somehow survive the brutal contrasts of long, harsh winters and short summers crowded with long sunlit hours, so that their growth is a slow, painful struggle to maturity. This sub-standard wood will someday be utilized as the valuable resource it is, as ever increasing demands make the utilization of new supplies of fibre mandatory, but its current fate is predictable: it will fall prey to the perennial forest fires that sweep the sprawling interior, and, more often than not, are simply allowed to burn themselves out.

Ninety-five percent of British Columbia's forests are Crown Lands, harvested under cutting permits issued for a specific time and subject to rigid controls. For this reason, it behooves operators cutting on public lands to very carefully stay within the guidelines laid down for them by the Provincial Forester. That cutting permit is not ownership and may be cancelled for cause, with a host of eager operators ready to snap up any permit that becomes available. For that reason, block cuts and other operations on Crown Lands are all cleaned up very well and the ground quickly prepared for replanting. As long as the permit holder abides by the regulations, that piece of land may be farmed by it indefinitely, a necessary situation in an industry that is presently implementing projects its planners probably will not live to see completed. Nobody wants a piece of unproductive land, especially since under the influence of a mild climate and generous rains that tract could be producing new forests and continuing dividends indefinitely.

Speaking of a mild climate while alluding to logging in British Columbia is not completely accurate. While this is the rule in the most spectacular logging areas, Vancouver Island and the coastal mainland, it is not by any matter or means the whole logging picture of this vast and infinitely varied province. British Columbia has vast inland forests and half a dozen mountain ranges where the weather is anything but benign. Inland, from Prince George and Quesnel to Kamloops and Revelstoke, the spruce, balsam, lodgepole and bullpine forests are harvested on a year-round basis under conditions that can best be described as brutal. There is every kind of logging carried out in this region but considerably more skidder logging than there is on the coast where the terrain and the size of the logs effectively inhibit this type of harvest. The coastal logger routinely deals with huge trees and so generally uses the high-lead method, which can effectively handle the largest tree that might be encountered. Since trees three metres in diameter are not unusual, his equipment must be scaled to their size, which means that it is heavy, expensive and subject to breakdowns from the tremendous loads it must wrest from the woods. Twenty-five millimetre chokers are common, and the logger's problems are cut to the same scale. The coastal logger has one advantage over his inland contemporary; he may be wet most of the time, but he is seldom in danger of freezing. His inland counterpart would not take a bet on that score.

The inland timber is generally smaller, although a spruce a metre thick is not uncommon. When a tree is felled, a rubber-tired or crawler-type skidder hauls the tree to the landing, effectively delimbing it in the process. At the landing, the remaining limbs are trimmed off and the tree bucked to a suitable length. More and more, this operation is done by a computer-equipped delimber which not only does a neat job of removing the limbs but also infallibly cuts the log to the right length and stacks it into the proper pile so that it can easily be loaded onto a truck for transportation. More and more, especially in the smaller timber of the interior, the operation is becoming mechanized with one operator of an expensive faller-buncher doing the work formerly allotted to four men.

The mechanized equipment is expensive, but it still represents a smaller investment than that of the coastal logger and has the advantage of being able to operate even in the ferocious winter of the inland forests. In fact, winter is often the preferred logging season because the snow not only protects the frozen land but makes hauling easier. Streams are spanned with ice bridges that only occasionally drop a truck into an ice-cold river. The crew adapts to the conditions and works, if not comfortably, at least efficiently under conditions that almost anyone else would label intolerable. No one familiar with British Columbia would ever make the mistake of assuming it is a beautiful never-never land with all looks and no muscle. It is a tough land and the men who harvest her forest bounty are tough men, yet they always seem to have the time to be polite, helpful, and cooperative; and here I speak from personal experience. They may not have time for tea, for they are busily building a Canadian empire based on wood and hard word; both, in this magic land, renewable resources. Anyone who has fallen under the spell of British Columbia's magic and her likable people discovers that his or her thoughts stray there quite often and always with a feeling of warmth, respect and sincere admiration.

Few countries of the world can face the twenty-first century with the equanimity of Canada. It is a country which has only begun to realize its potential; and when it does, it will occupy, in the community of nations, a place even more prestigious than it does today. It's natural resources are vast, and barely tapped; and in first place on that list is its forest reserve, if only because it is infinitely renewable. Canada is a forest nation; over two-thirds of this vast land are in forest cover, and this priceless resource has been assigned to the custody of dedicated men and women who are determined that the riches with which the nation has been endowed will be wisely nurtured. British Columbia alone contains more than half of all the coniferous wealth of Canada, and the regeneration of that forest wealth deservedly has a high priority on the provincial agenda. For the next fifty years, the bulk of the demand for Canadian lumber must be met by old-growth forests, and while these reserves are vast, they are not limitless. Like all other responsible timber operators, Canadians must look forward to the time when the forest products needs of their country will be met by regrowth timber grown under managed conditions as a crop. In this respect, British Columbia is already well on the way. Their system of tree-farm permits, which make replanting and the best possible care of the land mandatory, predicates that when the nation celebrates its two hundredth birthday, wood products will be in profusion and, more than likely, British Columbia will be leading the way.

British Columbia throws a spell over the visitor, a spell as willingly received as it is effortlessly cast. It is a spell compounded of the misty, salt-laden air of the Inside Passage and the cool bracing winds that have just lately passed an Arctic-Circle glacier. It is the roar of the Frasier River digging its deep canyon ever deeper and the long magic twilight of the Midnight Sun reflecting off ice-topped mountains. It is the blossom-laden Okanagan Valley and the lure of the thousand uncharted lakes. It easily blends the floral charm of Victoria with the cosmopolitan bustle of Vancouver, while only a few kilometres away thrives the ageless magic of cathedral-like groves and of new forests redolent with the promise of tomorrow. Often called the Sunset Province, British Columbia is the last place in Canada to see the sun go down. But as one faces east, looking across a vast space of thick, rich, verdant forests, the morning sun is also rising.

Logs ride the mill pond near Ladysmith. These have been towed sometimes for as much as a hundred kilometres from the centre of Vancouver Island.

A tree goes down in the Kelsey Bay Division of MacMillan Bloedel, Ltd. The central parts of the island supply most of the timber cut on Vancouver Island.

The operator of this grapple cannot even see the log he is grabbing but is simply following the directions given him by the spotter with the walkie-talkie. Production by this method is surprisingly good.

On the Fraser River, a hard-working tug smelling of hot oil and spilled coffee pushes and tugs its ungainly load of logs toward the river's mouth and the mill.

Majestic Mt. Rainier towers over an arboreal empire. Timber has been cut on the flanks of this mountain for over one hundred years, and loggers are now taking the third growth of trees, in an ever renewable cycle.

CHAPTER VI

WASHINGTON, EVERGREEN STATE

There is a local legend that explains why the Olympic Peninsula looks the way it does. When God was building the Cascade Mountains late in the day, so the story goes, some huge boulders accidentally slipped from His hands and tumbled wildly over this huge thrust of land. When He returned the next day to set things right, He noticed that the haphazard arrangement had a rustic charm unlike any other of His works. The rocks were a little bare and unfinished, but with a covering of trees and moss and crowned with a carapace of ice and snow, He mused, this place would have considerably more than a passing charm. As frosting on the cake, He covered it with a thick layer of fog, made the trees grow to heroic proportions and so the Olympic Peninsula was born.

The Almighty might have been indulging a bit of whimsy, or maybe He was feeling very generous the day He created the Olympic Peninsula, and included the whole state of Washington, for few places on Earth are as munificently endowed with a variety of environment as is this beautiful place. Within its confines one can find rain forests or deserts, snow-capped volcanoes or seemingly limitless prairies and a range of climate suitable for the growth of everything except tropical plants.

Washington also goes by the soubriquet of "The Evergreen State," and it comes by this appellation honestly. From the rain-soaked Olympic Peninsula, to the Cascade range and across the northern forest belt to the east-side Blue Mountains, the land is covered with a seemingly solid cover of forest. Better than half of this very large state is covered with trees in commercial size and quantity; in fact, one out of every six trees harvested in the United States grows in Washington. Blessed with the right amount of rain from the nearby Pacific and rooted in the rich soils bequeathed to it by its recently quiescent volcanoes, Washington was predestined by Nature to be a bountiful provider of forest products; and this fact has had a paramount influence in shaping the economic and social conditions of the land.

The western-bound logger who first came to Washington through northern Idaho felt quite at home in the forests of the eastern part of the state. After all, they had leveled pine forests in Maine, Wisconsin and Minnesota; and these forests were not that much different, albeit a bit on the large size. Even the eastern slopes of the Cascade mountains were taken in stride, although the lordly ponderosa pine must have evoked murmurs of admiration from even the most blasé faller. It was when they topped the Cascades and saw their first full-sized Douglas fir that they stared in stunned amazement and wondered what in tarnation was in the local liquor that could produce such illusions.

The "illusions" covered the western side of the Cascades in such size and profusion that it was inevitable that they would become the economic foundation for the growth of the region. Up to this time, white pine had been the standard by which all lumber was rated. In the Douglas fir of the Pacific Northwest, a new and much better standard was found. Strong, straight-grained, with superb milling and construction qualities, Douglas fir was hailed as the perfect timber tree...and the Northwest was covered with such prodigious quantities of it that the old-time loggers firmly believed that "We ain't never gonna be able to cut all this timber!"

The first sawmill to take advantage of this seemingly limitless supply was built by the Hudson Bay Company near Vancouver in 1827, when the Union Jack still waved over this territory. It was a primitive factory, and its product would hardly be acceptable today, but it was better quality than that produced by the sawpits that up to this time had been the sole suppliers of finished lumber. It started an industry that built a state and firmly planted Washington's economic roots in the products of its forests. Small sawmills began to rise around Puget Sound and, with increased competition and demand, the quality of the product became such that the Washington-milled lumber became the standard by which all others were judged. Henry Yesler's mill, established in 1852, helped build Seattle and Henry's not inconsiderable fortune. Pope and Talbot, a present-day forest-products firm with a very proper Maine background, established its first Washington sawmill in 1853 and is still using the same site. The completely-owned company town of Port Gamble, today a priceless gem of highly-prized, century-old homes sitting on immaculately maintained lots with a water view, is a direct copy of East Machias, Maine, except that the proper Congregational church in that town somehow became Episcopalian when it reached the West coast. The whole town is a National Historic Site; and the mill, whose pervasive buzz can be heard as a muted background sound all over town, has a long waiting list of people willing to take a cut in wages, if necessary, simply so they can get to live in one of those old hillside homes and be part of the extended family that is Port Gamble, for employment by Pope and Talbot is a prime requirement of residence. The large, modern mill at the water's edge still operates on the original site and now feeds on timber in its third round of cutting. It

At Port Gamble which is a copy of the Maine town of East Machias, the proper Congregationalist church in that town somehow converted to Episcopalian when it reached the West Coast. This Pope and Talbot owned town is a veritable gem, and on the National Register of Historical Places.

A slack line operation yards in small second growth timber on Weyerhaeuser land near Headquarters.

This land has already been harvested and replanted, and the new plantations show fresh and green in this photo. This is on Weyerhaeuser land near Castle Rock.

ranks as the oldest sawmill in continuous operation in the nation, well beyond the hundred-year mark, and employs numerous descendants of the original workers who first opened up this country at this same mill over a century ago.

Port Gamble was only one of many lumber towns operating on Puget Sound. Port Ludlow, Port Townsend, even Seattle, far down the Sound, all fed a seemingly endless stream of picturesque lumber schooners transporting finished lumber to the burgeoning cities of California, and later, mine props and timbers to shore up the galleries of the Silver Lode pits that fed three hundred million dollars into San Francisco in one roaring, tumultuous decade. When that demand cooled down a bit, it was more than offset by a demand for Northwest lumber that extended to the Hawaiian Islands and even China. When a ship from Alaska docked in Seattle in 1897 with "a ton of gold," another wild gold rush ensued. The smart money, remembering the lessons of the Forty-Niners, stayed in Seattle, supplied the Stampeders and acquired their riches supplying lumber to Alaska without suffering chilblains

By 1900, Washington was the nation's chief producer of lumber, a distinction it held until the vast stands of Oregon came into full production. Lumber was firmly established as the paramount industry in the Pacific Northwest and the regional economy was firmly based upon it. Demand was for flawless lumber and, since the supply seemed endless, that demand was met. Huge old growth trees were felled, and often only one cut that would produce clear lumber without a single knot or

blemish was the only part taken. Waste in those days was appalling; logs were left in the woods that would today have plywood companies wildly bidding for them. With the advent of the steam yarder, the "glory days of old-time logging" began. Those days, however, had their darker side. Little or no thought was given to preserving the ecology. Huge logs were dragged through the woods with the force of elemental battering rams, flattening everything in their path, leaving behind scenes of carnage that are hard to believe. Old pictures of logging sites resemble nothing so much as battlefield scenes from World War I after a heavy shelling.

Much of the public image of the present-day logger dates back to those "golden days of logging" which in retrospect were nothing of the sort. It was an age of brute force applied without consideration to some of the loveliest scenery in the world, and it sowed a bitter harvest that is being reaped even today. Worst of all, it is being applied to a generation of loggers who, if anything, decry the waste, carnage and inefficiency of that age more than anyone else, because no one knows better than they that it could have been avoided.

This is all hindsight; but at the time, it seemed the proper way to do things. Today, we know that those old-time loggers who thought "We ain't never gonna cut all this timber" were wrong, dead wrong, and can only find excuses for the old extremes by realizing that this was the thinking of the times. Nevertheless, the excesses of old-time logging, especially here in Washington State, are still flung in the face of an industry that has long ago mended its ways but is often still tarred with the dirty brush of yesterday. It deserves better than that, if only in the name of fairness; but the process of education can often be a slow and painful one. Nevertheless the process has been started, and the message it carries is that the present-day logger is as eager to maintain a viable environment as is the most ardent environmentalist, in fact, even more eager. After all, his very livelihood is dependent on it.

The broad chain of the Cascade Mountains sustains the major part of the logging in Washington State, although the broad coastal plains are once more heavily wooded. These were the first areas cleared of timber, and practically all the land that was not devoted to farms or settlement is once more covered with timber; this time arrow-straight second and third growth. This is the timber that is being cut at this time, and since the trees are in their prime, not their dotage, there is very little waste. What there is is being vigorously attached by an industry which has found out that total utilization is not only good ecology but also good business.

The Cascade Mountains, running in a hundred mile wide belt from the Canadian border to the Columbia River, are the scene of the major part of the logging in a state largely devoted to that activity. This grand range of mountains contains magnificent stands not only of mature trees but also extensive stands of second growth that have sprung up since this area was logged at the turn of the century. From rugged Mt. Baker in the north to broken-topped Mt. St. Helens in the south, the whole area is crisscrossed with logging roads, logging operations, logging towns and vigorously growing new forests.

Some of this country is so steep, so inaccessible, that even the steel fingers of the old railroad loggers could not reach them and remains today as an example of how the forest looked before man and his needs put in an appearance. These remote, pristine areas more and more are being incorporated into national parks and wilderness preserves that will be forever closed to logging, although some more accessible areas are coveted by both loggers and preservationists, and thereby is engendered much of the conflict which increasingly makes the logger's life more complicated.

Actually, the second-growth timber is so much better adapted to modern logging methods that more and more of it is filling the demand for wood products. There is still some old growth being logged; there is still a demand for the type of wood it produces even if it is from an overly mature forest past its prime, and it occupies land that would be more productive if replanted with a new, genetically improved forest. Nevertheless, the industry is unquestionably gearing up for the day when all the demands for wood will be met by second and third growth, both natural and that grown on tree farms. There is no doubt that the Cascade mountains

A self loader unloads a turn of small timber secured from thinning operation near Forks. This thinning is called "commercial thinning" because the wood taken from it pays the cost of the operation.

grow trees superlatively well! There are places in the Cascades where loggers are taking the third growth off the land, and planting the fourth generation of trees that these acres have borne since the advent of the white man to this region.

On the eastern slopes of the Cascades, the fir forests gradually give way to mixed stands of fir and pine, interspersed with western larch. As the rainfall diminishes in the rain shadow of the Cascades, so does the character of the forest change, until it yields to the pine stands that are characteristic to areas of lower rainfall. The ponderosa pine is the unquestioned king of this domain, and few monarchs have a better claim to rule than this magnificent, cinnamon-colored tree. A question that is often asked by people new to this area who are familiar with the smaller, darker-colored bull pine which is common throughout the eastern part of Washington state is, "What is the difference between ponderosa and bull pine?" After all, the needles are identical. Could it possibly be a mutation of the same tree? The answer is quite simple. Ponderosa is simply a bull pine in a favored location that has attained sufficient maturity to have shed its lower limbs and whose bark has changed from a dull, dark brown to a beautiful cinnamon color. The tree is usually tall and straight and mills into beautiful lumber that brings a premium price for casings, window frames and shelving.

The eastern slopes of the Cascades are clothed in a wildly mixed stand with Douglas fir predominating closer to the summit and gradually shading off to a mixture of larch and fir in the middle sections. This mixture is especially visual in the autumn when the needles of the deciduous larch turn color and proclaim their presence with splashes of vivid gold. As the rain shadow of the Cascades prevails, the stands gradually turn to pine and eventually disappear into the sunbaked plains of Central Washington.

The eastern slopes of the Cascades are largely federal and state land, so the stringent ecological strictures that have lately been imposed on the timber industry are definitely a problem, and one that is getting larger every year. Yet, somehow, in spite of the mountainous paperwork that is part of every timber sale, the yards of the busy mills at Naches and Yakima, which largely feed off the largess of the Cascades eastern slopes, are well stocked; and the industry somehow muddles through. It is a sign of the stubbornness and dedication to hard work that are so much a part of the logger's makeup. This is a rugged breed, determined to survive and continue a way of life that is so engrained that he will pursue it as long as there is breath in his body.

Besides growing superlative fruit, Yakima has another claim to fame. Right after World War II, its largest lumber mill, the Cascade Lumber Company, merged with an Idaho-based sawmill, the Boise-Payette Lumber Company, to form a new corporation: Boise Cascade. Blessed from the very beginning with sharp, venturesome leaders, it quickly blossomed into an industrial giant that easily qualifies as one of the largest and best-managed corporations in the Northwest and indeed in the nation. Although it was a late comer in the race for desirable timber lands, it quickly acquired forest lands that supply a large part of its timber requirements, all under intensive management that has earned it an enviable position in the industry. Partly through necessity, because the best land west of the Cascades had long since been bought up by the pioneer companies, Boise Cascade has acquired large holdings in the then largely neglected Intermountain Region and proved beyond a shadow of a doubt that this is indeed first-class logging country.

The northern part of the state, east of the Cascades, supports a vigorous forest growth, mostly of pine, although isolated pockets at higher elevation grow some very respectable Douglas fir. When I first saw this region and compared it to the lustier growth on the western side of the Cascades, I thought that the trees on the eastern side were appreciably smaller than the giants I had been photographing on the west side of the mountains. Eighteen years later, I must confess that much of this disparity has vanished. Maybe it is because there are more second-growth trees being harvested, or maybe it is that the second-growth on the eastern side of the Cascades is now as large as that being harvested on the coast. Whatever the reason, there is a vigorous logging industry going full blast in the eastern part of Washington State; and this activity constitutes a very considerable segment of the state's economy. The Colville Indian reservation is heavily forested and timber is one of the tribe's most valuable assets, especially when one considers that a good part of the 200,000,000 board feet of timber that this region produces annually comes from Indian lands.

The scenic Blue Mountains, beginning near Pomeroy, extend along the eastern side of Washington state and deep into Oregon. Heavily wooded with a mixture of Douglas, white and noble fir, spruce, western larch, lodgepole pine and ponderosa, the area has been extensively logged since the first days of white occupancy. On a map, there is only one paved highway crossing the Blues north of Interstate 84; but a knowledgeable person who can read a Forest Service map would have no trouble at all crossing these mountains on a network of logging roads, some of which have been in use for over a hundred years. The original timbers from which Fort Walla Walla was constructed in 1857 were cut in the Blue Mountains and hauled to the fort site by ox-drawn wagons, gouging ruts that are still visible along a route known as Government Mountain Road. Most of the old growth has been cut but the new growth has achieved a size equal to that which originally covered the mountains.

Another section of excellent tree-growing land that is seldom mentioned in current statistics is the region consisting of Cowlitz, Clark and Skamania counties. This was the site of the Yacolt Burn which in 1902 was rated as one of the largest forest fires to ever devastate the state. Recurrent burns in 1918 and 1929 pretty much destroyed the area's productivity, so that it has been the site of considerable rehabilatory activity. This has paid off and handsomely, for this area is once more covered with a forest of mature timber and supports a vigorous logging economy. The Yacolt was once one of the finest forests in the state and it is once more claiming its due. Nature is forgiving, otherwise the

A Weyerhaeuser forester checks the progress of a plantation established in the Blast Zone on Mount St. Helens after the great eruption of 1980. The new plantations are doing beautifully, clothing the gray landscape with a coat of verdant foliage.

A graphic example of the difference between managed and an unmanaged environment, land in the foreground was replanted after the volcanic eruption of 1980. Land in the background was not.

New plantations in the Blast Zone at Mount St. Helens. These plantings are five years old and already better than head high.

tree species we know would have long ago disappeared from the face of the earth.

Probably no place on Earth illustrates that fact...or just how destructive Nature can be...than the Blast Area at Mount St. Helens. For years this mountain reigned like a queen over one of the most densely wooded, old-growth forests in the state. Renowned for its symmetrical beauty, reflected in an azure lake of unbelievable perfection at its base, it was often referred to as America's Fujiyama. Artists and photographers often traveled into the wilderness surrounding it to portray its calm serenity.

That serenity masked a restless heart. Mount St. Helens had already experienced one eruption since white men came to the Northwest, and it is a well-known geological fact that any one of the Cascade Mountain peaks, each and every one of them a dormant volcano, could erupt at any time. This one gave plenty of warning: a series of minor earthquakes gave notice that magma was swelling under the peak and an ominous bulge on the mountain's flank, growing larger by the day, was watched with increasing trepidation not only by professional geologists but by the hundreds of loggers working in the forests within thirty miles of the peak.

When the eruption finally came on May 18, 1980, at 8:32 on a Sunday morning, it was with cataclysmic violence that stunned even the professional vulcanologists accustomed to this most awesome of natural events. An earthquake of magnitude 5 triggered one of the largest landslides in recorded history, and 1300 feet of the mountain's height was either blown to dust or cascaded into the Toutle River valley below. The massive landslide exposed the liquid core of the mountain and caused a laterally directed blast which leveled over 150,000 acres of private, state and federal forests, much of it virgin old growth. The pyroclastic blast, consisting of incandescent gas, pulverized mountain and superheated steam, was so powerful that, even many miles away, whole forests of huge trees were laid over onto their sides as though they had been matchsticks. To add to the devastation, the volcano poured out such fantastic quantities of ash that the whole denuded landscape in places was covered, sometimes to a depth of several feet. It was a scene right out of Dante's Inferno, except that here the dominant color was gray; the gray of an ubiquitous cover of gritty, tenacious ash that stretched clear to the horizon.

Eleven years later, the predominant color is still gray, at least in those parts of the blast area that have been set apart as the National Volcanic Monument, which is preserved in its natural state of devastation. In this area, thousands of acres are covered with a thick carpet of fallen trees all pointing in various directions from the volcano. Over the years, the bark has mostly weathered away from these trees leaving them a silvery gray, a fit complement to the gray surface of the earth. What is left of Spirit Lake is approximately one-third covered with logs, again gray, that are still floating but in the process of becoming waterlogged till they sink and add their leachates to the water. Given the marvelous recuperative powers of Nature, Spirit Lake will in time undoubtedly recover as will the land; but in the most highly impacted areas, that time could be decades, even centuries away. Nature eventually heals its own wounds, but in its own time, and Nature can afford to be profligate with time: it has an unlimited supply. Man, however, does not.

If ever there were a good example of the relative values of a managed rather than a natural environment, that example is furnished by the desolation of the National Volcanic Monument which was left in its natural state and the adjacent Weyerhaeuser lands which were the recipient of immediate and thorough man-made aid. The managed land has a vigorous growth of growing trees and is well on its way to again being a productive, beautiful and useful forest. It didn't happen by chance. The Weyerhaeuser Company sustained a staggering financial blow in the Mount St. Helen's eruption. Not only were 36,500 acres of variously aged timber badly damaged, but 26,000 acres of young trees were destroyed and an additional 5,500 of meadows, streams, and reforested land severely impacted. The mudflows that followed the eruption effectively wiped out or severely damaged three logging camps, miles of railroad and logging roads and practically all the bridges in the blast area. Damage to equipment alone was in the many millions of dollars, but the Company counts its blessings: fortunately, the blast came on a Sunday when no company woods crew were working. The loss of 57 lives to the volcano is a tragedy, but it would have been infinitely worse if it had come on a workday: there usually were many more than that working in the impacted area, and few could have survived a cataclysm of this order.

The dust had literally not yet settled before Weyerhaeuser began its salvage efforts. Ruined roads into the area were reconstructed, and an around-the-clock race against time began to salvage whatever was salvageable from the ruin of what had been one of the most productive tree farms and forests in the state. It was a scene of such utter desolation that only a logger, and one ever tougher than usual, would dare to tackle the problems it presented.

Fortunately, more than 1000 tough loggers were willing to give it a try, even if they had to write the book on salvaging as they did the work. Regular, steel saw-chains were supplanted by carbide-tipped chains which were changed as many as four times a day as they bit into logs that had gritty, hard siliceous ash driven into them by the cyclopean forces of the volcanic blast. The Green Mountain mill, almost completely isolated by the mudflow that had come roaring down the North and South Fork of the Toutle River, became the staging area at which 600 truckloads of logs were unloaded every day. The Longview mill, the ultimate destination of those logs, got to be even more adept at changing bandsaws as the gritty logs, often with particles of stone imbedded into them, were sawed into useful lumber. The operation was essentially completed by November 1982, by which time 850,000,000 board feet had been salvaged, and 20,700 acres had been cleared of fallen trees.

Along with the mature trees, 26,000 acres of young plantation trees had been destroyed. The Company was therefore faced with the task of completely replanting its holdings in an area where no one knew whether or not a seedling could even take root. Fortunately, the test plots that were almost immediately established indicated that the seedling not only would grow but in some cases at a better than average rate. The hard crust of the volcanic ash had to be penetrated and the seedlings planted in mineral soil. Often this meant digging down through volcanic ash that was so fine that respiratory face masks were required for anyone working in the blast area in any operation that would disturb the dry dust.

The ash cover actually acted as a kind of mulch, sealing in whatever water penetrated. The roots of the new seedlings greedily fed on this trapped source of moisture, and the trees GREW, and GREW, and GREW! By 1987, 18,400,000 seedlings had been planted on over 45,500 acres. Some of those first plantings, when I saw them in May 1991, were over thirty feet high. Nature will in time heal the wounds of the area left in a natural state; but, by the time the first extensive greening takes place, the managed forest next to it will already have produced usable wood from the first commercial thinning and be well on its way to the first harvest as a completely normal tree farm.

Logging in Washington goes on generally all year round with some seasonal fluctuations. Summer sometimes sees a shutdown especially during a bad fire season, but since this coincides with good vacation weather, no one gets overly upset over a work stoppage except maybe some superintendent behind on his production quota or a logger intent on keeping up his payments. Autumn is usually the best season: by then the bugs have settled down , the black wool underwear with its ever-present itch has not yet been donned and, until the late seasonal rains set in, the weather is ideal for logging. Winter does not usually suspend logging. In the eastern part of the state, with its predominance of skidder logging, it is even the preferred season.

In the spring, high water and the breakup of roads close some operations; but generally loggers tough it out in heat, cold, snow or mud and accept it all as part of the price that must be paid to get the logs out.

A special atmosphere hovers over the small towns of Washington's timber belt: Darrington, Forks, Morton, and Randle to name only a few. These are towns where the work ethic reigns supreme. Energy and enthusiasm are common; but lately even these optimistic people are beginning to wonder when the largely urban populace of the state will begin to realize that the good life they live is rooted in a utilization of natural resources and so begin to support movements that will guarantee access to those resources. The whole lifestyle of these towns is geared to forest products: if you need to have a chainsaw overhauled, there is no better place anywhere to have the work done, for in these towns the job will be done by men to whom this tool is an everyday part of their lives; and it will be done expertly. However, a word of advice from someone who has been there: the timber towns are a good place for an outsider to act very politely and not try to impress the natives with his position or importance. The people of these timber centers are accustomed to

judging a visitor by their own standards; and according to these, he may come up wanting. If, on the other hand, he shows that he can meet the local standards of achievement, no one will find more help and friendliness than he will.

Washington is headquarters for one of the nation's largest forest products concerns. Near Federal Way, the Weyerhaeuser Company conducts its worldwide enterprises in a modernistic building that blends into a wooded landscape, complete with swans and ducks swimming peacefully on an adjacent pond except when an occasional marauding eagle stages a lightning raid. Long a leader in forest research and reforestation, the company established the nation's first tree farm, its Clemons Tree Farm near Montesano in 1941, and has seen the idea grow into a system that is now standard in the industry. Weyerhaeuser's research and nursery facilities are state-of-the-art, as befits a company with a dominant position in the industry. When Frederick Weyerhaeuser came to the Northwest at the turn of the century, "Dutch Fred" embarked upon a vigorous campaign of acquiring forest lands, some already clothed in standing timber, and also large tracts that had been cut over by other companies and then, according to the custom of the time, surrendered for taxes. The policy has paid off handsomely, for today Weyerhaeuser owns over one and a half million acres of actively growing forests in Washington State alone with additional large holdings in Oregon. All the land is under intensive management with the result that Weyerhaeuser is in an enviable position compared to most companies. It is not tied to dependence on federal or state owned timber for its operations. This company is one of the last to run its own logging crews: its holdings are extensive enough that it can, and does, maintain permanent crews on a year-round basis. Not too surprisingly, it is also a favorite target of preservationists. The company has shown a willingness to listen to any reasonable demands but lately the demands have become so outrageous that even a company that wants to get along well even with groups not always too friendly to it is showing a resistance that is based on its determination to survive. Frederick Weyerhaeuser was a strong man, and his heirs have not only inherited his business acumen but also a strong streak of the determination that took their ancestor to a dominant position in the industry. A company as big and well-managed as Weyerhaeuser can be a redoubtable adversary, and one that preservationist's would be wise to approach with caution. It may be a gentle giant but one that it would be most unwise to provoke to anger.

Washington's magnificent medley of glaciated mountains, wooded valleys and sun-washed deserts make a strong appeal to any one exposed to it, especially if the exposure is prolonged for any length of time. Whether a person is penetrating its verdant rainforests, where the sunlight slants through the trees in green-gold sheets, or threading his way through the columned awesomeness of an old-growth fir grove, the magic is there. Lately, there has been a new and welcome addition to that magic. The visitor can now walk through beautiful new forests that have grown up in his

Loader equipped with a computer-directed cutting head which delimbs the small timber being worked here, cuts it to size and stacks it.

own lifetime, and which in their youth and vigor exemplify the progress that have been made in the industry in only a few decades. An appreciation of this splendor entails special obligations, since that splendor could be obliterated through misuse, and it is much too beautiful to be destroyed. Fortunately, this spectacle is the special concern of foresters who not only appreciate this wonderland but are dedicated to giving a good accounting of their stewardship.

As long as they do, the annual spring miracle which is the rebirth of life will gladden man's hearts; and Washington will forever remain the Evergreen State.

A high-lead show is the basic logging method of the big timber country. Centered around the mobile metal spar, it is an expensive but highly efficient way of yarding big timber.

In the Blue Mountains of Washington, a rubber-tired skidder equipped with multiple chokers drags the felled log to the landing, effectively denuding the log of branches in the process.

CHAPTER VII

OREGON, HIGHBALLER'S HEAVEN

OREGON!

The very name is evocative of greenish surf crashing into precipitous headlands, eternally snow-capped mountains towering over lush woodlands and some of the most mind-boggling scenery to be seen on this or any other continent. The natural beauties of the state are so well known that they embody everything that is majestic and scenic on the West Coast, but has another attribute, one not nearly as well known. This magnificently-endowed state is also the country's leading producer of lumber and plywood and is second only to California in the total value of its forest products.

Back in the days when the tides of colonization were surging westward, "Oregon" meant the whole Pacific Coast north of San Francisco. It was the subject of glowing reports by government scouts and explorers intent on developing this land and claiming it for the United States as a logical development of the "Manifest Destiny" policy that was so popular at this time. The majority of Americans had been won over to the idea that the United States should extend from the Atlantic Coast to the Pacific littoral and that every effort should be made to achieve that end. The acquisition of the Oregon Territory, in those days of a rather prickly national pride, was therefore pretty much a matter of upholding the nation's honor.

It was a magnificent land, and the United States was not the only sovereign power that coveted it. At Fort Vancouver in Oregon Territory, Dr. John McLoughlin, the Hudson Bay Company's indefatigable factor, presided over an empire of fur trappers and traders in the shadow of the Union Jack and was busily consolidating his hold on the territory with the view of making it part of Canada rather than of the United States. A very able and energetic administrator, he was quick to see the potential in the forests all around him and established a sawmill near Fort Vancouver, thus laying the foundations of what was destined to become Oregon's leading industry.

The coming of the American missionary, Dr. Marcus Whitman, to Wailatpu in 1836 demonstrated the feasibility of the Oregon Trail, for he had brought his lovely blonde wife with him a good share of the way in a wheeled vehicle. It also demonstrated something else: where a simple wheeled vehicle could go, so also could a United States Army cannon; so hegemony over the Oregon Territory was more than a wishful dream. By 1842 settlers began arriving; and in the next five years, the trickle became a flood which, only briefly interrupted by the Indian uprisings of 1847, secured the land for the United States and made it a state in 1859.

Few places in the world had more or better building material for the homes needed by the new settlers. In New England, the settlers had heard tales of Oregon's fabled forests: the tallest and most beautiful groves in the East were often compared to the legendary trees of Oregon. But just as the first settlers in American were overwhelmed by the trees of the New World in comparison to the Old, so settlers coming into Oregon Territory were stunned by what they found. Most of the yarns about the West were told by promoters who spread their verbal colors with such a wide brush that the settlers could be forgiven if they had expected to find trees similar to the ones they knew back home and not the super trees described by the early scouts into the new lands. To their astonishment, this was one story that not only had not been exaggerated but actually understated, simply for lack of adequate comparison.

Compared to a grove of mature Douglas firs, the largest and tallest trees on the East Cost are downright puny. The western side of Oregon is covered not only with Douglas firs of tremendous size but also supports forests of cedar, hemlock, spruce, white fir and larch, most of them grown to heroic proportions. It is an area well adapted to natural monocultures, and some of the pure stands are vast; but it also supports mixed stands of equal size.

About forty percent of Oregon is covered by forests of commercial size, although mere statistics can only hint at the grandeur of this forestation. Oregon has one of every five trees growing in the United States today; and with the success of the tree-farm system, that proportion is fattening every year. This is one place where mere words, no matter how evocative, fall woefully short; one has to see this country to realize just how heavy and extensive this forest domain really is.

Oregon-born loggers take this rank growth pretty much for granted, assuming that it is the norm, until they see other forests. Then they wonder how anyone else can take pride in logging what to them seems a downright anemic growth. Other regions may have as much rain or good soil, or even a warmer climate, but seldom do growing conditions come together as fortuitously as they do in the Beaver State. This is absolutely superb timber-growing country, and the state comes justly by its high ranking among timber producers.

The forestation starts at the western edge of the continent, usually a mixture of spruce, cedar, hemlock and fir, fed by the ubiquitous rain and fog and drained by the short but spectacular rivers of the Oregon Coast. From Astoria to Brookings, this three-hundred-fifty-mile stretch of spectacular littoral supports a dense growth of tall timber marching in a solid phalanx over the rounded hills of the Coast Range, a constant source of wonder to foresters, especially those not born to all this profusion. Only a few miles inland, the mixed stands are usually superseded by solid stands of Douglas fir. It may sound peculiar to the uninitiated, but these spectacular forests are the legacy of what we have been conditioned to believe is a natural disaster; these beautiful timberlands are the result of forest fires that regularly clearcut the old growth, and by letting in light, propagated a heavy growth of light-dependent Douglas fir. The wetter coast strip, not as susceptible to fire, is predominantly of the more shade tolerant spruce, hemlock and cedar.

The journals of the early fur trappers who first opened up this region to white occupancy repeatedly mention the huge forest fires by which this inland region was periodically clearcut. Following a cycle perfectly natural to fir, these charred areas came back to life and now support a luxuriant growth of trees in their prime years. This is considered "old growth," and the usual assumption is that it has always been there in its present condition; certainly the efforts of the preservationists seem to be to keep it in this condition in perpetuity. It is a forlorn hope: a Douglas-fir forest is an interim forest and if left undisturbed will eventually die off to be replaced by a climax forest of hemlock, which will endlessly perpetuate itself until something clears away the old growth and so makes a new, young, different type of forest possible. The present growth of Douglas fir is approximately the seventieth generation since the end of the latest Ice Age and is there simply because of Nature's clearcutting by fire. The logger maintains, with considerable logic, that his method of renewing a mature forest is not nearly as wasteful and destructive as Nature's; and the wood takes on a new lease on life as finished lumber, rather than being converted to ashes.

Scattered pockets of timber escaped these infernos and acted as seed trees to reclothe the denuded hills, and survive today as the largest trees in Oregon. An extremely widespread holocaust seems to have swept through Oregon about five hundred years ago, for no trees in the Coast Range, among them six- and seven-foot monsters, seem to be beyond that age. Whatever the reason, Oregon has the trees in the right size, quantity and quality to sustain the industry which has traditionally been the state's largest and is the backbone of the state's economic strength.

The rounded hills and wooded valleys of the Coast Range are very nearly ideal logging terrain –wonderful timber, good drainage and enough challenge to make it interesting. For that reason, wastage in Oregon logging is at a minimum. The timber is of an age when the diseases that so often plague a very old forest have not yet had a chance to take their toll, and practically the whole tree can be utilized because none of it is rotten. Therefore, the residue left in the woods, while ample to sustain a new generation of trees, is minimal.

Loggers from other areas, viewing the sound, strong, hundred-and-fifty-year-old timber of Oregon, grow green with envy, especially when they consider how much of their five-hundred-year-old wood stays in the forest simply because it is too rotten to warrant a trip to the mill. This generally good timber makes possible a speedy and efficient operation, which may help explain why Oregon loggers have the reputation of being the highballers of the industry, an accolade which they wear with pride, especially since they feel it is richly deserved.

Ever since the first days of logging in the state, the short, deep rivers of Oregon have served as highways to get the logs to the mill. Since the streams, originating in the nearby mountains, are usually short, the mills are generally at the mouths of the rivers so that the accumulated bounty of the river drainage may be utilized. That is very fortuitous, because this is usually where the towns are located, so a symbiotic relationship has long existed between the coastal towns of Oregon and its loggers. The logs are floated to the mill and often stored in mill holding ponds until needed. This practice is deservedly drawing the ire of the environmentalists: prolonged water storage leaches out wood sugars from the stored logs and if the circulation in the pond is weak, the tendency is to promote the growth of algae, thus effectively diminishing the amount of oxygen held in the water. Since this element is essential to fish and plant life, it is a problem that merits the attention it is getting. Old habits die hard, however, and many a mill still draws its supply of logs from a well-filled adjacent pond, although more and more of them are now sporting areators, which, by increasing the flow of oxygenated water in the pond, diminishes the problem of leachates. It is also a sign that a compromise that should be acceptable to all is earnestly being sought.

The hilly nature of the region makes logging by the high-lead method the logical choice. Since by its very nature this required a high investment, it has a tendency to restrict the activities of the smaller gyppo outfits, although newcomers to the ranks are frequent. There is another activity in this region where smallness...and extreme mobility...are not only an asset, but a downright necessity. This is the freelance work of shakebolt cutters, as raffish a lot as ever added color to a region or an industry.

Shakebolt cutters are the men who provide the cedar which eventually becomes high-priced roofing in trendy neighborhoods, especially, it seems, in fire-prone canyons in Southern California. As it reaches the mill, it is a board, twenty-four inches long and about an inch thick, split with a frow from a cedar bolt that has been expertly cut from a cedar stump or good-sized tree. And when I say "expertly" I am not exaggerating. The first practitioners of this art that I met each sported chainsaws with five-foot-long bars, and they were not affectations but actual working tools. When a likely piece of cedar had been spotted, a mark was made at the twenty-four-inch level and then a freehand cut made through a tree that could be up to sixty inches in diameter. When that bolt had been cut through, a tape was applied to the backside to check the trueness of the

In the Oregon Cascades, an early snowfall carpets the ground in a mantle of white and effectively delineates a stand of young second growth.

Ponderosa pine is simply mature bull pine in a favorable site which has shed its lower branches and acquired a beautiful, cinnamon colored bark. It mills into superb lumber with numerous applications in building.

cut, and very seldom was the deviation from one side to the other more than a quarter of an inch.

Oregon has several distinct timber-producing regions. Two of them, the Coast Range and the Cascade Range, are separated by the Willamette Valley. The Valley is mostly farmland or residential areas now, but once it held stands of trees; and, even today, in some areas a constant battle must be fought to keep Nature from reclaiming its own. Looking either to the sunrise or the sunset, the viewer sees tree-covered slopes, striking evidence that this environmental factor had much to do with determining the industrial makeup of the state.

Oregon is timber oriented simply because there is so much of it and the land is supremely adapted to tree growing. Trying to suppress this fact would be tantamount to having apprenticed Mozart to a cobbler or hiring Michelangelo to paint a pigsty. Fortunately, Oregonians generally recognize this fact, although in recent years the growth of urban populations, who are more apt to be environmentally uninformed, has resulted in ecological strictures that are changing the face of the industry. Still, simply as a matter of supply and demand, the state's economy for the next few decades should be tied to, or at least very much influenced by, the bounty growing at its doorsteps.

In 1971 the forest products industry in Oregon directly employed 83,232 people, who drew a payroll of $763,715,000 and manufactured wood products which sold for $1,984,214,000. Eighteen years later, although the industry was in a slump due to lack of building starts, it still employed 66,900 people who earned $1,550,000,000 and produced goods worth $3,900,000,000...and that doesn't include 15,000 log truck drivers not exactly renowned for being underpaid. In spite of extensive mechanization which has reduced the number of people directly employed in the woods, the industry is still Oregon's largest, especially when considering that over 150,000 people in the state are in ancillary industries dependent on the bounty of the state's forests. Six out of every ten railroad cars leaving the state carry forest products, which is not surprising considering that Oregon is the nation's largest producer of lumber, plywood and particle board. Oregon is fortunate in having a balanced economy, for agriculture and tourism are also big business; but the balance wheel is still the forest products industry. It paces them all, as it has for generations, and is fueled by the resource which, properly managed, is infinitely renewable.

On the eastern edge of the Willamette Valley, the foothills begin unfolding toward the Cascade Mountain Range. As the altitude and rainfall increase, the stands become almost solidly Douglas fir, and this is where the most extensive logging activity takes place. Seldom if ever, anywhere else in the world does an industrial activity take place in a setting of comparable beauty, for this is the domain of the Cascade peaks; snow clad giants proudly wearing their crown of ice and snow while towering over an arboreal domain of unparalleled grandeur. From the Columbia Gorge at its northern end, southerly past Mounts Hood, Jefferson and Washington, Three-fingered Jack and the Three Sisters, the whole state sings its song of beauty, with the unbelievably blue waters of Crater lake as a unfollowable encore.

Oregon built its reputation and its economy on the treasures of the Cascades. Fortunately, the treasures are still there and are renewable. The Cascades today are clothed with ideally-sized trees ready for another round of harvest, for much of this land was cut over at the turn of the century. This should at least put into proper perspective the arguments that "America is running out of trees." Fifty years ago I heard, over and over again, "The world is running out of oil, and America will cut its last tree in twenty years." Oil, being a fossil resource, may indeed in time be completely depleted, but as long as the sun shines and climatic conditions remain even reasonably as they are today, we will always have trees. Something else also seems to be guaranteed a long existence: prophets of doom, like death, taxes, and the poor will probably always be with us.

When I did my first logging book eighteen years ago, there were 556 certified tree farms in Oregon covering 5,377,834 acres. In 1989 there were 1020 farms covering 6,608,887 acres, and every one of them exuberantly growing healthy, oxygen-producing young trees. No wonder the Oregon air is so bracing that casual visitors begin thinking they should defy the anti-newcomer James G. Blaine Association, whose motto seems to be "Keep Oregon Green. Bring Money, Spend it. Then go back Home."

The Cascades and the Coast Range, while outstanding, are not Oregon's only timber regions. When Mt. Mazama blew its top five thousand years ago creating beautiful Crater lake, it showered a good part of Oregon with volcanic dust and pumice. The dust that travelled on the wind created distant fertile fields of prodigious growing power; but, at closer range, the volcano also spewed out enormous quantities of pumice rock that does not always sustain a vigorous growth of plant life. Fortunately, Nature is extremely adaptable. Combined with the light rainfall common in the lee of a mountain range, an ideal environment for one of the most beautiful and useful timber trees in Oregon was created. This is the domain of the ponderosa pine; and it's admirers, whose name is legion, will claim that it deserves to be classed right along with the Douglas fir as the perfect timber tree.

Tall, straight, and vigorous, this stately tree with its distinctive cinnamon-colored bark is the dominant tree of South Central Oregon. Its strong, straight-grained wood mills into absolutely beautiful lumber much sought after for applications where beauty as well as utility are important. Window frames and door casings, for instance, are often made of ponderosa pine, and the wood commands a premium price in this phase of the industry. Utility is not this tree's only asset: it is one of the most beautiful trees in America; and a stand of ponderosa pines, before it is converted into lumber that will convey the gift of beauty for an even longer time, lends a dash of beauty to many a hillside that would be considered scabrous without it.

Ponderosa is quite different from fir in its growing habits. A tree which thrives on comparatively dry land,

its stands are usually much farther separated with little or no underbrush. For that reason, ponderosa is well adapted to skidder logging, and this method is standard throughout the whole ponderosa belt. The sight of one of these skidders dragging a big turn of logs amid clouds of pummy dust is enough to make an environmentalist's blood run cold, but as in so many other aspects of logging, the first impression is not the correct one. Close inspection will reveal very little soil disturbance, for the logs seem to float in the slippery powder, and little harm is done to the environment.

From the air, Klamath Falls seems to be located in a semi-desert environment: at least that is the impression one gets from the barren hills encircling the city. That conclusion does not hold up under close scrutiny. Klamath Falls is the center of a very busy lumber and plywood operation feeding primarily on the large ponderosa stands in the area. The miracle of truck transportation brings logs from as far away as one hundred miles to the busy mills which are justifiably proud of the expertise with which they transform that fine timber into superior lumber and plywood.

There are extensive stands of ponderosa interspersed with Douglas fir, white fir and cedar all around Klamath Falls; but this is primarily pine country. The wide, open stands allow prescription cutting so that an extensively logged area looks as though it still were undisturbed forest, only a little smaller and thinner. This thinning out is actually quite beneficial: the added moisture and sunlight available to the remaining trees fosters a rapid growth that substantially shortens the growing cycle and helps produce a superior tree. Reforestation is standard practice: by this method a steady supply of new timber is available.

As an integral part of this program, Weyerhaeuser Company maintains a large nursery where millions of pine seedlings are grown every year. Constant experimentation has resulted in vastly improved strains specially bred to meet the peculiar needs of this region. Temperatures in the open stands of pumice soil often reach 140 degrees Fahrenheit at ground level so that mortality of a standard seedling on a difficult site would be very high. Even though ponderosa is a dry-land tree, exposure to these oven-like heats requires exceptional characteristics if that seedling is to survive. Patient researchers were always looking for that one exceptional seedling that did not wilt; and, today, they have a powerful new tool. Advances in plant genetics and breeding have made it possible for the right genes necessary for survival in a very tough environment to be artificially introduced into the genetic pool, and the resulting tree will pass on those characteristics to its numerous offspring. The super-ponderosa is already a reality; but the search for the ultimate tree goes on with unabated vigor, even though the researchers know that whenever they make a breakthrough it only becomes a platform from which an even greater effort will be launched. One researcher grinned as he gave me this information. "At least," he said, "I have job security. There is no way I can produce a tree that can't somehow be made better, so I'll never run myself out of work."

Medford is to the west of Klamath Falls and so

situated that it draws from the Douglas-fir stands of the Cascades as well as from the lower flatlands which support an extensive forest growth, often of wildly mixed stands. This is the land of the sugar pine, a magnificent tree that often grows to monumental size and produces one of the best looking logs in a region noted for superior timber. Boise Cascade, Medco and a host of smaller mills all help to make Medford a city with a definite orientation to the forest-products industry. They have plenty of material from which to draw: the land is mostly under intensive forestry, and the impressive forest stands of the region attest that the method is producing superior results. Even naturally-seeded areas have been thinned to an even-aged stand, so that, when these are eventually harvested by clearcutting, a new forest will be quickly regenerated.

All the timber-belt towns are forest products oriented; but the leader, where wood is king, is probably Roseburg. Eugene, with its extensive mills and manufacturing facilities, might dispute this a bit, but Eugene has other things going for it–the University of Oregon, for instance. In Roseburg, the many mills, the heavy traffic in logging trucks all attest that here lumber is king, and the townspeople are willing subjects. Roseburg thrives on lumber: and, while recent ecological restrictions may cast a shadow over the economic future, the general feeling is that the product they produce is so good, so indispensable, that somehow good sense and reason will eventually prevail, and their prosperity in the future, as in the past, will be solidly rooted in the forests growing all around them. Since the supply is renewable, they can logically look forward to many bright tomorrows.

It is the same all the way north through the evergreen mountains where the upheaval of the coast Range and the Cascades close ranks with the Calapooyas and into the Willamette Valley at Cottage Grove, the All-American City. Busy Springfield and energetic Eugene are all influenced by the green gold growing at their doorsteps. Since supply usually follows demand, many of these cities, Portland, Salem and Eugene especially, have developed substantial heavy industries catering to the demands of the lumbering industry. And everywhere, in the small towns of the timber belt, the ancillary service industries sell and maintain logging and lumbering equipment, giving these small towns an economic stability they would not otherwise enjoy. Coos Bay is the nation's largest log exporter, while Astoria, at the mouth of the Columbia River, loads a steady stream of log ships, mostly headed for wood-hungry Japan.

The small towns along the coast do a thriving business in tourism, especially during the busy summer months: beauty is a saleable commodity, and the coast connecting these towns has it in spades, but places like Reedsport, Florence, and Newport would be tourists watering holes for three months of the year and not much more if it were not for the solid underpinning of their economies supplied by the forest products industry. Beauty is a marketable asset, and these towns sell it effectively; but this is the frosting on the cake. The foundations of those towns are firmly set on logging, and anything that unduly restricts this activity poses a threat to the economic well-being of these communities. A good example of this principle if Port Orford, on the southern coast of Oregon. This town had its day in the sun as the processor and shipper of the famed, straight-grained cedar which made its name synonymous with quality. With the depletion of mature trees, Port Orford languished, kept alive as a town by tourism drawn by its spectacular setting; but only lately has it shown signs of regaining some of its former vigor. The reason? The second-growth cedar is now attaining marketable size, and Port Orford is once more becoming a town with a solid economic base.

The coastal rivers of the region are justly famous for their scenic attractions, but they also provide some sensitive ecological situations which were largely ignored when this region was first logged. The slopes are often so steep and the rains so heavy and pervasive that logging by the usual high-lead method would...and has...produced scars that have taken many years to heal. Some ingenious methods have been devised whereby the rich bounty of those hillsides can be harvested without wreaking an ecological disaster. One very picturesque method, much in vogue eighteen years ago, was a huge helium-filled balloon which, through a clever arrangement of cables, could be moved over these ecologically sensitive slopes and waft a respectable turn of logs to the landing without disturbing the soil in the least. It was colorful, but expensive, and economically feasible only if the stumpage rate was ridiculously low. Such sales are a real rarity these days, so now the job is usually done by powerful helicopters which may not be as colorful but are faster and more efficient.

Oregon is not only the nation's leading lumber producer but also paramount in that most versatile of building materials, plywood. The size and quality of the trees prevalent in Oregon make ideal peeler logs the rule rather than the exception, and each year a larger proportion of this ideally-suited wood is converted to a versatile building material. The plywood industry is well established in Oregon not only because of the plenitude of raw material but also because of the excellent research and development facilities the state affords. The research has not only kept Oregon in the forefront of the industry's industrial development but also assured that, when it must switch to the smaller logs of the second-growth crop, its raw material supply is assured. This research has occasionally taken on some bizarre twists such as the clandestine research project at Georgia-Pacific's Coos Bay plywood plant that resulted in a spectacular technological breakthrough. Recently transferred there from the South, Jens Jorgensen became convinced that some of the methods in standard use in Oregon could be utilized to peel and bond the resinous wood of the quickly-growing southern pine. Surreptitiously finagling a few carloads of logs, he began to experiment, and by the time he had unravelled his supply, had solved most of the technological problems involved and laid the foundations of a thriving new industry in the South.

The particleboard industry is also a significant part of the forest products picture. As more and more uses are found for this versatile material, Oregon is its

The short, swift rivers of the Oregon coast have been highways over which much of the state's forest bounty moves. Here, on the Coos River, a boom boat herds a pod of logs into a raft which a tug will move to the mill, a practice which was discontinued in 1991.

A fast growing spruce and hemlock forest on the Oregon coast allows sufficient sunlight to pierce its canopy which maintains the abundant undergrowth.

logical producer. There is a brand-spanking new Boise Cascade plant in the Grande Ronde Valley that was not there eighteen years ago which now converts into particle board sawmill residues formerly consigned to the beehive burner. Each technological advance that makes use of the greater part of the tree not only improves the ecological picture but also strengthens the economic position of the entire industry. Oregon is a pacemaker in wood technology with good private research facilities as well as the renowned laboratories of the University of Oregon and Oregon State University. The Corvallis-based Oregon State University, especially, has an excellent College of Forestry whose laboratories have a reputation for excellence and whose graduates feel that, when they have a degree from this college, they have a vested right to take their rightful place in the forefront of the industry.

In the eastern part of the state, there are extensive timber-producing areas normally classed as part of the Intermountain region. It is a different type of timber than that prevalent in the coastal areas and harvesting methods are quite different, but it is an important and growing segment of the state's economy. This is the area around John Day, a town of three thousand with six good-sized lumber mills. Baker, La Grande and Elgin boast large modern mills, all drawing from the extensive forestation of the Blue Mountains, while Wallowa and Joseph feed on the heavy growth of the Wallowa Mountains.

The Tillamook Burn was probably the best known forest fire in America since the days of Wisconsin's Peshtigo holocaust. As little as thirty-five years ago, snags were still standing in great numbers in this area, mute testimony to the searing fires that swept a region as large as Rhode Island and so devastated the land that most people viewing it doubted that this sere, blasted land would ever again grow trees. The region had been hand-planted, and today one of the most beautiful and potentially productive forests in the world has developed on those once burned and barren hills. On July 19, 1973, the Tillamook Burn officially became the Tillamook Forest and proudly took its place as one of the world's most beautiful woodlands. The trees are up to fifty-feet high, growing in joyous abandon and are so thick that they are ready for their second commercial thinning.

It is the way of the forests. Oregon has been burned over many times since the end of the Ice Age, and each time the land has flowered anew. Today, as long as good sense and a pragmatic usage of this land prevails, the logger takes the wood for man's use, opens up the land to the sun and allows the forester to nurture the trees that spring from the fertile earth. If the pioneers were around to see this recurring miracle, they would marvel at all the beautiful timber and reaffirm their belief that this is indeed the Promised Land.

Honeyman State Park, just south of Florence, Oregon, is a beautiful stand of second growth any time of the year but takes on an additional beauty in the springtime when rhododendrons are in bloom.

These beautifully shaped trees, usually Douglas fir but also often of noble fir, are an increasingly common sight in the Northwest as more and more tree farmers cash in on the boom in plantation-grown Christmas trees.

Although the coast redwood is the tree that most often comes to mind when California logging is mentioned, there is actually much more Douglas fir cut in the state. Most really big redwoods are safely ensconced in parks.

In the redwood logging museum at Scotia, these massive bullblocks give some idea of the tools used in the days of steam. Some of these monsters weigh well over a ton, and were formerly hung from a tall spar tree.

An old steam donkey; one of the most massive, powerful machines ever devised by the mine of man. This contraption, mounted on skids, could winch itself across rivers, even lift itself bodily out of canyons.

CHAPTER VIII

LOGGING THE GOLDEN STATE

California, as its boosters will proudly tell you, is the state that has everything, and indeed the Golden State can live up to almost all of the claims its proud sons and daughters will make for it. In this welter of related accomplishments, there is one legitimate claim to fame that is seldom mentioned. The accomplishments of the southern and central portions of the state are lovingly listed, but very seldom is it mentioned that California is the largest producer of lumber and forest products in the Union. Mention this fact, and our proud booster will say, "Of course! The redwoods!" and feel that he has stated the whole case.

There is no doubt that the redwoods are a very definite and extremely important part of the lumber industry in California, but it may come as quite a surprise that there is considerably more Douglas fir cut in California than there is redwood. The bounty of the state is such that it has representation in practically every form of wood commercially harvested on the West Coast, and it has it in quantity and quality that not only command respect but also supports a vigorous year-round operation. It even has some forms of logging, indigenous to the region, that are uniquely its own.

Just as Oregon bears a stereotype of a rain-soaked, tree-covered state, California bears an equal burden but shows the opposite side of that image. Easterners, especially, brought up on a diet of Hollywood movies, think of California as a semi-desert land of endless sunshine and orange groves that achieves its amazing fertility only through the miracle of irrigation. Those same Easterners probably would be astounded to learn that two-thirds of Oregon is a high desert where even the hardy juniper has to fight for its existence and that the northern third of California gets rain sometimes measured in feet and sports a thick cover of trees with never an orange grove in sight.

Mention California trees and the redwoods immediately come to mind, and with good reason. If ever there were a tree that could command universal awe, that tree would have to be a California redwood, either the massive giants of the Sierras or the equally impressive and taller coastal redwood. These two cousins are the largest and tallest trees on earth and are exceeded in age only by one other tree: the bristlecone pine, which, naturally enough, is also a California native.

The first white man to see a full-grown coastal redwood must have seriously pondered whether or not he should tell about it. As a matter of fact, the first explorers who reported these trees were accused of being monumental liars. It was only when the totally reliable Franciscans came back not only with good descriptions but also accurate measurements of the giant trees that the stories began to be believed.

Even so, nothing takes the place of actually seeing one of these giants, for this is a case where even the most vivid description does not do justice to the massiveness and majesty of this gigantic plant.

My first sight of the redwoods came in 1945, when, still in a wartime uniform, I toured through the coastal groves in the company of the most winsome colleen Ireland ever bred. We were on our honeymoon and probably even the Gobi Desert would have seemed attractive at that time; but the fact that each time I see the redwoods, the spell they cast becomes deeper, is proof positive that I was beguiled by the beauty of the groves as well as that of my little Irish bride. Viewing the redwoods is an experience bordering on the spiritual; and it is very easy, at such a time, to sink to one's knees as though in a vast arboreal cathedral. The gesture is not out of place; thousands of people have had the same reaction, for God lives in these trees.

The coastal redwood grows in a narrow strip along the Pacific Coast from Southern Oregon to, roughly, the Big Sur, and even farther south in isolated pockets. It is the world's tallest tree, with several known specimens in excess of 360 feet. It is exceeded in circumference only by its cousin, the giant redwoods of the Sierras, which can measure up to 85 feet.

The scientific name for the coastal redwood is Sequoia Sempervirens which translates loosely to "ever-living sequoia." The name is well deserved. By virtue of a thick, high-tannin bark that is virtually fireproof and bug-proof, the sequoia comes virtually unscathed through forest fires and bug epidemics that would obliterate other species. A redwood stump quickly sprouts a new growth of upright canes, and if left undisturbed, will soon have a circular growth of new trees, all feeding on the extensive root system of the original tree. Almost all of the redwood logging done today is on the second-growth of trees first cut around the turn of the century. Some of the regrowth from the first trees cut by white men has attained a size where it is the object of protection from preservationists seeking to save the "old growth" redwoods. Redwood is one of the fastest growing of all trees. Near Scotia, in the heart of the redwood belt, there is a redwood plantation of experimental trees. Some of these trees are seven years old and forty feet tall...and these are growing from their own root systems. Numerous seedlings sprouting from a cut stump do almost as well; and in the favorable moist, cool climate of the redwood belt, regrowth is downright spectacular. On a favored site a

These massive trees grow in a narrow coastal strip from southern Oregon to the Montery Peninsula and, in isolated pockets, even farther south. They are the world's tallest trees and one of the longest-lived.

Theses logs may look pretty huge but by redwood standards are only medium sized. These are residuals, trees that were too small to be considered when the region was first logged almost a hundred years ago.

redwood can easily attain a height of 150 feet and be four feet in diameter in 60 years. As the first settlers who tried to clear land for farming in the redwood belt soon found out, it is practically impossible to eradicate. It just keeps coming back! It is well that it is so, because if ever a tree suffered by being too perfect, that tree is the redwood. It is a tree of awesome beauty that demands protection and it mills into beautiful lumber that demands utilization.

Tall, straight, sometimes a hundred and fifty feet or more to the first limb, it has a majesty, especially in the clustered groves to which it is partial, that inspires awe and respect, not only for its size but also for a particular kind of beauty that is unique to this species. The beauty is not only skin-deep. The reddish, straight-grained heart-wood is highly resistant to rot and mills into some of the most beautiful lumber imaginable. All through the wine country, before stainless steel made them obsolete, there were huge aging vats and tanks made of absolutely perfect redwood staves, some of which had been in service for many decades with no sign of deterioration. Nowhere is the dilemma the logger faces of destroying beauty in the name of utility more in evidence than in the redwood country, and it is completely understandable that large and enthusiastic groups have been formed whose avowed purpose it is to save the redwoods forever.

The first man who decided to cut down a mature redwood must have been one of the brashest, or maybe the most determined, human being that ever lived. Imagine cutting down a tree eighteen feet in diameter with a double-bitted axe and a hand-drawn, twelve-foot saw! Then just imagine dragging that saw against the friction of a cut nine feet or more long!! Just chopping in the undercut sometimes took days, and there are numerous photographs of tall men lying down full length in some of those cuts. And all this work was done while balancing on a springboard a dozen feet or more above the ground. A logger's work has never been easy, but when you think of the work necessary to cut down a large redwood, it makes you realize that those early redwood loggers were MEN!

They still are, but some things have changed, and practically all for the better. In the first place, very little of the largest redwood is being cut nowadays. There is only one mill in the world, that of Pacific Lumber Company in Scotia, that is equipped to handle a log as large as ten feet. The occasional log that comes in bigger than that, usually a blowdown salvaged from one of the parks, must be split before it can be run through the headrig. Most of the really large redwoods, especially on the easily accessible coastal plain are in federal and state parks where thousands of awestruck visitors every day can see what the redwoods looked like when the white man first came to this region, and, regrettably, often kill them with kindness. One of the major factors in the deterioration of redwood groves is the compaction of the soil that takes place at the foot of major trees as hordes of awe-struck tourists mill around them, all looking for that one perfect picture-taking spot that will capture the majesty of these trees. Barricades around the larger trees help to preserve them, but it is undeniable that the human adulation the redwood groves receive has not contributed to their well being and, indeed, is a major cause of their deterioration.

The first white settlers of California came into the southern part of the state, and that region was comparatively well settled and known before the wooded northern section got any attention. When it did, it was shrugged off as very scenic but of little value. It was a tangle of trees so massive that it would take years of labor to clear even a small opening in the redwood jungle; and, even when that was achieved, the soil was not particularly disposed to produce worthwhile crops. There were plenty of fertile if somewhat parched acres farther south and the bulk of the settlement took place in those areas. The lands adjacent to the redwoods, however, were another matter; and their settlement created a demand for lumber which was superbly met by the heavily forested areas of the well-watered North. An added impetus was the influx of population brought on by the 1849 Gold Rush. Not all of the Forty-Niners found gold, metallic gold, but most of them, once exposed to the other possibilities that the Golden State offered so liberally, never returned to their original homes. Instead, they set their roots in the fertile soil of California and rapidly built the agriculture and industries that ultimately made this the most populous and wealthiest state of the Union.

That growth demanded lumber, large quantities of lumber, and it was only a matter of time before the forest wealth of the northern part of the state began to be utilized. Northwest lumber built San Francisco and most of the cities that sprang up in the aftermath of the Gold Rush. The industry already had a foothold in the Northwest, and transportation by water from the new ports of that region gave direct access to San Francisco, the main center of activity for the Mother Lode country. Nevertheless, there was some penetration of the local timber country of the north; and some ports, notably Crescent City and Eureka, began shipping locally finished lumber to the busy construction centers of the South so that by 1855 lumber was solidly established as a viable industry in the timber belt of northern California.

While redwood was the dominant timber of this area, it was approached warily. There was plenty of small Douglas fir and cedar in the vicinity and that was the first timber cut, simply because it was easier to fall, transport and finish. Some of the smaller redwoods were cautiously harvested; and as the sterling qualities of this magnificent tree began to be realized, it was inevitable that the larger trees began to receive the lumberman's attention.

The technical problems attendant to harvesting trees of this size were more than formidable; they were staggering! The problems not only had to do with the size of the trees, which presented problems in falling such monsters, but also in moving the fallen giants to the mill. The redwood country has few streams large enough to transport logs twelve feet or more in diameter by water; and live, old-growth redwood is often so dense that it had to be buoyed with smaller, lighter wood before it could be floated to the mill. For several decades the technological problems attendant to logging large old growth redwood were so formidable

Talk about total utilization! At the site of the Day Forest Fire near Birney, a portable chipper converts half burned logs to hog fuel which will power a co-generation power station in a nearby mill. The surplus power is fed into the regional electrical power grid.

that the vast arboreal resources of Northern California were largely unused.

When the California logger eventually tackled the large, old-growth redwoods, they found out that the methods that have been adequate with the smaller timber did not always work with the gigantic sequoias. For one thing, redwood is quite brittle, and the first efforts to fall the large trees often resulted in a mass of short, broken, splintered logs that were a parody of a tree that had been majestic when it was standing. That problem was solved by a method still used when falling a large redwood. A series of small berms is pushed up in the path of the tree to be felled, designed to cushion the fall of the tree, so that the trunk will be reasonably intact after the impact of falling. Because the fall of the tree must be precisely gauged, another innovation peculiar to the redwood country evolved. A pair of hinged sticks, called "gum sticks," was inserted into the undercut, and a sighting along the apex would predicate where the tree would fall. Apparently, the system worked, because with the new falling methods few redwoods were shattered, although it still happened on occasion much to the chagrin of the cutters who had spend days cutting down a tree whose worth was materially lessened if it was reduced to a mass of fragments.

There were other problems attendant to the logging of old-growth redwood other than their size. The remarkable vitality of the redwoods is such that the tree is practically indestructible, but not immune to injury. Many an old, majestic tree, upon being felled, turns out to be a hollow "chimney," a seemingly healthy outer shell surrounding a burned out heart with a large part of the tree unusable. This condition was so prevalent in old-growth redwood that for many years these trees were measured according to the "Humboldt Scale," in which 1000 feet of scale was actually a realistic 600 board feet of usable lumber. As in other parts of the country, the old, overmature tree is not the most desirable timber.

Once the tree was down the work had just begun: the tree had to be sectioned and the pieces moved to the mill. Slow moving bull teams furnished the motive power, and hempen ropes and massive chains secured the tree sections to the teams. It was brutally hard work for the loggers, but nothing compared to the agonies of the patient oxen who, under the lash, were forced to move loads weighing many tons over improvised skid roads, often knee deep in mud, which, from the oxen's viewpoint, probably improved the movement of their gargantuan loads. In an era when little or no consideration was given to the feelings of animals, it must have been the animal equivalent of the days of human slavery and every bit as reprehensible. It did get loads to the mill, but the range was limited; and many a mill closed for lack of available timber within sight of ample, though in those days unavailable, reserves.

Technological problems are usually solved by technological means, and it was three advances in the logging industry that made the enormous resources of the redwood belt available to man. Up till the advent of the flexible steel cable, massive hempen rope and large-linked chains had been used in moving logs out of the woods. They each had failings that were cured by the advent of the extremely strong, more easily maneuverable woven wire rope. With the availability of the stronger cable, steam yarders spooling thousands of yards of two-inch thick cable came into use; and coupled with the advent of the logging railroad, completely changed the face of the industry

An example of the monstrous steam-powered machines used in the redwoods to move cut logs to a place where they could be loaded can be seen at Scotia, near the logging museum Pacific Lumber Company maintains in that town. It is an awesome piece of machinery, dwarfing anything in use today. Mounted on wooden skids, it could pull itself to its destination by means of the thick cables spooled on its oversized drums; and once there, firmly anchored down, through an intricate system of cables and enormous blocks it supplied the titanic forces necessary to move cut redwood logs to a loading site. It dragged monstrous logs through the woods like gigantic battering rams, knocking down small trees in its path as though they were straws and left behind a trail of unbelievable devastation. In a matter of a few decades, it had almost completely superseded the patient bull teams, especially when the steam loaders were coupled with the steam logging railroad and so made possible the utilization of redwood stands some considerable distance from the mill.

With the new tools at their disposal, loggers attacked even the largest redwood stands in earnest, and old growth redwood lumber became a readily available commodity. Logging camps grew into small villages and the northern part of California became an active part of the lumber industry. Eureka became the logging capitol of the state, with over a dozen mills processing the huge logs of the area, and lumber barons built ornate homes that flaunted their wealth and the prosperity of the region.

Even a locale as rich and productive as the coastal timber belt of California has its limits, and these were beginning to be reached, and even exceeded. The beauty of the redwood country was rapidly being replaced by the ugliness that the logging methods of the times fostered so liberally, and it was only natural that concerned citizens should band together to save some of the natural beauty of the redwood country before it was completely obliterated. Impetus to this movement was added in 1914 when an important transportation link, the Northwest Pacific Railroad was completed, and visitors from all over the country flooded in, some of them people highly influential in the federal government. They wanted large sections of virgin redwoods saved; and the lumber industry, notably the Pacific Lumber Company, which owned large sections of old growth redwoods, was caught in an environmental uproar.

Fortunately, industry and conservationists agreed to work together. Large sections of prime redwood land were bought or traded, and the major logging companies refrained from cutting some of the more spectacular and easily accessible groves until money could be raised to buy them. This included some of the most renowned groves; Rockerfeller Forest and

Founder's Grove were acquired in this way, as well as the "Avenue of the Giants;" and to this day, acquisition of desirable groves by state and federal parks have made the Redwoods National Park the most expensive park in the whole federal system. On a dewy summer morning, with the sunlight slanting in sheets of greenish gold through this arboreal Eden, it seems like a bargain.

That their efforts were successful is amply demonstrated by the beauty of the redwood country today. Travelers along U.S. 101, the coastal highway that threads through the redwood belt, pass through miles of state and national parks where the virgin redwoods are forever preserved in their original state. The "Save the Redwoods League" in conjunction with private and state organizations has bought or traded thousands of acres of prime redwoods that will be forever preserved so that future generations can marvel at this, one of Nature's most marvelous productions, fresh from the hands of the Creator. Anyone with any appreciation of beauty will admit that this is a good and even noble task, and breathe a silent prayer of thanks to those who had the foresight to save this treasure for the enjoyment of generations yet unborn.

While the coastal redwood is unquestionably the dominant tree of the well-watered coastal strip, there are other trees in this area, notably Douglas firs, that in their bulk and height are easily mistaken for the more massive redwoods. In the northern reaches of California, redwoods and firs seem to co-exist quite easily, although each reaches hungrily for the sun. In this contest, the fast-growing redwood usually wins, but there are enough fir survivors to give the majestic park-like stands a decidedly mixed character, undetected as this is to the casual eye beguiled by a seemingly sold phalanx of lordly redwoods.

Much of the present-day logging consists of thinning the rank regrowth that has sprouted from lands harvested as recently as thirty years ago or the much larger second growth that followed the first harvest, as much as a hundred years ago. The Pacific Lumber Company, which traces its origin to 1869 and owns 194,000 acres of forest land, 80 percent of it redwoods, practices vigorous forest management on its widespread acres, so that its large mills will have a perpetual supply of timber supplied mostly by its own land. The company has never bought federal or state-owned timber, relying solely on its own resources; and the system has worked so well that they intend to continue this practice. On plots where the original old growth was removed at the turn of the century, they are now removing residuals–trees too small to be considered at the time of the original harvest but which have grown in the intervening years to a size that merits removal to the redwood mill at Scotia. Those trees profited by the additional light and nutrient made available by the removal of the original growth, and their rate of growth has been phenomenal.

Redwood is one of the fastest growing of all trees. A cut stump will in a matter of days sprout a vigorous crop of seedlings; and these, feeding off the extensive root system of the cut tree, will grow at a truly amazing rate. All through the redwood belt, there are clusters of trees growing in a semicircle. Examination will show that these have sprouted from a common stump; and since the new trees can be up to six feet or more in diameter, the display is remarkable, to say the least!

It is standard practice to thin out second-growth stands, taking out the smaller trees to give light and air to the smaller trees. Each thinning removes 50 percent of the volume and produces about 35,000 board feet to the acre. The remaining stand will grow faster, straighter, and produce timber which, at harvest, will have practically no waste and will be of the optimum size and quality for efficient processing. While the alluvial flats subject to frequent flooding support most of the old-growth groves that are mostly held in park, it is the hillsides that provide most of the commercially grown timber. A favored site can produce a tree 150 feet tall and six feet in diameter in 60 years; and for that reason, most of the redwood logged today comes from second growth that was never allowed to reach the size of the hoary old giants one sees in the parks.

The redwood country has a long tradition of logging and loggers. Scotia, in the heart of the redwood belt is still a company town with all the houses and business enterprises owned by the company. Apparently, the company is a benevolent landlord, because many of those snug, hundred-year-old houses are occupied by descendants of some of the original mill workers who worked there in the 1880s. My guide to the redwood country, Ed Lewis Sr., is a third-generation logger, and his son, Ed Lewis Jr., carries on the family tradition by running four sides for Pacific Lumber. Ed told me with a grin, "When I started logging for Pacific Lumber over thirty years ago, my bosses were all older than I was, then for quite a while they were the same age, but now they're all younger than I am." Working uninterruptedly for the same company as an independent contractor for almost forty years says quite a bit about working relationships between these mill owners and contract loggers.

On a hill overlooking Scotia, a tall, old-growth redwood towers over the already tall second-growth. Ed Lewis' great grandfather logged this area in 1900 and left that old monarch crowning the hill. In 1970, his grandson, Ed Lewis Sr., thinned the second growth, taking out some trees already four feet in diameter. Again, the old tree was spared. The area is now ready for a second thinning and Ed Lewis Jr.–the fourth generation to log on that land—will probably do the job. He has already passed the word to his crew that anyone even looking crosswise at that tree had better start running....

Most of the work in the redwood country is let out to contract loggers although Pacific Lumber still employs about a hundred loggers on company sides. Remnants of what used to be large logging camps are still in evidence, notably the old cookhouse adjacent to the Louisiana-Pacific plant at Samoa which has been made into a top attraction where modern-day tourists can eat the way loggers did back in the days when most of them were bachelors with no one to cook for them. At Carlotta, the old loggers' hotel has been rejuvenated with a large dining room featuring family-style tables and a menu that would rate rave notices in any epicure's book. It is well-patronized by local loggers who

"Lining 'er up." In the Trinity Mountains, a logger sizes up a leaning Douglas fir so that he may fall it in such a way that he can properly buck it to the desired length.

He made it! This tree has quite a bit of butt-rot in it but also some very fine lumber. The faller now becomes a bucker and measures his log so as to get the best possible scale.

133

appreciate not only the quality of the food but the size of the servings.

Even with the restrictions imposed by ecological considerations, and they are many, logging and forest-related industries are still the mainstay of the Northern California economy. The land is so superbly adapted to the growing of valuable species of trees that putting it to any other use would be the waste of a valuable natural resource. This is understood in the timber belt, but it is an idea that many of the urban dwellers of the sunny, arid south have a hard time understanding. Since they control the greater part of the votes in the state, to say nothing of the money, the people in the timber belt often feel a bit frustrated. Education is the answer, but education traditionally has been an often painful process.

While the coastal belt and its redwoods are the most spectacular part of the California timber country, it is not by any matter or means the only region that grows marketable timber; in fact, it is only one medium-sized segment to a very large pie. Nothing illustrates this better than a trip along State Route 299 from Eureka to Redding. This route crosses the Trinity Alps and winds through heavily forested terrain the whole way. In a three-hour trip along this route, I counted 58 logging trucks, 51 of them loaded with quite impressive Douglas fir, 2 with mixed loads and 5 loaded with pine. This tally does not include dozens of unloaded logging rigs which merrily barreled by me as I plodded along at the legal 55 mph limit. The fir all seemed to be headed for Eureka and the pine toward Redding; but no matter how you look at it, the economy of this region is definitely tied to forest products.

The forest cover gradually changes as one leaves the coast. As far inland as 20 miles, there still is an occasional redwood; but soon the predominant species is fir, and it stays that way until the lighter rainfall regions around Redding bring on a heavier growth of pine. Redding and Red Bluff have large mills, and the Sierra Pacific Industries mill at Anderson is state-of-the-art. While this area is not as wholly dependent on timber as the coastal belt, there still is a large and viable industry here, feeding off the largess of the Trinity Mountains and the wooded areas around Burney.

The Trinity Mountains are rugged country and, predictably, the men who log this area match the mountains. Steep mountain land is usually logged by the high-lead method, although the tall steel towers so prevalent in the Northwest seem to have been replaced with smaller rigs that nevertheless get the job done. Wherever the terrain permits, large grapple skidders, often moving quite impressive loads, drag Douglas and white fir to the landing. Some of the most beautiful logs I saw were of sugar pine, which is a welcome addition to any timber sale since its beautiful lumber brings a premium price for specialized building applications.

Thinning has been raised to the status of a fine art. Every commercial woodland is routinely thinned; but so skillfully is the work done that when the operation is completed, the thinned area looks more like a park than an area that had just been logged. As on the coast, about 35,000 board feet are taken out in the thinning operation, and the resultant rapid growth will bring that area to harvest by clearcut in about twenty years. The area is immediately replanted, usually to a mixed growth that matches the original cover. Natural regeneration also contributes to a heavy reproduction, so that thinning is not only good forestry but also good business. The operation is heavily mechanized. Power feller-bunchers lay the small trees down in windrows; they are dragged to the landing and quickly processed. Nothing is wasted. A portable chipper converts even the branches to hog fuel which is trucked to the co-generation plant at Burney, which supplies not only enough electrical power to run that quite large operation but also feeds into the local electrical power distribution grid.

A good example of total utilization was taking place near Burney. The Day Forest Fire had ravaged several thousand acres; but, as is usually the case, myriad of dead, partially burned trees had been left standing. Gary Graham, a gyppo (his words, proudly!) working for Roseburg Lumber, was clearing that land, dragging the partially burned logs to a central landing. Anything having a sawlog left in it was cut out, segregated and sent to the mill at Weed. The rest of the tree, even the partially charred remains, went through the chipper. The stream of hog fuel issuing from that machine was pretty dark, but it was all combustible and would be sold for a profit. The cleared land would be immediately replanted and in a short time would once more sport the covering of emerald-green trees that is its rightful due. With the help of man, a process that would take Nature many years would be completed in half the time.

California, unquestionably, is a bountiful land. It can boast of something as gigantic as the redwoods or the fact that ninety percent of all the pencils produced in the United States are encased in the incense cedar that grows here. Its forest resources are immense and in the hands of foresters determined to give it the best possible care. Its loggers, like loggers elsewhere, are a rugged breed, proud of their expertise and grimly determined that their sons will have a chance to follow in their fathers' footsteps if they so desire. The pride that is so endemic in the whole craft shines like a beacon in the Golden State, and why not?

This is logging country and these men are loggers. They have every reason to be proud.

CHAPTER IX

INTERMOUNTAIN, INLAND EMPIRE

Whenever the talk in the western part of the Pacific Northwest gets around to logging, as it often does, the swapping of hard information or tall tales is apt to concern either the coast or the Cascades, for with most people these are the only areas worth mentioning. The sprawling territory farther east, stretching clear to the Rocky Mountains, is known to contain trees but is not ordinarily considered to be logging country of any consequence.

This is a major misconception. The Intermountain Region may not have trees twelve feet in diameter, but it has millions of two-foot trees and brawny men who not only know how to harvest them but also wear the name of "logger" like a badge of honor. An area that produces over two billion board feet of finished lumber every year and shows a steady increase in production can hardly be ignored. Make no mistake about it, this is logging country; and these men are loggers.

The Intermountain Region is roughly that area between the Cascades and the Rocky Mountains north of California. It takes in the eastern part of Washington and Oregon, as typified by the heavily wooded Blue Mountains and Wallowas, the Idaho Panhandle and that part of Montana bisected by the Continental Divide. It is a fascinating country of much diversity and has evolved logging methods quite different from those common on the western side of the Cascades.

Areas on the leeward side of high mountains always suffer from a lack of rainfall, but the once arid Columbia Basin, in the rainfall shadow of the Cascades, is now green with irrigation and grows wonderful crops of practically everything–except trees. A northern fringe of timber, mostly pine, supports some logging; but generally the woods look a bit anemic until the Spokane area is reached. Toward the Idaho border the trees grow larger, and the Coeur d'Alene, Pend Oreille and Priest Lake region is heavily forested. There is no question but that the Idaho Panhandle is timber country. The forestation is heavy and the small towns of the area very definitely draw their sustenance from the lumber industry. Every river deep enough to float a raft of logs is lined with mills, either presently operating or, in their gaunt abandonment, testifying that at one time the lumber industry dominated the economic life of the region.

Probably the most famous of these is the storied St. Joe River whose beauty lures a host of appreciative boaters every year but is also the artery by which the local resurgent logging industry moves its logs to market. The region around St. Maries and Avery was once heavily forested with old-growth pine, cedar and fir and supported numerous mills, most of them situated on the river to take advantage of the easy transportation it afforded. In time, the old growth was cut off and the mills languished or died completely. The second growth has now reached the size where it once more supports a viable industry, so every few days a raft containing three million board feet or more of bundled logs is towed to the mills at Coeur d'Alene by a pair of hardworking tugs that somehow bend their ponderous loads around the sinuous bends of the river without running aground. The log booms were assembled next to pilings sunk into the river before anyone working on that raft was even born, testimonials to the fact that man has been using this gorgeous river for some time without destroying its beauty. In fact, the pilings of long-deserted mills and booming grounds are so natural a part of the landscape that they seem to have grown there. St. Maries is very much a lumber town, proud of its heritage and determined to continue in the way of life that has sustained it for decades.

The loggers in this area and in the Kootenai Range to the north profitably log timber that would be scorned by the coastal loggers accustomed to five-foot-thick Douglas fir. They wrily refer to themselves as "twig benders," but make no mistake about it, these men are excellent loggers who exemplify the logger's famed adaptability: they accept the environment as they find it and shape their logging practices to fit local conditions. In so doing, they are demonstrating the prime requirement for any species' survival–adaptability. These men will survive and they will survive as loggers, not as something else decreed for them by militant urban preservationists.

The timber may be unimpressive in size, but the woodlands are thick and extensive. A white fir three feet in diameter would be considered a big one and almost certainly would be rotten. A two-foot tree would be more representative and productive of more board footage, while anything above four feet, and they do occur, would present acute loading problems. Although such loads are becoming increasingly rare, there are occasional loads on the west side consisting of three logs only, or even a single monstrous butt cut. In the Kootenai Country, the average load would be closer to fifty logs and would probably contain a smaller volume of wood than that contained in the coastal haul. This is not all bad; they log lots of lodgepole pine in the Kootenais and precious little of that very versatile wood on the coast.

In the Intermountain, the mainline on a yarder is maybe three-quarters of an inch, on a loader it is five-

Large tracked machines of awesome power are used to skid massive redwood logs to the landing. The same path is used to move multiple logs so that a skidroad is soon established.

eights, which would be considered strawline on the coast but perfectly adequate here. Coastal choker setters, struggling with inch-thick chokers, would have no love for the often very nasty brush through which those slender chokers must be maneuvered. In this country of comparatively small trees, the heavy, expensive equipment of the west side isn't needed; and while there is some high-lead logging done in the rougher areas, the usual method used is skidder logging. Rubber tired tractors and crawler skidders drag the logs to the landing, in the process breaking off most of the branches. At the landing, a few quick cuts clear off any remaining branches; the log is bucked to the proper length and swung into the proper cold deck by a loader that would be considered on the puny side on the coast but is entirely adequate to handle anything that would be encountered here.

All this talk about small trees might tend to make one believe that all Intermountain logging is in inconsequential timber. Nothing could be farther from the truth. I remember seeing a show near Chewelah in Washington State where a good-sized skidder was hauling in a turn of three logs, each log at least two feet in diameter and at least a hundred feet long. That timber was straight, sound Douglas fir and would have been considered beautiful peeler logs on the coast. The nice part of this was that this was the norm for this show rather than the exception. Intermountain cannot compete with the coast in terms of greatest size, but it can and does compete on an even basis in terms of quality.

Skidder logging is done in all regions except Alaska,

but in the Intermountain it has been refined into a high art. Large, crawler-type skidders may drag in a turn of as many as fifteen logs while smaller, double-jointed, rubber-tired skidders that look as though they always are on their way to an accident, will haul in a somewhat smaller load. The rough, jolting ride effectively tears off most of the branches, so that a practically denuded pole is delivered to the landing. The sight of this load coming in would make the average preservationist's blood run cold; but the method is founded on a pragmatic assessment of all the factors involved, ecological as well as economic. Many turns are needed to make up a load, and the labor involved in cutting off hundreds of small branches would be economically prohibitive. The skidders take the same path to the landing, so that a road of sorts is quickly established and the soil disturbance involved is not nearly as extensive as one would imagine. It is also note-worthy that the old skidder roads are usually the first to sprout a crop of new trees once the work is completed. This is the same principle involved as the farmer turning over the soil to create a new seedbed and accounts for the fact that regrowth is always heaviest along the course of a former skidroad.

Not all types of terrain are amenable to this treatment. If the soil is particularly thin or all the humus has been burned out of it by a particularly hot forest fire, the soil, once disturbed, would erode rapidly and degenerate into gullies that might never heal. In this case, timber growing on an ecologically sensitive slope might never be harvested, or if it were, probably only with the use of some method that does not disturb

A feller buncher snips off a tree with a set of hydraulically operated shears, then neatly lays the cut tree down into windrows where the skidders can move a whole pod to the landing.

the soil, such as helicopters. They are an expensive procedure that usually is not economically sound unless the stand is either very good or so clogged with debris that harvest is essential, if only to defuse a potentially disastrous fire hazard.

In these east-side forests, we have a paradox: the region's ecology is being altered not by the direct depredation of man but by the protection he is affording the forest. For untold generations, this region experienced–almost annually–small, naturally occurring forest fires that did a good job of cleaning out the debris that had accumulated since the preceding fire and regenerated the lodgepole pine by subjecting the cones to enough heat to pop out the seeds. The very successful fire suppression methods of the modern forester have allowed dangerous quantities of flammable materials to accumulate on the ground, waste that in a wetter climate would have disintegrated by the natural degenerative processes of the forest floor. But this is a drier world; although the forest produces about four tons of debris per acre each year, the degenerative processes decompose only two tons, leaving an accumulated mass of flammable material each year that is equivalent in thermal value to three hundred gallons of gasoline. In the pre-fire-protection years, this accumulation was regularly removed by the perennial small blazes that swept the forest floor, with the result that major conflagrations occurred only when conditions were right for them. Unfortunately, conditions were right altogether too often, and large forest fires were frequent.

The idea of preventing wildfires was basically so good that it achieved wide acceptance. The problem was that as a result of the suppression of the small perennial fires, a massive accumulation of twigs, branches, bark and fallen trees was piled up next to living timber, awaiting only a well-placed lightning strike to touch off an inferno which would consume even the thickest-barked tree. The forester does what he can to avert disaster; but in his heart he knows that unless the accumulation is removed, someday he will have a holocaust like the devastating Yellowstone Fire, which was so hot and fierce that the ground was burned clean of all humus; and what was left is an almost sterile soilbed that will take decades to once more become a viable seed bed for trees unless it is the recipient of some very special and expensive care.

The Yellowstone Fire was a classic example of what happens when man tries to govern the forests without taking into consideration the natural requirements of that woodland. If ever there was a forest that needed burning, that certainly was Yellowstone. For forty years, fire had been suppressed in a largely lodgepole-pine forest with the result that the trees had grown to maturity and beyond with practically no new growth started, since lodgepole pine needs the heat of a forest fire to pop the seeds out of the cones and so ensure a new crop. The problem could have been alleviated in Yellowstone by...horrible words!...logging the decadent forest and burning the slash, which would have provided the heat necessary to ensure a new generation of trees without devastating the landscape. Can you imagine the hue and cry that would have arisen if this logical and sensible solution had been applied, or even suggested? The cries of "Greed!" because some timber would have been salvaged and presumably sold at a profit? Instead, the natural devastation it left behind is far uglier than any clearcut would have been. At least a clearcut would have been green again within five years while some of those blackened acres will not be green again during my lifetime, and I fully intend to live at least three more decades.

That same problem faces foresters today; they are faced with a dilemma where they lose no matter what they do. In the Selway-Bitterroot Wilderness Area, a roadless section closed to mechanized travel, the Forest Service is experimenting with the idea of letting wilderness fires burn themselves out. They might as well, since they have no choice. Fighting fires in rugged, dry wilderness areas where there are no roads over which mechanized equipment may be driven is sheer suicide, as quite a few casualties in this area will attest. In a wilderness, fire is a perfectly natural way of life, Nature's way of clearcutting an old forest so that a new one may be propagated. The whole eco system is founded upon it and since this is a "natural area" it should be allowed to run its destructive, fiery course. After all, wilderness areas are supposed to be unmanaged and nothing is more unmanaged than a forest fire.

To generations of foresters raised with the idea that fire–any fire–is a catastrophe, this seems sheer heresy, since the greatest innovation in forest protection over the last fifty years has been the magnificent work done in the suppression of wildfires. Compared to the Peshtigos and Tillamooks of yesteryear, present day outbreaks are pretty small affairs, although they still can happen, as Yellowstone will attest. The big reasons are the quick action that results whenever smoke is sighted and the network of logging roads that makes modern fire-fighting equipment available before that half-acre brush fire can mushroom into an inferno covering several square miles.

Millions of acres of beautiful, productive forests are standing today that would have become blackened snags without the intensified efforts of the fire prevention campaigns, such as the Northwest-born "Keep Green" movement and Smokey the Bear. Instead, these woods flourish as a living tribute to the hard work, accomplishments and satisfactory results of controlling unwanted fires. That doesn't mean that fire is entirely out of place in our woods, an idea that makes some leaders of the fire prevention programs go up in smoke. Our woods, especially the drier forest lands, are ecosystems in which fire, or some other means of reducing flammable material, has a definite place.

This is where the logger comes in. By removing wood and breaking up the continuity of the flammable chain, the logger replaces fire or a bug kill as a means of renewing an old forest and promoting new growth. If for no other reason, this makes his work a worthwhile endeavor. Unfortunately, the general public has yet to understand the logger's link in this chain of events; although once accepted, this concept may very well swing public opinion in his direction. A good part of the blame for this lack of knowledge on the part of the general public can be put squarely on the shoulders of the forest-products industry. They have been so certain that they are doing a worthwhile job that they have believed these truths are so self-evident as to need no promulgation. That is not the case. The work that the logger does, its worth to the general public and the logger's place in the ecological chain have never before been made known emphatically enough. If this book does nothing else, that will have been an excellent reason for writing it. So to emphasize by repetition, we have a choice. We can let the logger systematically break up the flammable chain or let forest fires do the job. It comes down to a simple statement: log it, or burn it.

Meanwhile the experiments with uncontrolled fires in the wilderness areas are being watched very carefully by foresters, for the outcome of this daring innovation could influence the future course of fire prevention or fire usage. While the forests of the Intermountain are quite different from those of the coast, there are still enough similarities to make the knowledge obtained from this experiment applicable to all regions.

Although the Intermountain has largely been spared the spotted owl problem, there are other areas of ecological concern, some of them grave enough to seriously threaten the well-being of the region's woodlands. A case in point would be the serious spruce budworm infestation that threatens the spruce and fir growth of the Blue Mountains of Washington and Oregon. This insect feeds on the new shoots that sprout in the spring and thereby prevents the tree from putting on any new growth. After a few years of this treatment, the tree dies.

The west sides of these states are quite familiar with these pests and have usually countered them with a little judicious spraying; but on the eastern side, vigorous legal action by preservationist groups has tied up such action in court to the point where little or nothing has been done to combat this scourge. The preservationists say that the solution to this problem should be left to nature, since a natural solution would not have the adverse effect of a pesticide. What they seem to overlook is that nature's solution would be to let the forest die, thus starving out the bugs and solving the problem, but also starving out the loggers who subsist on this land. While the preservationists seem to think this would be a wonderful idea, the loggers view this solution with considerably less enthusiasm. Meanwhile, the bugs merrily proliferate and the forests take on a decidedly shabby look, just one more example, and a sad one, where the interference of pressure groups has resulted in a weakened, ravaged forest.

The Intermountain has within its domains almost every type of coniferous wood except southern pine and sequoia. The lower slopes are pine country with some gorgeous specimens of ponderosa, and the well watered regions sport some really impressive cedar. The largest concentrations of white pine are in the Idaho Panhandle, with some very impressive stands in Montana, and the plebeian but very versatile lodgepole pine seems to grow everywhere. Spruce, noble and white fir, an occasional hemlock and the ubiquitous Douglas fir make up most of the balance, with a little largely-ornamental Engleman spruce crowning the higher elevations. In the fall of the year, the bright yellow splashes of color blazing from the mountainsides proclaim that western larch is also well represented in the woodland inventory of the Intermountain.

When the rules were either non-existent or written by the timber barons, even the steep slopes of fragily soiled hills were logged with no thought of the consequences. The resulting erosion made reforestation not only difficult or impossible but also produced scars that are still pointed out as examples of how the logger is ruining the country. Many of these areas are being rehabilitated with modern methods so that places that had not grown trees for fifty years are again wearing a mantle of green. The particularly hot and fierce forest fires of the region usually leave behind a seared land that requires special attention if it is to be rehabilitated because the dry nature of the soil makes it possible for the fires to bake out all the humus, thus effectively sterilizing the land.

The modern logger on Forest Service lands who must render an exact accounting of his stewardship to the ever watchful Forest Service harvests with one eye on the profits that will allow him to stay in business and the other on environmental damage which could close him down. The Intermountain does not have a spotted owl problem, but it does have another one; and as my Montana friends wrily pointed out a much bigger one, grizzly bears. Since the bears are a threatened and protected species, a bear taking up residence on a logger's sale or even some distance from it can effectively shut him down. There are even rules that keep mechanized equipment off certain roads during that time when the bears have romance in mind. Their mere presence certainly has an effect on the peace of mind of even a tough Montana logger. The logger is blamed for many things; but interfering with the love life of a grizzly bear is low on his list of priorities, even if he is blamed for it. He's used to that: he is often blamed for scars in ecologically-sensitive areas that were there before he was born, so he can be forgiven if he gets a bit defensive now and them.

The days when a man would irretrievably desecrate a hillside and get away with it are gone, and good riddance! Even on his own land, the manner in which a man treats his land is now a matter of public concern and anyone who maltreats his acres is liable to be spending so many hours in court he won't have time to rape any more land. Streams flow through miles of environment, both public and private; and what a man does in his own domain directly influences his neighbor and his neighbor's land. One of the greatest benefits derived from the awareness of ecological problems is the weight of public opinion that can be brought to bear against an inefficient operator, so that he may mend his ways.

The favored logging season for the Intermountain seems to be winter; in fact skidder operations seem facilitated by snow, and frozen roads hold up quite well under the pounding of log trucks headed for the cold-decks at the edge of the logging sites. Spring turns those roads to quagmires and effectively brings logging to a halt. In anticipation of this, the mills have built up

In the Blue Mountains of Washington, a light carriage riding a three-quarter inch mainline spools out chokers powered by a small diesel engine. This equipment would be considered puny on the coast but is entirely adequate for this size of timber.

This neat, efficient show near Valley, Washington, utilizes modern hydraulic loaders to load a powerful, large-capacity truck, only one example of how machinery promotes a more efficient operation.

This long-boom loader building a nice load is a holdover from another age but proves that time-tested equipment is not only adequate, but often desirable. The skill of the operator running that grapple is the deciding factor.

Winter is often the best time for logging in the Intermountain, since the snow and the frozen surface facilitate moving the logs without disturbing the soil.

huge stacks of logs during the winter months, and it is upon this supply that they feed during spring breakup. Usually the log decks are built at the head of rock-ballasted roads or even at the terminus of a paved road which guarantees the mills a steady source of supply.

While winter is the favored season, that doesn't mean the logging is easy. Winter in the Intermountain can be downright ferocious, with blizzards lasting for days and twelve-foot drifts common. The contractor must have a significant investment in road-clearing equipment, for if this lifeline is closed off, he may as well start thinking of unemployment compensation. The Intermountain logger is conditioned to these conditions and probably takes a perverse pleasure in knowing that weather this brutal would stall a coastal logger while, to him, it's all in a day's work and part of the mystique that makes the Intermountain logger the tough, proud man that he is.

The isolation of the Intermoutain country from other major logging centers has fostered logging practices peculiar to this region; practices that are founded in the solution of local problems and adapted to local conditions. The logger on the landing, who may have to walk the length of a felled log, may be wearing the traditional logger's caulked boots; but the other members of the show may very well be wearing heavy outdoor boots...without caulks. Caulked boots are traditional for a logger; it gives him secure footing on a felled tree, but when you're in snow up to your hips a large part of the day, those steel-spiked boots transmit cold to the feet and so are supplatned by warm insulated boots. Some of their terms would puzzle a coastal

logger. An Oregon logger knows that a "sawyer" is the man who runs the headrig in a sawmill. The Intermountain logger is just as positive that a sawyer is that man on the crew who falls the tree, the equivalent to the California "cutter" or the Washington, Oregon, Alaska or British Columbia "faller." Likewise, some of the coastal terms seem peculiar to the Intermountain logger. On the coast, a "busheler" is a faller on piecework; to the Idahoan, that might mean a man paid to sack potatoes by the bushel. It's a different world, but these Intermountain loggers can hold their own with anyone, because they have a firm understanding of the methods and techniques of their area and the ability to handle any type of logging job. Their basic idea is one they share with loggers everywhere: harvest the crop, regenerate it and stay alive.

With the large number of trees that must be processed to make up a load, it was only natural that mechanization would find a fertile field in the Intermountain. Feller bunchers are in increasing use, wherever the ground will permit it. If the terrain demands a high-lead system, it is liable to be a small, tractor-mounted tower of maybe twenty-five feet rather than the towering "tin spar" common on the coast, although occasionally, where the terrain demands it, you will see a tall steel tower as large as anything in the Cascades. One of the most beautiful loads of logs I saw anywhere was loaded in Montana with a long-boom crane equipped with a mechanical grapple. That operator had thirty years' experience with that type of machinery, and the things he could do with that old fashioned grapple would have put to shame the operator of the latest high-technology hydraulic loader.

It is really a wonderful experience to watch a skilled crew going about its work without tearing up half an acre just to move one tree. Every motion is synchronized within the crew. The sawyer lays down the trees in such a way that the skidder operator can hook onto them with minimum effort; the bucker gets the most scale out of each log, and the loader builds a load that will allow the truck driver to move the greatest volume compatible with safety regulations. It is a game played with gigantic toys and the loggers of the Intermountain play it extremely well. Some of the best logging I have seen anywhere in gathering material for this book was in the Intermountain, but it is only fair to report that this region also had the worst example of the type of logging that the industry eschewed fifty years ago. The loggers of the Intermountain are good; but like loggers everywhere, they aren't all choirboys.

The Selway-Bitterroot National Forest covers a good part of the Intermountain area. It also has a wilderness section which was badly impacted by the gigantic 1910 fire, the smoke from which was seen as far east as Chicago. It was ravaged again in 1912, and the land was so badly burned that it is just now recovering. It is a land of spectacular scenery and lately has been discovered by hordes of adventuresome types eager to see a pristine wilderness. The Lolo Pass Highway, from Lewiston, Idaho, to Missoula, Montana skirts this huge forested area, giving ready access to tourists. A great, unused reservoir of timber is held forever in this wilderness area which is forever closed to logging and rightly so. Some areas of wilderness must be allowed to exist and this is one of the best. Legend has it that the workers on the Lolo Pass Highway, which was finally pushed through in 1962, experienced some of the best trout fishing in the world, since they largely followed the Lochsa River which flowed out of the wilderness area and was completely potable. With the advent of the highway, the Lochsa still flows gin-clear, but drinking from it today would take on all the aspects of a somewhat sporting proposition.

Farther south and west, the headwaters of the North Fork of the Clearwater support large stands of white pine which feed the world's largest white-pine sawmill, the Potlatch plant at Lewiston, Idaho. Throughout the whole region, the impact of new technology and ecological restrictions has had an effect. Some towns have lost their sawmills, the victims of changing technologies and improved roads that make the transportation of logs to a larger, distant mill economically feasible. Other mills, especially the small, privately held ones, grimly hang on, fighting the trend by improving efficiency, using every sliver of wood and praying a lot. The logging camp at Headquarters, formerly the second largest in the contiguous United States, is gone, although the area is still an active timber-producing area serviced by loggers who live mostly in the neighboring small towns, although some still commute to and from Lewiston. There is change; but in the small timber towns, teenage boys still serve their apprenticeship in the woods under the critical eyes of their fathers and carry on a tradition as old as the white occupancy of this land.

Clear up to the Canadian border, the whole country is timber oriented. Bonners Ferry is the hub of the Northern Idaho timber country, while some distance to the east, Colville, in Washington state, services an area that every year produces over two hundred million board feet of high-grade pine and Douglas fir. The area is of sufficient importance that large corporations, notably Boise Cascade, Louisiana-Pacific and Plum Creek, have made heavy investments in timber lands and new processing facilities. Plum Creek has erected a state-of-the-art sawmill at Arden which saws some of the most beautifully finished lumber I have ever seen. Boise Cascade, always an innovator, has erected a large plant at Kettle Falls, which not only meets all its own power needs by burning biomass but also generates enough excess power to light the adjacent town. The experimental plant has been so successful that it has attracted national attention as an indicator of how our future power needs can be met without depending upon expensive and unpredictable foreign oil.

The Blue Mountains have extensive stands of white fir, spruce, Douglas fir, larch, ponderosa and lodgepole pine and have been extensively logged for over a century. These are enthralling mountains, and the Forest Service very wisely has placed logging operations well out of sight of the few paved roads that penetrate this wilderness. Consequently, most people are unaware of just how extensive logging operations carried out here really are; but well-stocked log piles at Joseph, Elgin, Pilot Rock and Walla Walla testify that the forests of the area are a good part of the economic mix that fuels the prosperity of the region. Elgin has a large plant, erected by Boise Cascade Corporation, which seems to specialize in processing the lodgepole pine which grows profusely in the Blue Mountains and which, up to a few years ago, was not particularly important as a lumber tree. Then it was discovered that the small tree made an excellent, lightweight, quite strong stud and that the residue had good value as chips for producing the light-colored kraft paper which is the specialty of the large Boise Cascade pulp and paper mill at nearby Wallula.

One of the advantages of the Intermountain is that in this region a person can get into the logging business with considerably less investment than is necessary in the Cascade area. It still is a place where a determined gyppo with old, but still usable equipment can get a start; and there is a good pool of skilled labor which can supply his manpower needs. Missoula, Kallispell and Libby, in Montana, are all logging centers; and some of those operations are large by any standards. In those areas, and indeed throughout the Intermountain, it is not unusual to see equipment forty years old, or even older, still working, still doing the job and representing an investment well within the scope of a person willing to forego the new Mercedes and the lakeside villa until he is established and his second-hand equipment has been replaced with state-of-the-art loaders and delimbers. One such gyppo, who was told that his thirty-year-old log trucks were not that impressive, came back with the perfect answer. "If I want to impress anyone," he said, "I show him my financial statement."

The recent advent of chipboard, stud mills and pulp

operations have had a salutary effect on wood utilization. If a log has any appreciable amount of sound wood left in it, it will be trucked to the mill, whereas not so long ago that same log would have been left to rot in the woods simply because it would not have paid its way out of the woods. The same thing applies to small timber. A log as small as four inches across the small end is transformed into high-quality studs and the residue becomes paper chips. The light colored wood of the Intermoutain produces a naturally light-colored kraft paper which is highly prized because of its ability to take and hold superior printing and, therefore, brings a premium price on the market. A few years ago, the log that produces this superior material would not have paid its way out of the woods because no pulp mill was close enough to guarantee even a modest profit.

It is a sad fact of life that economics play a major part in wood utilization. If a mill is nearby and the hauling costs justify it, that cull log that is useless for lumber will be utilized by the pulp mill. If no market exists for boarder line material, that log stays in the woods and enriches only a limited area with the products of its decay.

The future of this region is especially bright. Intermoutain country is rich in scenic beauty, comparatively undeveloped and has a growth potential that is finally being realized as evinced by the new flood of capital being poured into this region, especially by large corporations not exactly noted for making unresearched investment. New technology favors the small trees as we move out of the period where emphasis was mainly on the utilization of the large, old-growth tree and into an age of complete utilization of the smaller, second growth. This fits the type of tree most prevalent throughout the Intermountain region, and not a few far-sighted investors are betting that this is the region where the investments they are making will have their most spectacular future growth. The time is coming, and rapidly, when the fiber in a tree will be more important than its physical dimensions because technology has already begun to divorce the industry from the limitations imposed by fixed size. Particle board is already supplanting plywood in many building applications and particleboard can be made from any sized trees. Research along this line indicates that within a decade wood technologists will be able to reconstitute a board of any dimensions from fiber of trees that are now completely ignored. And with its varied terrain, Intermountain can count its trees in great variety and look forward with confidence to a bright and prosperous tomorrow.

Hydraulic loaders are pretty much standard on a modern logging show, although the average gyppo will work with whatever equipment he has on hand or can afford. This show is in the Blue Mountains of Washington.

This log deck is built up at the edge of the St. Joe river in Idaho. The logs, strapped into bundles with steel ties, will be formed into a raft and towed by a hard-working tug to the mills at Coeur D'Alene.

This feller buncher is a comparatively new development which has revolutionized logging in small timber. Using either hydraulic shears or a carbide tipped rotary saw, it cuts the tree and stacks it in neat windrows.

CHAPTER X

TOOLS OF THE TRADE

The <u>Bible</u> has long had a deservedly cherished place in the hearts of Americans. To some, it is a source of consolation and inspiration, to others a piece of literature beyond compare, to still others the literal word of God. Archaeologists and historians have found the places and events described in it to be highly accurate, but few people realize that it records the first extensive gyppo operation of which we have a reliable record. The fifth chapter of the first Book of Kings records that Hiram, King of Tyre, entered into an agreement with Solomon, King of Israel, to furnish a considerable volume of fine fir and cedar as well as some skilled artisans for the temple Solomon was building at Jerusalem. For his services, Hiram received twenty thousand measures of flour, twenty thousand jars of fine oil, plus a few cities here and there. Thus Hiram takes his place in history not only as a fine builder, but also as the first gyppo.

Hiram delivered the logs on time, mostly by laying the lash across the backs of twenty thousand slaves, and cajoling along the ten thousand draftees Solomon had consigned to his tender mercies. History does not record the kind of performance Hiram got, but it is reasonable to assume that twenty good men with modern equipment would have easily outproduced his crew.

Slaves were readily obtainable in Hiram's day. Their numbers were limited only by his army's ability to capture them and his commissary to feed them, after a fashion. The modern logger substitutes horsepower and sophisticated engineering to get the job done and he does it with infinitely greater efficiency. Even the most brutally driven slave is no match for a tireless machine.

Ever since primitive man practically gnawed down his first tree with a hand-held sharp rock, the search has gone on for a better way to do the job. Adding a handle to that rock–the first primitive ax–was a big step forward; and for thousands of years this tool was gradually improved and became the basic way of felling trees. To this day, the ax symbolizes a woodsman, even though that very useful tool plays a relatively minor role in modern logging. The frontiers of America were cleared of trees by axe men; the more efficient saw did not come into general use until a way of rolling steel into a thin strip was devised, which, with the addition of teeth, became the falling saw, the fabled "misery whip" of old time logging.

By comparison to the colorful era at the turn of the century, modern-day logging is pretty drab. With the glamor and excitement reminiscence attaches to that roaring time, it is well to remember some significant facts. Old-time logging turned magnificent, smooth-faced, iron-muscled young men of twenty into hard-handed, stoop-shouldered, iron-muscled old men of forty, assuming that they survived that long. Putting two young giants at either end of a twelve-foot misery whip and watching that steel ribbon bite its way into a tree may have been exciting for the observer, but was lung-bursting work for the poor devils pulling that saw.

When I researched my first book on modern logging, I tried to get some figures by which a comparison could be made between the amounts of wood that had been cut since the dawn of time using hand tools versus the amount cut since the advent of power machinery. Predictably, I was unable to get any accurate figures simply because, in the old days, no accurate figures were kept. So, an educated guess is about the best that can be done. Considering that man has been fashioning wood with hand-powered tools for at least ten thousand years and infinitely longer if we consider the fashioning of spear handles and dugout canoes, it is a safe assumption that more wood had been cut by hand than has been by power tools, even though modern power saws are rapidly closing what must have been an immense gap. A tour through our own Northwest forests, with their innumerable huge stumps notched with springboard holes, reminds us that the old-growth forests that covered the land a century ago were felled by hand tools.

With the advent of steam-powered yarders and locomotives, the inventive Yankee mind soon turned its attention to the more efficient sawing of those big logs. Since steam was the first mobile power source, early steam saws were located at the landing where the yarder's boiler could motivate those first cumbersome monsters. They were weird and wonderful contraptions, and some of them even worked, but legend has it that the first men operating these things are remembered reverently in the logging fraternity as the most inventive, fervent and prolific purveyors of profanity the woods have ever produced.

The real breakthrough in portable power saws came with the gasoline engine. Calling these saws "portable" is allowing considerable license, since they weighed about one hundred and thirty pounds, and even among loggers, it took a special breed of man to hold one of these sputtering monsters up against a tree, especially while balancing on a springboard. A few men could–and they became the first power-saw fallers. Some of the best stories and legends in the logging fraternity have to do with the titanic contests between

Unquestionably the greatest improvement in logging since the invention of the axe, the modern chainsaw is the logger's indispensable personal tool, and the good logger treats it accordingly.

woodland John Henrys who pitted their muscle and expertise against the new sputtering giants. They usually won, unless the chosen tree was a really large one, simply because the more mobile hand team would be three-quarters through that tree before the power-saw men could get their sputtering monster settled down to cutting wood, or even started; but little by little, the power saws improved. It must have been a very sad day for the men who had spent a lifetime tuning up a Swedish Fiddle when they realized their smooth music had been superseded by modern jazz.

Logging has seen many improvements since it became an industry, but the greatest of all is unquestionably the power saw. Everything else, mobile spars, power loaders, even the indispensable bulldozer, is simply an advancement over existing methods. The power saw was so revolutionary, and had such an impact on the industry, that it must undoubtedly be classed as the single greatest advancement in the art of cutting wood since some unknown genius tied a sharp rock onto a handle, and so invented the ax. The power saw, in its era, was the last major breakthrough in woods mechanization; but its impact was such that it must be rated first in all the improvements that have come along in the last century. The only appreciable change that I have seen in power saws in the last eighteen years is that the modern saw is lighter and has safety features routinely built into it that were just beginning to be known back then. It is still heavy, especially towards the end of the day, but nowhere near the hundred pound weight of its progenitors. Its efficiency is such that it can easily cut through a tree in

ten minutes that would have taken a good team a half day to fall in 1910. Compared to the old days, there aren't nearly as many fallers and buckers in the woods today, but the volume of timber cut per man is immeasurably greater.

During this same time, a marked change in the basic power that had ruled the woods for fifty years came about. The first trees felled commercially in the Pacific Northwest were hauled to the sawmills by oxen–patient, slow-moving animals with large appetites and limited range. Timber more than a thousand yards from this plodding motive power was safe, unless it happened to be near a stream which could furnish transportation. The bull teams lasted a long time because few people thought a better way would ever by devised, and none was, until in the 1880s, with a shrill scream and a rattle of gears, steam crashed the woods. It is one of the few sorrows I have in life that I missed the age of steam in the woods. As late as 1973 there was an old steam donkey engine operating in a quarry near Tacoma, and anyone hearing the pulsating rhythm of that machine laboring under a full head of steam would understand what an exciting, pulse-pounding age that must have been. From 1880 to the late 1930s steam ruled the woods, and incredibly powerful machines using it were developed. Viewing a modern logging show, one would easily believe that the complex system of a high-lead operation is the result of jet-age technology, but in fact it is only a refinement of methods initiated in the days when the steam donkey was king.

The steam donkey was a gigantic machine spooling thousands of yards of one-an -a-half inch steel cable on

This loader, working on the Olympic Peninsula is capable of lifting a five ton log and placing it onto a truck so gently that the truck will not even be jolted. Here it is being used to move a carriage which in itself weighs several tons.

its monstrous drums and riding a sled of huge logs solidly bolted to its frame. The places to which this improbable combination was winched, pushed and tugged defy description. There are samples of this huge machine still preserved in museums, and even today, there is nothing that even comes close to equaling the massiveness of these monstrous machines. That this gargantuan piece of machinery could pull itself up 45-degree slopes is very hard to believe. That it could cross rivers and even lift itself bodily out of canyons stretches the bounds of credulity. It was the proud boast of the donkey puncher that he could take his machine any place a lokie could go; and the lokie engineers claimed that if a blackberry vine could cling to a hillside, so could a Shay.

Logging in the Pacific Northwest really came of age with the advent of the steam logging locomotive, the "lokie." Superbly adapted to the job it was meant to do, it was about as tough and well-designed a piece of machinery as the inventive American mind has ever produced. Usually, but not always of narrow gauge, the tracks followed the best available grade, although they cheated a bit when a particularly tough ravine had to be crossed. Considering the rough terrain through which most of these early logging railways were constructed, the big wonder is that they moved their monstrous loads at all over the steep grades and high trestles of the mountainous ranges. Accidents were frequent and often spectacular but were taken as a normal consequence of doing business. Many of the trestles the old time logger erected, in defiance of most engineering principles, are still standing and were so sturdily built, using the

material at hand, that many of them would still bear the monstrous loads of the steam age.

The railroad's steel fingers reached up every draw and yarded in timber from a thousand yards on either side. There were some high spots beyond their grasp, and these were "left as seed trees." Maybe this was done intentionally, but the logging ethics of that time refute that suggestion. There were no seed trees left in the areas the loggers could reach, so it is safe to assume that whatever stands escaped the rapacious clutch of the timber barons were saved more by physical limitations than by the goodness of their hearts. The logging ethics of the day dictated that every salable stick be removed and the devil take the next crop! Fires in the enormous debris left in the loggers' wake were accepted as "normal," unlike today's slash fires which are very carefully set and controlled.

The old-time logger probably figured that in his fast, stalwart steam donkey he had the ultimate logging machine. Who would have dreamed that those foul-smelling diesels would ever take the place of a team? But they did, and for two simple reasons: they were mobile and they packed more horsepower into a given space. This is one thing that hasn't changed a bit. The diesels were the prime source of motive power eighteen years ago and they still are. A diesel powering a loader or a yarder can be mounted on crawler treads and be transported or even move itself to the logging site with a minimum of effort. If there is no road, another diesel, this one with crawler treads and pushing a bulldozing blade, makes one. Diesels are everywhere in the woods, on yarders, loaders, caterpillar tractors, trucks–

everywhere a strong, dependable power source is needed. Small diesels are even carried on mobile carriages riding high-lead mainlines and spool out their chokers on radio command. It is started at the beginning of the shift and shut down at the end of the workday, during which time it reliably furnishes power; on command and with a minimum of maintenance. While they don't have the personality of Babe, Paul Bunyon's fabled blue ox, they do have the horsepower, and modern logging depends upon reliable, intelligently applied mechanical force.

Just as the steam era logger was astounded to have his machines supplanted by new and improved equipment, so the present-day logger may be astonished at changes that will make his current equipment obsolete. Ecological restrictions will be the driving force behind this change. If present experiments with the transmission of electrical energy without wires are successful, and it is only a matter of time until they are, we may see electrically-powered saws taking the place of today's gasoline-powered models. The days of the internal combustion engine in the woods, with its attendant fire potential and use of a volatile, highly-explosive fuel are numbered, although that number may very well be a quite substantial one. Something will have to take its place, but it is doubtful that even the most stringent ecological regulations would ever drive loggers back to the two-man saws.

Another improvement in the long, gradual improvement of lumbering equipment is the modern logging truck. The gasoline-powered logging truck first appeared in the Northwest woods over eighty years ago, but today's powerful, streamlined haulers bear only a superficial resemblance to those old solid-tired, chain-driven progenitors. Today's haulers would laugh incredulously at the idea of a thousand yard range for a haul, for many of these men travel a hundred miles or more from the logging site to the mill yard and make two trips a day, even at that distance. The carrying capacity of today's logging truck is far in excess of the legal load limit set for public highways. Therefore these men feel they are carrying a "light" load and make up for lack of capacity with speed.

That doesn't mean that he is driving carelessly. The log truck driver has been the subject of numerous legends, all stressing his fortitude and skill in guiding his iron steed around the hairpin curves and dangerous grades of a logging road often hacked out of the precipitous side of a mountain. I rode on one such road in Montana, where a glance out the window was unobstructed by anything but thin air for at least six hundred feet straight down. That driver took his truck, loaded with over thirty tons of logs secured only by a few binders around hairpin curves, at a carefully calculated speed until he got to the freeway; then it was right up to the legal limit, and on the occasional downhill,

This Canadian-built machine runs a log through a delimbing head with spiked, power-driven rollers. The result is a log shorn of limbs and easily fitted into a neat load.

153

Mounted on a Komatsu yarder, this Steyr delimbing head not only removes the limbs from a log, but also cuts it to length with a computer controlled rotary saw. Then it neatly stacks the denuded log.

quite a bit beyond.

Actually, these highly-skilled, well-trained men may seemingly bring a devil-may-care attitude to their jobs, but that is only a mask, for inwardly they are acutely aware of the many problems of their precarious trade and approach them with respect. A rash or reckless trucker doesn't last very long; the dangers along his route will see to that. The person who survives and prospers is apt to be the careful craftsman who has pride in his trade. He maintains his truck with scrupulous attention to detail and has an ardent desire that his grandson will inherit his job. The modern log truck, with its multiple wheels and enormous tractive power, is a wonderful instrument, but the motivating force behind its success is unquestionably the spirit of élan of the man or woman who drives it.

The whistle punk was one of the most colorful members of the old-time logging crew. His tugs on a light wire actuated the steam whistle on the yarder and so conveyed signals to everyone on the show. This worked quite well while the work in progress was close to the yarder, but got progressively more chancy as distances stretched out to a thousand yards. Nowadays, signals are flashed by a portable radio transmitter carried on a belt allowing the rigging crew boss not only to signal the yarder but also to talk to the operator. They have a number of brand names, but the name Talkie Tooter has become a generic term. That is what it is called when it is working well, which is most of the time. It is, however, a marvelously sophisticated, complex electronic device with over five thousand soldered connections, anyone of which, coming loose,

can cause it to cease functioning, in which case it is called many names, most of them highly scatological. More and more, compact portable radio transmitters are coming into use, so that any member of the logging crew can talk to practically anyone else on the show. This is one change that has occurred in the last eighteen years, part of the communications miracle which has increased safety to a marked degree.

Radio plays a vital part in the success of a modern logging show. Every side I saw was completely radio equipped: the foreman's pickup, the yarder and loader, even bulldozers had transmitters as well as receivers. If the crew members drive to the logging site in their own pickups, there is a CB radio in operation all the way to the logging site, spelling out the truck's position as it proceeds. This instant communication is one of the greatest improvements in modern logging, for before the widespread use of radio, face-to-face communications often between members of the crew separated by a considerable distance took up time that would have better been utilized in getting out the logs.

Eighteen years ago, grapple logging was a comparatively new system just getting established in the business. Time has proved the worth of the system and it is now in common use especially in British Columbia. In this system a grapple riding on a slackline is positioned over cut timber by an operator who may be as much as a half mile from the spotter, who is stationed with a walkie talkie at the point where cut logs must be picked up. Using a very stylized and precise set of signals, the spotter tells the operator where and when to drop his grapple, and the log is quickly reeled in even though the grapple operator cannot see the log he has picked up. The system depends on a good rapport between operator and spotter, but once such a team is established their production can put to shame the best team of choker setters available. It is especially useful in rough or swampy terrain where the conventional setting of chokers would entail even more than usual maximum effort.

Another feature of modern logging that has stood the test of time is the use of helicopters. It was a well-established way of logging ecologically-sensitive slopes way back in 1973; but in the intervening years it has blossomed into a practically indispensable tool, especially in view of ecological restrictions that would otherwise prohibit logging on well-stocked, but sensitive, slopes. The chopper, with its ability to waft logs off even the most controversial site with no soil disturbance, has endeared itself both to loggers and environmentalists, who see in this expensive but very efficient tool a way of placating both parties in environmental disputes. To justify heli-logging, the site must by very productive, the stumpage low, and other conditions absolutely perfect, for those double-bladed flying bananas don't operate for free, and it takes very rich timber to justify their usage.

That is only one aspect of helicopter usage, but there are other aspects that have made this machine an integral part of the modern logging scene. Ask the injured logger whose life was saved because a chopper was able to get him to medical facilities where the intricate work necessary to achieve this end could be done, and you will have an enthusiastic endorsement of the flying ambulance. Ask the beleaguered operator working deep in the brush who needs a critical part flown in, and whose part is delivered onto the landing within a half hour, and you will have another fervent booster. But most of all, talk to the forest fire crew surrounded by a wildly spreading blaze, and whose only avenue of escape is by air, and you will find people who will tell you that the helicopter is the biggest improvement in logging since chainsaws.

These are dramatic instances of the helicopter's usefulness but of equal importance is the everyday flexibility the chopper brings to a logging show. A chopper can string haywire, transport personnel or inspect an entire operation. It can be used in seeding, fertilizing, aerial surveying; but probably it's biggest contribution is the feeling of security it brings to an isolated work crew. This is especially true in Alaska, where the work is usually done miles from any sophisticated medical facilities. A logger working there knows that, if he is injured, the chopper can become a flying ambulance that will get him to the hospital in time to make the repairs that will enable him to continue a productive life in the woods.

One of the changes that has come about in the last eighteen years is the disappearance of balloon logging. It was a colorful operation, moved wood off slopes that would otherwise never have been logged and could do some things that no other system could quite duplicate. Apparently, those fringe benefits were not enough. The helicopter was more mobile and less expensive, so balloon logging is now largely a memory, albeit a very colorful and vivid one.

The steam era saw the advent of the high-lead system, a method of logging that has stood the test of time. In the Pacific Northwest and any other place with large timber and terrain not suitable for skidder logging, this is the system that gets the trees to the landing. A high-lead show required the stringing of a large, strong steel cable to the far end of a logging site, which, securely attached to a large tree, and well-guyed to stand the tremendous loads to which it will be subjected, becomes the mainline over which all the trees felled within a considerable distance parallel to it will be transported. The other end of the line is fastened to either a spar tree or a mobile metal spar. A powerful diesel located in the yarder furnished the power that moves the carriage along the mainline and drags the logs to the landing. A variation of this system, called a slackline, features a mainline that can be lowered to make the chokers available to the setters. Still another system was developed in the Alps to move heavy timber down from high elevations. Called the Wissen System, it depends largely on gravity. The system works very well and is used in the Northwest in places where the steep elevations necessary for it to function are available.

When the old-time logger moved to a new location, the first thing he looked for was a tall, stout tree that could be topped, rigged with a heavy bull block, and suitably guyed, to serve as a spar tree at the center of the new landing. There are still a few spar trees in use, but their days are numbered. Not only does the mobile, telescoping metal spar offer a more versatile and completely dependable tool but it is always there when you need it. The telescoping, self-mobile, metal spar can be moved to a new location, guyed, and in operation in less time than it takes a good man to top a tall tree and rig the necessary hardware. Also, good tree toppers are hard to find, and getting scarcer all the time as the old timers finally reach the end of their careers and are not replaced. Although the tin spar is very expensive and prone to freakish ailments, it still is a big improvement over the spar tree, mostly because it can be put into the right place at the right time; and practically all well-equipped companies have one or more. Small gyppos have ambivalent feelings about them. When a gyppo is just starting out in business, he has a tendency to regard them as a pretentious luxury and points out that many spar trees can be rigged for the cost of one tin spar. Of course, as soon as he has accumulated enough capital to make a down payment, those objections are somehow forgotten and he happily goes into debt for one of those capricious, telescoping beauties.

In smaller timber, especially in the Intermountain, a small version of the mobile tower, known as the "Idaho Jammer," mounted on its own mobile tracks, is in wide use. With about a thirty-foot elevation, it is usually quite adequate to run a slackline, especially if the timber is on the small side; and while not nearly as impressive as the towering tin spar, it has a large and devoted following who point out that it does the job, and anyone using a sledgehammer to swat flies is wasting a lot of time and energy. Both the large spar and its smaller counterpart are used with mobile carriages, radio controlled, which ride the mainline, can stop on command and spool out chokers as needed. A small diesel engine mounted in the carriage usually provides the power to spool out the chokers, but it is the force supplied by the yarder's main engines that actually move the logs to the landing. Some of the smaller carriages rely on gravity to drop their chokers, but they are a vanishing breed. Much more common is the large carriage weighing several tons which, on radio command, will spool out chokers in three directions and is a very reliable piece of equipment.

The other large piece of equipment on the landing is the loader, the direct descendant of the smoke-belching steam donkey. This rig may not be as colorful but it is a lot more practical. Powerful, smooth-running, it is usually equipped with a hydraulic grapple which can pick up a five-ton log and place it onto a truck bed so delicately that the truck isn't even jolted. A loader is usually scaled to the size of the logs it will be loading so that they are huge on the coast. In the Intermountain, an old-time, long boom derrick with a mechanical grapple, run by an experienced operator is entirely adequate. Loaders, often called "shovels," are the darlings of the men who have mastered them, and the bane of those who have allowed themselves to be mastered, which may explain why loaders almost always have a name, by some coincidence, usually feminine.

In British Columbia they have developed a very interesting variation which has considerably increased the loader's efficiency. Above the boom a supple twenty-foot log about ten inches in diameter is clamped in metal brackets. This "snorkel" as it is called, carries the weight of the grapple–only the actual lifting is still done by the regular boom. With long practice, yarder operators have developed the ability to throw their grapples in much the same manner as a fly fisherman casts his fly. A word of caution, culled from personal experience: Don't ever bet a case of good Canadian beer that the operator cannot cast his grapple the length of a football field, especially downhill, and reel in a designated log. Some of those Canadians will do anything to win a bet, even achieve the seemingly impossible, and not just lucky once, but time after time.

The major change that has taken place in logging equipment in the last eighteen years is unquestionably the tremendous strides in mechanization. In a mechanical show, the loader today may be equipped to do a couple of other jobs that formerly took the complete attention of two men. When the skidder brings in a turn of logs, the loader's grapple will pick one out of the pile. A series of toothed, power-driven rollers will pull that log through a delimbing head where all remaining branches are neatly shorn off, measure that log with laser beams, then accurately cut it to size with a hydraulically-driven saw. Only then does the traditional work of a loader come into play: the cut, denuded log is neatly stacked into its proper category. That delimbing head is completely computer controlled, and all the operator needs to do is punch the right button. I saw one operation in the Intermountain where such a set-up, teamed with a feller-buncher, consistently loaded out fifteen to twenty loads a day with an eight-man crew. This progressive gyppo had bet on mechanization, invested over a million dollars in new equipment and

was now reaping a richly-deserved harvest.

No enumeration of logging equipment would be complete without mentioning skidders, those double-jointed perverse machines that successfully wed the strength of ten elephants with the agility of a mountain goat. Skidders seem to be a natural progression for youngsters enamored of All-Terrain Vehicles who think that in the skidder they have found the ultimate ATV. A few days on the job quickly bring disillusionment: while the skidder can in fact go practically anywhere, the fledgling drivers soon learn that the idea is to snake the logs out of the woods without tearing up the landscape or knocking down valuable young trees. Eighteen years ago the skidder was already a well-established tool, usually a medium-sized cat with a winch and multiple chokers. At the site of the felled timber, the operator became a choker setter, attached his steel cables to two or three logs and headed back to the landing. On the larger shows with a multiplicity of skidders, the choker setting was done by men delegated to that job, leaving the driver free to take a break while the logs were being attached. In any case there was a time-waste involved that has been eliminated with the newer, grapple-equipped machines. These are usually rubber tired, although the massiveness of redwood logging usually dictates that there the skidders are crawler tractors scaled to the size of the logs they move. The fledgling skidder operator soon learns that if he has any hot-rodding tendencies left after the first week on the job, he's liable to be setting chokers after that. The machine he is driving can cost well up into six figures; it is a complex, beautifully designed machine which must be carefully maintained, and above all, driven safely, even over the rough terrain that is routine in his job. Any competitive instincts he may still have can be dissipated in contending with the other skidder operators to see who can bring in the most logs.

A natural adjunct to skidder operation is the feller-buncher, one of the greatest technological changes that has taken place in Pacific Northwest logging. Machines using hydraulic shears to cut the small pine timber of the South were just getting a start eighteen years ago, but they have been developed to the point that they are now a major component of the logging done in the Northwest. A feller-buncher is a massive, track-mounted machine with curved steel arms that can wrap themselves around a tree and hold it steadily while either a carbide-tipped rotary saw, or a pair of hydraulic shears cuts the tree at ground level. The cut trees are laid down in windrows, so that when the skidder reaches them, its grapple will have a pod of trees already assembled for transport. It is infinitely more efficient than the old choker operation and much safer because no one is at ground level. Feller-bunchers can presently handle a tree of up to twenty inches in diameter, but, as usual in logging machinery, plans are already under way to make this very efficient method of logging applicable to even larger timber.

A major part of the total cost of logging is road building. In King Hiram's day that was done by thousands of slaves wielding mattocks; today, the major part of the work is done by a bulldozer. This ugly, snorting machine can move more rocks and earth in

A grapple equipped skidder is a natural adjunct to a feller buncher. With its hydraulic grapple, it gathers in the pods laid down by the cutting machine and hauls them to the landing where the delimber will process them.

one day than a thousand men using picks and shovels. It is a truly universal machine and probably the first piece of mobile equipment a logger acquires when he gets into the logging business, for a good bulldozer with a stout blade and a good winch can do a great part of work entailed in logging. It can build roads, clear a landing, snake out logs and can even be rigged to load a truck. Many a logger' wife complains, and justifiably, that her husband's bulldozer is a strong rival for his affections. That may very well be so. A good cat is always willing to serve, even if it must sometimes be coaxed into action with some well-chosen pet words and a few strategically-placed kicks.

Fire is an important tool, as has already been described elsewhere in this book. Another controversial tool is fertilizer, which can greatly stimulate the growth of trees and thus reduce the time cycle between crops. Under closely-controlled application undesirable brush growth can be controlled with chemicals, although this practice is coming under very close scrutiny by the ecological watchdogs. A great amount of research is being concentrated on natural enemies to woods-threatening species with the aim of substituting this method of control for the use of pesticides; and advances in this method indicate that this will be the chosen control measure of the future. The chief problem with most control methods seems to be the ancillary effect that always seems to emerge when one species is stimulated, usually to the detriment of other flora or fauna. The spruce budworm problem that is currently (1991) plaguing the Blue Mountains is a good example. The budworm could be controlled with massive uses of

pesticides, but the side effect on fauna would allegedly be so severe that the problem goes largely untreated, while various ecological groups wrangle over what treatment, if any, the "natural" infestation should receive. Meanwhile, the bugs merrily propagate, and a whole forested region is in danger of being stripped of its trees, clearcut by bugs and ravaged by fire.

The last eighteen years has seen a tremendous growth in the use of computers, and the forest products industry is in the forefront of the research that every day uncovers more usage for that versatile machine. In the head offices of all the large companies, banks of computers are constantly digesting the vital statistics of a complex industry and making them available at the touch of a key. For instance, a running inventory of the amount of salable timber available at any time can be obtained in a matter of seconds, simply by punching the right keys. Computers are integrated into the design of machinery, whether from bucking a log to the right length at the landing or sawing that log for the greatest possible scale at the mill.

Research into the best forest practices is an ongoing study, and all the knowledge gained from these studies is fed into the omnivorous computer to become part of the knowledge bank from which the whole industry can draw. Forestry has come a long way from the days when everything had to be checked experimentally because there was no bank of knowledge available. Now, experiments that formerly would have taken years are fed into a computer, and in a matter of minutes a remarkably accurate print-out is in hand.

The technology of cutting wood and caring for the

A smaller version of the towering tin spar, mounted on its own mobile carriage, is quite adequate for a high-lead or slackline operation in small to medium-sized timber. Very popular in the Intermountain region.

The massiveness of the machinery used in coastal logging is well illustrated by this Madill carriage. Weighing several tons, it rides the mainline, carries its own power plant, and can spew out chokers in three directions on radio command.

forests has come a long way from the days of King Hiram. It will continue to do so, possibly with a smaller cadre of workers, but those workers will have a higher output per person, be better educated, better paid and have the best tools that modern technology can produce. Already, earth-orbiting satellites keep an eye on our forests, and their cameras and sensors can spot a problem from space long before it is apparent on the ground. New machines are on the drawing board and will continue to increase the efficiency of the workers. The typical logger of the future may very well be a college graduate, skilled in running the complicated machines that will do most of the work now done by hand and accorded a degree of respect not always achieved by his hard-working, modern counterparts.

One thing is certain. As long as trees grow and their wood is utilized by mankind, there will be men and women who will harvest those trees, using tools of ever increasing efficiency. And they will still call themselves, and proudly, loggers.

The much maligned, much discussed, much criticized northern spotted owl, is really quite a nice bird, unless you happen to be a mouse. This one is a third generation, radio-collared bird who seems to prefer a man-made nest over one that it would build itself. This bird has adapted.

CHAPTER XI

THE EMPEROR HAS NO CLOTHES

One of the most popular and best known of Grimm's fairy tales is that of The Emperor's New Clothes. Not only is it an entrancing story, but it has a moral tucked away in it that can be applied to many different situations. So it is quite in order to apply it to a present-day ecological problem that plagues all of us and specifically the forest products industry in the Pacific Northwest.

Briefly stated, the emperor was fascinated with new clothes. They took a greater part of his time, since he changed his outfit a dozen or more times a day, and were more important to him than the welfare of his people or the needs of his country. Anything that was new, no matter how bizarre, was sure to attract his interest, even if it meant a serious drain on the royal treasury.

An obsession such as this one was bound to attract shady characters who saw, in this peculiar fixation, a way to line their own pockets. In this case, it was two "thieves" as Grimm described them, although today we would be more apt to describe them as "con men," who devised a scheme that took advantage of some phases of human nature that we all possess but are not often ready to admit.

These con artists began to spread the news that they had discovered a way of weaving cloth that was so fine that it would be invisible to many people. Only a person who was completely honest would be able to see this new cloth and the clothes made from it. Just as they had expected, a royal summons to the palace was not long in coming.

For a very considerable sum, they persuaded the emperor that they could weave him clothes that would make him the envy of all the kings of the earth and that even Solomon in all his glory would not be as well arrayed as he would be. They set up a loom in the city and could be seen busily weaving far into the night and asking anyone who came by if they had ever seen cloth as fine as that which they were weaving. Since they had already made liberal use of the media of their day to let people know that only someone who was completely honest could see the new cloth, a steady stream of visitors left the premises enthusing over the wonderful new fabric that was being woven.

The day finally came when the emperor's new clothes were to be fitted, and the emperor and his chancellor were admitted to the fitting rooms where the emperor was fussed over mightily by the two con men who energetically cut invisible cloth and sewed assiduously with needles pulling invisible thread. The old chancellor, loyal to his emperor but also very fond of his well-paying job, assured the emperor that he was indeed the picture of sartorial elegance and that at the great parade tomorrow he would be the envy of the world.

The great day came, and the emperor, outfitted from head to foot in his new clothes, pranced down the main avenue of the town to the admiring cries of his dutiful subjects, all of whom were trying to outdo each other in praise of the emperor's new clothes. Then a little child, probably one who hadn't been let in on the secret, let the cat out of the bag.

"Mommy!" he said, "The emperor is stark naked! The emperor has no clothes!" And the emperor realized he had been played for a fool, for no one can be more honest than a little child who had not yet learned to tell lies and who relies on what he sees far more than on what he has been told.

The story has more than a few modern implications and nowhere more than in the relationship between the forest products industry and the preservationist forces seemingly bent on destroying it. For over thirty years, in the guise of saving the environment, a host of legislation and regulations have been passed, all garbed in what we are assured are the finest clothes ever devised. Many people have unquestionably been convinced, and even those who have not are supposed to meekly accept this nonsense.

What started out as a benign movement, helpful to the environment and therefore enriching the lives of all the people, has become a Frankenstein monster with a life of its own, which can, and unless it is brought under control, assuredly will destroy its creators. A constant stream of misinformation, fed by a media system which will not give up what it perceives to be a rich lode of story material, would make us believe that our lives would be much richer if we were to let our forests revert to their primitive state; if we never cut down another tree more than a hundred years old; that snails, worms and obscure little birds are more important than people; and that we desperately need to lock up several million more acres into yet another wilderness preserve. It's time that someone calls a spade a spade and comes right out with it. **THE EMPEROR HAS NO CLOTHES!**

I will be the first to admit that this will not be a universally accepted idea. For at least three generations we have been spoon fed a steady diet of propaganda about "saving the Earth" and "having regard for the environment." Certainly no thinking person would object to these ends. I certainly would not, for I am a passenger on this great space ship we call Earth, and I want to live on a planet that is ecologically healthy. I

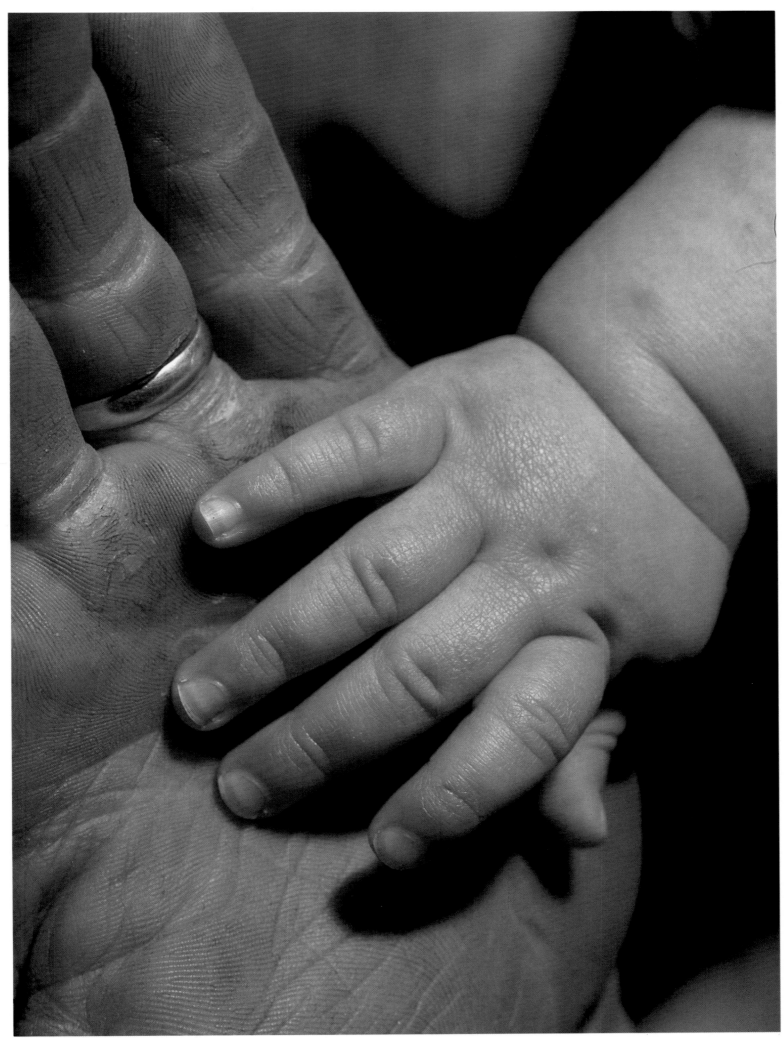

Earl Marcellus is a hard-working, callus-handed logger who absolutely adores his beautiful little daughter. Her future is in his work-hardened hands, and that pretty much controls the way he views restrictions that threaten his daughter's well-being.

also want it to be productive of a high quality of life: I deserve it: I've worked for it, and I feel it is my just right. There are millions of people in these United States who consciously or subconsciously feel exactly the same way. We want a healthful environment in which to lead a life where we can enjoy the fruits of the labors which have provided us with a standard of living that is the envy of the world. At first, we may seem outnumbered by a brainwashed majority, but that is nothing new: Columbus had to convince a roomful of doubters when he proposed his epic journey, and most of them thought he'd never come back because he would fall off the edge of a flat Earth.

There are all kinds of axioms about judging any piece of advice or legislation by the effects it produces. The <u>Bible</u> puts it as succinctly as any when it says, "By their fruits you shall know them." Judging by the mess the often well-intended legislation of the last two decades has produced, the efforts to save the environment by judical fiat have produced far more problems than they have solved. It's about time we stop kidding ourselves about this problem, face facts and then do something about it.

First and foremost, there is no question but that every effort must be made to protect the environment which is our home. Among all the forms of life that have peopled this Earth since the dawn of time, man is the only creature who has developed the means by which he can exterminate life on this planet and render it as unfit for human habitation as the moons of Jupiter. He is also the only life-form that can change his environment, for better or for worse. This makes him unique, for all other life-forms must live by the sternest, and to our way of thinking, the most cruel dictum of Nature: adapt or perish.

Scientists who have made a study of these things tell us that this is the most basic natural law governing the propagation of a species. For over a hundred million years or more, depending on where you want to start in the chain, the dinosaurs were the dominant life form on this Earth, and later studies have indicated that they were a far more sophisticated and evolved species than we had previously thought them to be. A change in climate doomed them, although certain isolated species then living, like the shark, the Komodo dragon and the crocodile, were able to adapt to changing conditions, and so survived. The woolly mammoth, as magnificent an animal as ever roamed the Earth, was marvelously adapted to life on the periglacial steppes; but when the glaciers retreated, it could not adapt and left only his fossils to show that he was once lord of his icy domain. In our own time, the elk, once a prairie animal roaming the Great Plains, was swept westward by the tides of civilization, till it found a haven in the mountainous wildernesses of the West. It adapted, and thrives to this day. Some species survive, others do not. The law is called survival of the fittest; it is a basic, fundamental law of nature and cannot be repealed or amended by judical fiat.

Those same scientists come up with another fact that at first glance seems improbable but which on further thought is completely believable. Ninety-nine point nine percent or even more of all species that have

ever existed have become extinct. The ones that have survived have demonstrated an ability to live and reproduce under changing circumstances, and so rightly deserve a place in the life scene. When, by means of legislation, of which the Endangered Species Act is a prime example, we attempt to preserve a species that Nature says must adapt or perish, we are flying in the face of one of the most inexorable laws of nature, and we are doomed to certain defeat. That natural law has stood the test of time and is not about to be defeated by human legislators who should be more cognizant of Nature's inexorable laws.

This does not mean that we should blithely tolerate all circumstances that can lead to the extinction of a species, especially if that species has significant impact upon the welfare of mankind and man is responsible for those circumstances. That was the intent of the Endangered Species Act, and if this very laudable aim had been intelligently followed, the law would have produced the end for which it was intended. Instead, this law became the darling of opportunists who saw in it a way of forcing their own peculiar brand of salvation upon the general population. These people rather obviously have gained control of what had been intended to be a movement that would have made the Earth a better place for mankind and turned it into a juggernaut that has seriously impacted a way of life and left a path of misery and destruction in its wake. In their hands, the preservation of some obscure worm or tadpole in its original habitat is important enough to halt the construction of a hydro-electric or irrigation program that would have bettered the lives of thousands of people. I have nothing against worms or tadpoles, but I maintain that people and their welfare are far more important and should have priority, even if it means that the worms should either adapt or perish.

Saying that legislation which is the law of the land and is largely accepted at face value by a large majority is flawed legislation is not an easy thing to do, and it has not been done without serious consideration. The right to dissent, however, is a cherished American right, guaranteed by the Constitution, and becomes less a right than a duty when the legislation it seeks to amend has proven, by the fruits of its application, that it cannot produce the effects for which it was intended but has instead brought in its wake a flood of human tragedy and suffering. Such a law is a bad law, and should be either repealed outright, or seriously amended. **<u>THE EMPEROR HAS NO CLOTHES!</u>**

Don Quixote found out that tilting at windmills can be a dangerous pastime, and I have no intentions of imitating the Man from La Mancha. When I suggest that one of our most sacred cows has been milked by people who have no inherent right to do so, I should be ready to defend my thesis, and I do so gladly.

First, and foremost, there is no doubt in my mind that this Earth would be a much more healthful planet if mankind took more seriously the stewardship it has assumed with its dominant place in Nature. Any legislation that will implement that end without also bringing in a flood of human misery is good legislation and should be supported. If, on the other hand, those same regulations result in serious human suffering and social dislocation, then a hard, stern look should be given to it, for the welfare of humans far transcends the welfare of any other species. This is the problem facing many forest products oriented communities today.

Up until a couple of centuries ago, the resources of the world were not seriously taxed. The planet easily supported the billion or so human inhabitants living on it, and the natural pollution they produced had little or no effect on the composition of the atmosphere, to take only one aspect of the changes wrought in nature by human occupancy. Population was balanced by disease, famine, war and natural disasters, things which we view as abhorrent but which are natural checks on a regenerative rate which was imprinted into our reproductive cycle eons ago when only one child in ten survived to his or her first year. Life was simple; and vast portions of the world were available for new habitations, so that mankind was well on its way to heeding the biblical admonition to "increase and multiply, and fill the Earth." There was still plenty of room for expansion, and no noticeable harm was being done to the environment by the lifestyle of the times.

Then came the Industrial Revolution and a quantum leap in science. In the following two centuries, advances in medicine and agriculture alone practically eliminated two of the factors that had kept the population in equilibrium, and a new kind of civilization developed. With machines doing work that had previously been done by people, wealth increased and with it a demand for creature comforts unheard of a few centuries ago. As has been previously stated, "There ain't no free lunch." Every single one of the creature comforts we take so much for granted exacts their toll from Nature, and if we want those comforts, we must be prepared to somewhere pay a commensurate price. By the beginning of this century, it became evident that the tab was being presented, and it was a stiff one.

The demands of this new culture, and the strains put upon it by a series of catastrophic wars have seriously depleted the natural resources of the Earth and polluted our environment to the point that it presents a great and ever growing challenge to the welfare, and even survival of human and other life on this planet. This is the condition that triggered the environmental movement, and there is no denying that the movement was, and is, not only a good idea, but one that is essential. Remedying and reversing the trends that have been poisoning our planet is necessary, but it should be done with care. To repeat the analogy already made in this book, a pinch of salt in the stew increases its flavor; but dump two pounds into it and you have something completely inedible which should be thrown out. Unfortunately, too much salt has already been added to the ecological stew, mostly by people who have no skill in that type of cooking. It is time that legislation now in effect be judged by the effects it has produced, and if those regulations have not benefited mankind, then we should have the fortitude to admit that mistakes have been made, and set about rectifying those errors. If the leaders of the Soviet Union can admit that communism, a social experiment affecting the lives of millions of people, was a failure and set their minds to the task of rectifying the errors it produced, we can, and should.

A prime example of this in the Pacific Northwest is the brouhaha over the northern spotted owl. A shy, innocuous bird supposedly dwelling only in old growth timber, it was propelled to the front pages of the nation's media when preservationist groups claimed that less than two thousand nesting pairs of these birds existed in the old growth of the Pacific Northwest and California and that their continued existence was threatened by the continued logging of old-growth forests. A report, supposedly by the best authorities on this subject was presented to the Fish and Wildlife Service along with a demand that, under the specifications of the Endangered Species Act, logging in old-growth forests should be forbidden, or at least severely curtailed. In June 1990, the Fish and Wildlife Service agreed and laid down severe restrictions that effectively curtailed logging in over eight million acres of national forest and private lands.

There was jubilation in the preservationist ranks. At last, a weapon had been found that would forever preserve old growth in its pristine state and send those hated loggers scurrying to the unemployment office like whipped dogs with their tails between their legs. The fact that most of them had never even heard of a spotted owl before, and that most of them wouldn't know one if it perched at the foot of their beds and hooted at them, was conveniently forgotten. Even loggers who had worked forty years in old growth admitted that, in all that time, they had never seen a spotted owl; and if it disappeared from the face of the Earth tomorrow, their lives would not be affected one iota. Nevertheless, by the implementation of a well-intended law, they were faced with starvation for themselves and their families and the end of a way of life that they enjoyed as the pursuit of that happiness guaranteed to them by the Constitution.

It could be understood, if not condoned, if some logger, faced with unemployment because a couple of small raptors had set up housekeeping on his timber sale, invested part of his last paycheck in shotgun shells and went owl hunting. It would be a very simplistic solution to a quite complicated problem, and an illegal solution at that. But a logger faced with the problem of making payments on his home and new pickup might not be too concerned over whether his solution to the problem violated some law foisted on him by suburbanites who had never worked for a living with their hands. A couple of blasts from his shotgun, and he would have earned the undying gratitude of his family, several hundred mice, and he could go back to making an honest living.

The living was unquestionably honest, the work he was doing was useful and in demand, but this direct solution to his problem would have been wrong. He would have violated the law of the land, committed a felony which could earn him jail time, and would not have solved his problem, at least on a long-term basis. That solution could only come by changing the law so that he could go back to making an honest living.

Changing a law, even a bad one, in the face of an entrenched bureaucracy with a stake in the status quo, can be a long and often painful process, as the inhabitants of the timber belt are finding out. One thing, however, is certain: loggers do not view legislation which decrees starvation for them with any degree of affection and will go to any lengths to have that law changed or repealed. They have found out, the hard way, that simplistic solutions, such as blowing owls into bloody tatters, are only a temporary solution, so they are becoming a bit more sophisticated in their assault on what is assuredly, especially to them, stupid legislation.

The regulation that forced them into unemployment was based on what was, at best, a flawed if not downright incorrect report. The original report which triggered the implementation of the Endangered Species Act claimed that there were only about two thousand nesting pairs of spotted owls left, and that old growth was essential to their propagation. **THE EMPEROR HAS NO CLOTHES!** Both those claims are completely false, and since the regulation was founded on this report, it is an "edifice erected on a bed of sand." Since this edict went into effect, additional thousands of nesting birds have been reliably reported, and the clinching factor to the claim that the original report was badly flawed is that practically all of these nesting pairs were found in second and third growth. Not only does the spotted owl exist in far greater quantities than was first reported, but it has evidently adapted to existing circumstances and is now raising healthy families in the new forests that have sprung up since its original

A logger's daughter who from an early age will grow up with a love of the woodlands and a desire to perpetuate a way of life that has given her a happy childhood. She is more important than any owl.

habitat was first harvested. The spotted owl has adapted to its new environment, and so is a species that will survive. It is not nearly as threatened as the logger who allegedly brought it to the brink of extinction. **COME ON, YOUR MAJESTY, GET SOME CLOTHES ON!** You look silly out there with no pants on!

In forty-five years of tramping the woods of the Northwest, I had never seen a spotted owl, in fact, the species was completely unknown to me. That doesn't make me any different from most of the outdoorsmen I know; only one, with a special interest in ornithology admitted to knowing of the bird before it achieved its present notoriety. And do the preservationists who claim to be the champions of this "Endangered Species" have any love for it? If you believe that, I know where there is a nice little piece of swamp land that would make a tidy little investment...no, the target was old-growth forests. If they would have to profess a love for crocodiles to achieve their end, they suddenly would have been enamored of long snouts and formidable dentification.

Since there is really no problem with the survival of the spotted owl as a viable species, how is it that the law has not been changed? The premise on which the regulation was passed is badly flawed if not downright incorrect, and the implementation of the law is causing the loss of thousands of jobs, with consequent misery and social dislocation. And to what effect? Who is profiting? Certainly not the logger, who is out of a job, or the environment, suddenly cut off from funds formerly dedicated to its improvement. Who then, is profiting from all this turmoil? It is only fair to delve into this mess and find out why this patently improper legislation is still the law of the land and the factors that keep it in place.

The United States is no longer a basically agricultural nation. Less than ten percent of the people in this country make their living by working on the land, although one hundred percent draw their sustenance from it. Recent surveys that show that a majority of Americans think that bread is made from oatmeal or have no knowledge of where milk comes from ("From the supermarket, in a carton.") would be laughable if they were not so frightening. So it is not unusual that the average urbanite has little knowledge of the part forest products plays in his everyday life. Most Americans have only a vague concept of what would happen if the forest products industry were to be shut down or forced to operate within the parameters laid down by even the more moderate preservationist groups. This knowledge might sink in when the urbanite goes to his local lumber yard, grudgingly prepared to pay ten dollars a piece for a couple of studs, only to find that the business has long ago gone bankrupt from lack of patronage at those prices. And when he goes to the supermarket for a few rolls of that plebeian but useful staple, toilet paper, he would fume to find that he must shell out a couple dollars or more for each roll because toilet paper, made from wood, if it is available at all, is in short supply. Incensed, he drives home (to a wooden house, built years ago when wood was still available) in an automobile (made of steel, and running on gasoline, both made from irreplaceable natural resources) to write a fuming letter (on paper, or course; he still has a few sheets left over from years ago) to the editor of the local newspaper which cannot print his letter because space in the paper (printed on newsprint, made from wood) is very restricted; the paper is now down to two pages, printed once a week.

Along with this lack of knowledge of whence many of our basic staples originate is a monumental ignorance of how the forests of the Northwest contribute to the regional economy and how that economy would be impacted if the woodlands are not properly utilized. The knowledge might belatedly sink in when urbanites are asked to pay new taxes to replace the funds formerly provided by the sale of timber on public lands when, through the implementation of legislation he supported, those lands are closed to logging. Throughout the timber belt in the Northwest and California, the counties share in the proceeds of timber sales on public lands builds and maintains schools and roads; and if that source of revenue is cut off, someone, somewhere, is going to be asked to take up the slack. When the most sensitive nerve in the human anatomy, the pocket-book nerve, is impinged, public scrutiny of the laws that led to this may result in a decided change in public opinion and a return to the old, painless way of financing through utilization of a renewable natural resource that would otherwise go unused.

Loss of tax money is only one of the many woes that would accrue to the timber belt if the present restrictions on logging are allowed to continue. Whole towns in this region have their entire economy solidly rooted in the forests at their doorsteps, and there are no viable alternatives for their continued existence. Towns like Forks, Darrington, Morton, and Randle in Washington State alone would cease to exist without the forest products industry which is their main support. Others, like Aberdeen, Hoquiam, and Raymond, to name only a few of many, would have their economies so severely impacted that they would become a drain on the state treasury rather than contributors to it. The situation is identical in the Oregon and California timber belt, and the ancillary effect that would result from a severe curtailment of the timber industry would not be confined to the timber towns alone but would spread throughout the whole region. We would wind up with a lot of unconcerned owls, a few ecstatic preservationists and many more destitute, unproductive and highly unhappy people.

The unemployed logger is not happy to be sitting at home drawing unemployment compensation when he could be in the woods doing the job he best enjoys and being a useful, tax-paying member of society. His worse fear is that it may take years to unscramble the mess in which he presently finds himself; and in that time, his way of life may disappear. The fear is not unfounded. During the thirteen or so years of Prohibition, in the wine country of California skilled coopers and viniculturists, put out of work by an unenforceable law, necessarily had to find other ways of making a living. Some of them reluctantly gave up the skills it had taken them years to acquire and went on to a much diminished quality of life. Others, determined to survive and fill a demand, turned to bootlegging and became wealthy.

When it was finally admitted that the Noble Experiment was a disaster and the law was changed, it took at least a generation to build back the skills that should never have been lost in the first place. The human race is not going to give up the use of wood, even if it were to become illegal, and it would be a rational thing to have someone in the wings ready to supply the demand once it is realized that it is essential and must somehow be fulfilled.

This may sound a little far-fetched to someone who has little or no contact with loggers. If you were to talk to them, as I have, sample their fears, face their problems, listen to their grim determination not only to survive but also to keep the way of life that they so desperately love, you would realize that this is simply a statement of a factual situation. They battle to save their homes, their towns and their way of life; and they are confident that in the end reason and good judgement will prevail, and they will survive.

They certainly will survive, because they are the warp and woof of the fabric that made America a great nation. They will have lean times, but a nation that survived the Great Depression has the toughness to outlive this period of national insanity. Already, grim jokes reflective of their mood are circulating throughout the timber belt. Asked how he and his family expected to survive an extended period of unemployment, one logger said grimly, "Well, we expect to eat quite a bit of big-eyed chicken." I sincerely hope that was a joke.

The better way would be to engage in a vigorous campaign of public education, to make sure that their representatives in Congress are responsive to their wishes, and most of all to get their message across to the urban dwellers who have too long been listening to the siren song of those who think that forests are meant to produce only scenery and owls.

When the first restriction on logging in spotted owl habitat was set up, over eight million forested acres subsequently boosted to eleven million were affected. Alarmed by the massive economic impact this would have not only on the timber belt but also on the national treasury which receives part of the proceeds from forest sales, this was later trimmed back down to eight million acres; but the restrictions are still severe enough to cause massive disruptions in the industry. If, in Western Washington state a pair of nesting owls is discovered on a timber sale, a radius of 2.2 miles is impacted, over 9000 acres, 40 percent of which must be preserved in a pristine state. This is wonderful for owls, but not so good on humans, who justifiably feel they too are a threatened species and should be furnished equal protection under the law. A sign-carrying youngster put it in words in a logger's rally protesting the new regulations: "Do I have to grow feathers and eat mice before my government will protect me?"

The point is well taken. A good, laudable movement has somehow fallen under the influence of vested interests who have everything to gain and nothing to lose by keeping the ecological pot boiling. Make no mistake about it, the preservationist movement has become big business, with billions of dollars at its disposal and some very high-powered people drawing fancy salaries ensconced in places of power that are not even slightly disposed to give up. Their knowledge of silviculture may be flawed, but they are masters at playing the public relations game; and that influences votes a lot more than a logical argument. Some of these sharp, extremely intelligent operators have their fingers on the public pulse and are so adept at manipulating public opinion that they can arrogantly influence legislation along the lines they prefer, whether or not that legislation is beneficial to the environment or the people who depend on it for sustenance. They are not about to give up their well-paying jobs, even if a few hundred thousand people are forced into a lesser standard of living as a result of their efforts. A bureaucracy that is loathe to admit that it can make mistakes plays neatly into their hands and perpetuates the farce, even after it has been amply proved that the implementation of these rules does not achieve the end for which it was intended but instead causes a welter of human misery and economic ruin.

What can be done about it? The intelligent person, forced into a corner by his opponent, assesses the tactics that got him there and if they are superior to his own, adopts them. I do not mean to adopt the misinformation that has been so common in the preservationist camp, for once that is exposed it redounds to their discredit. I mean the logger should become sophisticated in using the channels of public information so that his side of the story is told, and not just to loggers or the people in the timber belt. After all when he preaches his sermon there he is preaching to a church full of true believers. His message should be delivered to the masses of unbelievers out there who need to know that the logger is a decent, hard-working man who genuinely has the good of the environment in mind and is willing to put forth the hard work that it takes to keep the Northwest the beautiful, productive land that it is.

What a good part of the Northwest does better than anything else is grow trees. Those trees are a crop, a useful productive crop, that can bring economic prosperity and a good way of life to the whole region. It should not be allowed to lie fallow with very limited benefits but rather should be used for the good of man, and, under careful management, generate a new crop of trees as long as the rains fall and the earth gratefully receives the kiss of the sun. Then, and then only, will the Pacific Northwest continue to fulfill the destiny for which it was created.

In the meantime, it would be a wonderful idea to **GIVE THE EMPEROR A NEW SET OF CLOTHES,** one that every honest man, woman and child can see and rightfully applaud. It sure would beat the way it looks now.

Steve Kerns, wildlife biologist who has made a study of the spotted owl covering several years, uses a directional finder to locate a radio-collared bird. Steve has found that the owl has adapted to second and third growth and thrives there.

All over the timber belt, signs announcing that "This home is supported by Timber Dollars" have sprouted. This one is near Forks, Washington..

This well-trained Belgian draught horse can maneuver a log out of the brush with minimal damage to the environment. Slow, but still in use.

A bug-kill dominates a new forest springing up to take its place. By human standards, Nature is often bitterly cruel and her laws inexorable.

Although the problems of the logger are largely unknown in the cities, they are well known in the timber belt, as this sign adjacent to Interstate 5 near Centralia, Washington, will testify.

Loggers have been forced to surrender a bit of their cherished independence to present a united front to the forces arrayed against them. This rally was held in Olympia, Washington, and was attended by loggers from all over the Northwest.

A vigorous, managed forest on land that only a few years ago was being damned by preservationists as an example of how the logger was "ruining the country."

CHAPTER XII

THE RENEWABLE RESOURCE

Minnesotans are fond of repeating stories about one of their favorite adopted sons, Frederick Weyerhaeuser, whose timber empire had its roots in their state and which for many years was his home. Most of these stories have to do with his successes, but the one most repeated recounts his most spectacular missed opportunity. "Dutch Fred" never did anything halfway and his falls from good judgement could be as spectacular as his successes. As the story goes, Weyerhaeuser each workday would stand by the window and count the railroad gondola cars passing by his timber holdings. After each counting, he would shake his head sadly.

He was remembering that when he bought the timber rights on a large hilly tract of land he was also offered the mineral rights for one hundred thousand dollars. He declined because the tract's boundaries could not be definitely pinpointed. His timber cruisers reported that "his compass acted awful crazy on that Mesabi Range." Now, Weyerhaeuser was counting gondolas carrying ore from one of the world's richest iron deposits.

In his time of seemingly limitless natural resources, it probably never occurred to the timber baron that the trees on that hilly range, if kept in perpetuity, would ultimately be worth even more than its vast deposit of rich ore. The resources of the Mesabi, rich as they were, are now largely depleted, but its forests could have produced wood and wealth indefinitely because of a characteristic unique among natural resources. Trees, being a living organism, are infinitely renewable. Iron ore is not.

If wood had been unknown to the world and some chemist had invented it, with all its amazing characteristics, he would unquestionably have been regarded as the world's greatest benefactor. Wood is such a widely-distributed material that we take its versatility and quantity for granted, often forgetting that the supply is not guaranteed, and is dependent upon conditions that may either increase or decrease its availability. History is replete with instances of good and bad forestry. The heavily wooded slopes of Switzerland and the Black Forest of Germany have been intensively used for centuries and still are remarkably productive woodlands. The famed cedars of Lebanon, however, are presently in short supply due to lack of reforestation and the feeding habits of the ubiquitous goat. This animal is very popular throughout the Middle East for its hardiness and because it is a walking food factory; but actually the Moorish goat, which deforested Spain, Crete and a large part of Morocco, is responsible for more deserts that any creature except man. In biblical days, Israel was a "land of milk and honey" and partially forested, as was Greece. The timber disappeared from these lands because what was taken off was not replaced, a mistake which is being belatedly admitted and rectified through intensive forestry. With a crash program, Israel is regaining the forests that have been absent from the land since the time of the Crusades and is reaping side benefits from increased water supplies and the beauty that is natural to forested areas. All over the world, people are realizing that the forests are a resource of inestimable value and can be made even more so through intensive forestry.

Because of their characteristic of renewability, our forests are unquestionably our most valuable natural resource, along with the land on which they are nurtured. Anything else–iron, copper, aluminum, oil, stone, clay–once used up is irreparably gone. The living forests, combining carbon dioxide from the air with water and minerals from the ground, through the miracle of photosynthesis, produce wood, a substance with so many uses that civilization as we know it could hardly exist without it. Only the Eskimo culture had managed to live without a reliance on wood and wood products, and even in their frigid clime the occasional log that washes up on their barren coasts is highly prized and every sliver is utilized. All other societies use wood, and the more advanced the culture, the more wood it consumes.

Up until the end of World War II, not much thought was given to conserving America's resources. They had been so huge as to be considered limitless, but the tremendous demands of the war brought the realization that even the vast resources of the United States could be depleted, and serious consideration should be given to husbanding them. Among these, of course, were our forests. Actually, some far-sighted companies, Simpson, Weyerhaeuser, Pope and Talbot, and Crown Zellerbach, to name a few, had long ago realized that their continued economic health depended upon a reliable source of supply and had acquired and paid taxes for years on lands that were already growing the next crop of trees.

Weyerhaeuser Company in 1941 instituted a policy that was to have far-reaching consequences for the whole industry. For the first time, timber was considered a crop which should be planted, farmed and harvested like any other crop to make room for yet another cycle of tree-growing. The industry was quick to see the value of this idea and it was widely copied. Nurseries where selected seedlings could be grown under ideal conditions were established and replanting after harvest became standard procedure.

Forestry had for centuries been an honored profession in Europe and some parts of Asia, but there were areas of questionable knowledge, especially in regards to the forests of the Northwest. For instance, shortly after the tree-farm idea took root, a plantation was planted and sowed with Douglas-fir seed of unknown antecedents. The trees came up gnarled and twisted, a travesty compared to the beautiful forest that had been expected. The seed was assuredly Douglas-fir seed, but from a different environment and altitude than the location in which it was planted. In those days, who cared, or rather, knew? Seed was seed. It must have been quite a sobering experience for the tree-farming pioneers who so laboriously started this new planting and saw it develop stunted and twisted.

It was not a completely wasted effort. From it came the realization that seed for a new planting must come from reasonably the same altitude and preferably from the same tract as the one being replanted. Genetic adaptations to the various soils and climates become part of the genes of that seed and grow very well in conditions adapted to it, but not necessarily in what is to the seed a foreign environment.

That principle is well understood now and is taken into consideration when selecting seedlings for replanting. All public agencies and most of the large companies maintain their own nurseries where millions of young trees are grown and transplanted under ideal conditions to seed beds well adapted to that particular strain. The resulting plantations have a head start on naturally seeded areas and show it dramatically. A five-year-old plantation is normally head high, while a naturally seeded area of the same age may not even have gotten a start, especially if it should happen to be competing with a dense stand of red alder which in most of the Northwest is more than likely. Douglas fir, for instance, puts out a good seed crop only once in seven years; therefore it must compete against brush that may have had as much as a six-year head start. Douglas fir needs sunlight to grow properly, and there is precious little of that at the bottom of an alder thicket. A good part of the scattered seed crop may result in suppressed seedlings that will never amount to anything because they are shaded by the competing underbrush. Also, a haphazard seedling may result in bad spacing and a crowded, slow-growing stand. All these conditions are controlled by hand planting, which is one reason that it is now the normal way of regenerating a crop, except in Alaska, where the natural regrowth is so thick that thinning takes the place of planting.

A modern industrial forest is established with the idea that within a definite time, give or take a few years to account for vagaries in the weather, it will be harvested, just the way a field of ripe corn or wheat would be. Part of the emotional turmoil that accompanies the harvesting of a beautiful woodland can be alleviated by posting permanent signs, from the very inception of the new forest, that tell this story. This helps fix firmly in the public's mind that it is a commercial crop that was planted for a specific purpose. In contrast, the shock engendered by the harvest of a naturally seeded stand stems partly from the conviction that this grove sprouted naturally, and it should be allowed to run its span of life and die naturally. However, when a forest is regarded in the same light as an agricultural crop, corn is often used as an example, the way is paved for its ultimate utilization. It has been found that one of the best ways to stress this crop's destiny is to announce, early in its life, the time of the next harvest.

It should be remembered that the economic factor that makes the forest products industry viable is the constant demand for its products. "Profit" seems to be a dirty word in some circles, especially in the minds of those who have never been able to achieve one, yet this is the motivation that has created the comforts and conveniences taken so much for granted in our modern society, even by those who decry the word. Personally, I have nothing against the word; in fact, I have a distinct liking for it. It is the natural result of the work and effort a person puts into a project and in my way of thinking "profit" has a much better ring than "loss."

Whatever profit is ever realized by the tree farmer is certainly well earned. No one assumes a greater gamble, spread over the greater part of a lifetime, than the tree farmer, who plants a crop on which he will receive no income for up to thirty years when he makes his first commercial thinning. If he realizes a profit at all on that crop, it will be when he is a very old man, because a crop is usually harvested fifty years after planting. He must necessarily be a patient man who realizes that the crop over which he has labored will be harvested by his children or even grandchildren. Meanwhile, he runs the risk of windstorm, bug kill and forest fires, and even that, in AD 2051, there may be a depressed market for wood. This is gambling on the grand scale, yet the odds aren't as great as they would seem, for tree-growing conditions in the Northwest are so ideal that almost any plot of ground in the timber belt will in time sprout a crop of seedlings, some of which will almost certainly grow to maturity.

On the other hand, that same plot may have a tendency to reproduce alder faster than it does fir. This tendency can be combated in several ways. The hardwood crop can be killed off with selective herbicides, although this method is coming under close scrutiny from the ever-watchful ecological watchdogs, or, like the homeowner afflicted with a luxuriant and persistent crop of crabgrass, he may have to learn to love it. Another, and increasingly attractive alternative, is to let the hardwoods grow to maturity, and harvest them as a profitable crop. One of the main changes that has taken place in the last eighteen years is the increased utilization of hardwoods. It was always known that alder made good firewood, but it is only recently that this hardwood is being sawed into dimensional lumber, or even peeled for a very decorative plywood that has extensive uses in the furniture market. Weyerhaeuser even has a mill at Longview that cuts alder to dimensions, and the wood is of sufficient economic interest to merit research into its propagation. Experimental stands of this wood have been established, and it is generally conceded that the fine white paper of the future may very well be made from what was, up to a few years ago, considered a king-sized nuisance.

Weyerhaeuser Lands near Longview, that are managed like a farm whose crop is timber. This land, properly managed, will produce timber in perpetuity without depletion, part of the miracle that makes the forest products industry possible.

If the growing of evergreens is still the prime motivation, a little persistence will usually pay off. Any tract that has once grown conifers can be made to grow them again and, under modern forest management, better and more rapidly than through unmanaged conditions.

On a logged-over site, the common practice is to burn the slash and rotten logs as soon after harvest as possible. Replanting is done with nursery-grown, two-year-old seedlings, so that the new plantation has at least a two-year start on naturally seeded trees. Those new trees need that head start, for the first few years are perilous. The seedlings are susceptible to extremes of heat and cold and are in constant danger from deer and other animals who seem to regard a new plantation as a delicious new dish planted for their benefit. But with luck a five-year-old plantation is head-high already showing signs of the beauty it will wear for the next five-and-a-half decades. That new growth is also necessary if the conifers are to outstrip the brush that is vying with it for a place in the sun. Fortunately, the conifers, growing at the rate of two feet a year, usually win.

In a few years the plantation has become so dense that thinning is necessary if the optimum growth is to be achieved. This is a straight expense, because the wood removed, under present market conditions, is too small to be profitably utilized. This very well may change in the next few years, as the drive to divorce lumber from the physical limitations of its source continues, but at the present time, it remains in the woods. In the Puget Sound area the disintegration of this debris is very rapid, as little as two years, and in

Alaska it is not at all unusual to see a hemlock a foot thick reduced to a bunch of stringy fibers in a matter of months. The dominant trees, freed of competition, assert themselves and spread their canopies to the sunlight which is necessary for the process known as photosynthesis. Through the action of green chlorophyll and sunlight, water and minerals from the soil are combined with carbon dioxide from the air and produce wood. A by-product, and a vital one at that, is oxygen, the life sustaining element in the air we breathe. Thus, a tree not only produces a substance, wood, which is so ingrained into our culture that we could not get along without it, but it also clears the air of a good part of the pollution that has resulted from the burning of massive amounts of fossil fuel. Scientists have warned for years of the "greenhouse effect" caused by an excess of carbon dioxide, a global warming that could have dire consequences and require some far-reaching changes in our way of life. Every time a tree is planted, not only is a valuable natural resource propagated, but the atmosphere is improved not only by the regeneration of oxygen but also by the useful removal of a pollutant from an atmosphere that is vastly improved by the change. A tree in a thinned grove has a chance to do just this, for it is during the tree's active growing stage that the greatest amount of oxygen is generated. When that grove is harvested, it will be easy to tell the time of the thinning, because those growth rings will be conspicuous by their size. The tree of the future was planted about twenty-five years ago and in a favorable site had attained a growth that by present standards is nothing but phenomenal. I photographed that stump so as to have concrete evidence of what is a really significant development. That Douglas fir had twenty-seven growth rings, and it was twenty-four inches in diameter, an ideal size for processing. If all trees grew this well, and it is the avowed aim of the forester to ensure that they do, our Douglas-fir supply would be at least doubled because this tree grew to optimum size in half the usual time.

The next step, carried out when the trees are between thirty and forty years old, is called commercial thinning because the wood removed is of sufficient size to pay for the operation or, on a good side, even show a modest profit. This has been elevated to the status of a fine art in California, where it has ardent devotees who claim that a good stand can be even further improved by an additional thinning, over and above the first commercial one. The added growth, they claim, not only pays for the second thinning but the park-like stand that results defuses the preservationists' prize argument, that logging is a synonym for ugliness, thus creating a better public image for loggers. They just may be right. Some of the double-thinned stands I saw in California were so park-like it was difficult to believe that these were commercial woodlands and profitable lands at that. While California seems to be in the forefront in this practice, it by no matter or means has a monopoly on it, for I have seen instances of this same practice all over the West Coast and one of the prettiest examples of all in the Intermountain region.

This is only one example of how public pressure is influencing modern silviculture. In several places where I researched this book, I was shown new clearcuts that didn't look at all like the conventional clearcuts, but more like a severe selection thinning. In essence, that is what it was. In some places it was called a block cut, but everywhere it was admitted to be a compromise between the demands of the preservationists and the needs of the logger. In this method, the smaller but promising trees are left standing, the area thoroughly cleaned up by piling the debris into large burn piles, and in general, consideration given to the appearance of the stand after it has been harvested. Reaction to this method from landowners is a mixed bag. Some decry the additional cost of harvest and subsequent smaller profits, while others view it as a short-term loss but long-term gain, for it cools much of the resentment the general public has developed to clearcuts. It is a known fact that this resentment has resulted in restrictive regulations that cost a lot more money than the additional cost entailed in doing a neat job.

Every few years, an aerial application of urea pellets gives the trees a substantial growth boost in the form of soil soluble nitrogen. This is a concerted scientific operation, with soil samples lifted from the various parts of the forest and the correct application made according to need. Fertilization was a controversial method of silviculture up to a few years ago: opponents pointed out that it was very expensive and raised nitrogen levels in the treated lands and adjacent streams, sometimes to the detriment of other species. Proponents argued that while it was expensive it was cost effective, and with proper application no serious deleterious effects resulted. The argument has largely been settled.

Fertilization is routine on some privately held lands, and the large companies with these holdings are not exactly noted for indiscriminately throwing away money or entering upon a program such as this one without through research. They do it because it results in a shorter growth cycle and healthier trees.

The development of a young forest is watched as closely by the forester as that of a favorite child, for in many respects, that is what it is. The progress is charted and information fed into a computer which keeps track of may things, including growth and the amount of wood in any specific plot at any one time. These trees will be harvested in their prime, just beyond their fastest growing time, and will have remarkably little waste. Free of knots and scars, these thoroughbreds will make superb logs and first-class lumber or peeler material.

A parallel may be drawn between managed and naturally grown forests and today's present-day beef cattle and the stringy longhorn steers of Chisholm Trail fame. Those cantankerous old steers may have been extremely picturesque, but their meat was proverbially so tough it took a strong man to chew the gravy. Place them alongside today's blocky grain-fed steers and you have a good comparison of yesterday's sometimes magnificent tree grown in the wild and the predictably magnificent tree grown under controlled conditions.

As more and more cutover forest land comes under intensive management, people will become accustomed to the beauty of a healthy, even-aged stand. Trees are not planted in rows anymore; they are planted in such a way that each tree has room to grow, but a natural looking stand is one of the objectives of the planting. More consideration is being given today than there was eighteen years ago to replanting a stand to the same varietal mix that was on it in the first place. These trees will never attain the majesty of an old-growth forest, because they will be harvested in their prime; and a beautiful old-growth stand, for all of its majesty, is an old forest and usually decadent. Majesty seems to be something that comes with maturity, in forests as well as in mankind. It doesn't make good economic sense to keep a forest three hundred years past its prime simply for the aesthetic effect that can be achieved by allowing timber to reach a decadent old age: there are enough examples of that in our national parks to satisfy anyone but the most rabid preservationist, and while they serve their purpose by providing beauty, they are not in the business of providing wood for the benefit of mankind. The young, renewable forest can grow five crops in three hundred years and while it may not be as majestic, the wood it produces will enrich the lives of many people, and will be useful enough in a very practical way to offset any lack of aesthetics it may suffer. This does not, in any way, denigrate the value of old, preserved forests as aesthetic attractions. Our modern life, with its myriad pressures, certainly demands some method of relief; and the peace and quietude of an old sylvan grove is the best available buffer for the keeping of man's sanity and his sense of balance. Thus balance, is the key word. There should be enough old groves retained in their

A thinned stand in California. This stand has just sustained its second commercial thinning, and will now grow at an astounding rate because of the additional light and nutrient available to the remaining trees.

original state to provide forever this antidote to the pressures of urban life, just as there should also be a realization of the needs of our culture and how they must be satisfied. Civilization has brought many amenities to our modern way of life and few people are willing to give them up, even if it levies a toll on Nature, as witness the automobile; but always remember, "There ain't no free lunch." In the case of forest products, we can largely have our cake and eat it too, if we make the best possible use of our renewable forest resources. That means intensive forestry. Silviculture has become standard practice on virtually all large private and public land holdings, because industry and foresters know that given our present rate of consumption, we would eventually run out of wood and so would our way of life. It's as simple as that. With intensive forestry and full utilization of our resources we can live our full lives on a healthy planet for an indefinite span of years...and that is a goal of every forester I know.

None but the most rabid and illogical preservationist objects to intensive forestry responsibly applied to private lands, for that is the reason why those lands were acquired. There is still some bristling, especially on the part of a newly-fledged conservationist to applying these same methods to public lands even when it has been amply proved that their application results in a healthier forest. The cornerstone of their belief seems to be "natural growth" which seemingly is the most desirable of all ways of life since it is applied to every thing from hair to children. Interestingly, it is only a matter of "natural growth" until an awareness of the problems facing our timberlands seeps in; and therefore it seems that a better future for our forests is predictably

in store.

A tremendous amount of research into the propagation and growth of trees had already been done eighteen years ago, but that research has, if anything, intensified in the intervening years. New avenues of improving existing strains have been opened and are being eagerly explored. The old methods are not being discontinued by any matter or means, but new and powerful tools such as gene splicing are being used, so that the desirable characteristics of some trees can be implanted and be immediately available rather than waiting for years under the old method of cross breeding. The span between the time when a new and improved species is developed and is ready for planting is being immeasurably shortened, and computers now can accurately predict the way a new species will perform, at least some of the time. Nature's secrets are complex and not always amenable to being unraveled, but progress is being made in quantum leaps, to the ultimate benefit of all the industry and mankind itself. I fully expect to live to see the tree of the future grow to maturity and it will be a beauty!

Industry is not putting all its eggs into one basket, although it is betting heavily on the new methods to produce the super-tree. The old methods are still being used, mainly as a backup to what is at best an untried science. Superior trees, irreverently called "sexy trees" by researchers, are still used as seed donors, and carefully controlled crossbreeding is being done. Reproducing trees in this way is a slow, tedious process, but by selective cross breeding and grafting, scions of superior trees are propagated in great numbers. The resulting seed is planted, and once again the best trees are propagated. If some unknown glitch should happen in the gene-splicing process, the industry will not be left without some superior scions to propagate the next generation of superior trees.

Results of many years of careful breeding are already showing up in the nurseries, where thousands of vigorous seedlings with fast-growing characteristics are now ready each year for transplanting. It is an ongoing search; for, although much new knowledge has been acquired, there are still many of Nature's secrets to be explored. The knowledge already gained shows conclusively that the tree of the future will be taller, straighter, faster growing, better shaped and better adapted to the demands of modern technology than anything occurring in nature by accident. It is the same thing as the genesis of corn, or cattle, except that in trees the research and its attendant changes can take a long time, even a generation. Nevertheless, it is my firm belief, based on what I have observed first-hand that at least one generation of those super-trees has already been planted. They are not the last word, for this is a never-ending research, but the research that has taken place within the last ten years has already produced seedlings that will grow up with most, if not all, of the desirable characteristics that have been bred into them. Their progress is being watched by people who have put years of their lives into this effort, and I doubt that their efforts have been in vain. As a general rule, they are not the type of men and women prone to failure.

There always seems to be a logical exception to any rule, and there is one to the rule that replanting is now standard regenerative procedure. That exception is Alaska, where little or no replanting is done, simply because nature does the job and very well at that. The dominant species of timber in Southeast is hemlock, a shade-tolerant climax forest species that comes back so well naturally that no replanting is necessary. Just cut a hemlock and the abundant moisture and the seedling characteristics of this tree are such that, in a matter of weeks, young hemlocks are sprouting. This is true of Southeast, but in its northern reaches and in the interior, the regeneration cycle is so long, anywhere from one hundred to two hundred and fifty years, that anything to shorten it would be welcome. Some day, when this huge but presently largely untapped reservoir of timber is tapped, the same amount of brains and hard work that have been dedicated to the better growth of its southern cousins may be directed toward the northern tree with predictably remarkable results. Science has produced grape species that thrive in Canada, hundreds of miles north of their usual range, so why not trees? As yet there is little or no replanting in Alaska, even in the northern part of Southeast where it would be most desirable.

Many side benefits accrue from young, vigorous new forests, some obvious, some a bit more subtle. For at least forty of its sixty years, it will be a thing of beauty, affording shelter to wildlife, preventing erosion, helping to build a water-retaining soil bed and combating pollution by pouring out life-giving oxygen as a by-product of its youthful growth. Watershed protection...beauty...oxygen, such benefits bring a warm glow of achievement to the forester who has made it possible, but some other aspects of his achievements bring another kind of glow, especially when he sees his plantation turned into a kind of animal smorgasbord. Deer like to browse on new trees, porcupines consider them a great delicacy, and bears will walk a mile for a meal of sweet new cambium. A new and growing problem is the snowmobile, which makes the snowbound plantation an ideal spot to pick out a beautifully shaped Christmas tree without benefit of payment. Sportsmen have long known that the best place to hunt deer is in a clearcut, because this is where the deer congregate for the abundant feed. The fact that they reach their hunting grounds over a logging road and that their venison is by courtesy of a logger are facts that are mostly conveniently ignored.

Most of the large companies make their lands available to sportsmen, with access over logging roads restricted during the hours when logging trucks are operating but open in the late afternoon and on weekends. Logging roads, penetrating as they do some very remote vastnesses have allowed access to areas formerly impenetrable to all but the most avid hunters or fishermen. Forest service roads, being public land, are open at all times unless a really dangerous fire season forces a closure. One of the best investments a really adventuresome person can make is in a good Forest Service map, for it will open up a new world of adventure over roads that are surprisingly good, especially considering the difficulty of the terrain over

This Montana clearcut has been harvested according to the new guidelines that are becoming common in the management of forests. The trees remaining in this stand will be harvested a few years hence in a complete clearcut.

which most of them are built. Traffic increases dramatically during hunting season but this is at least partially balanced by a marked decrease in logging activity at this time. Most loggers, being avid outdoorsmen, have their personal deer all picked out, but getting that elusive buck into the locker may take a few days. Production people, well aware of this, figure on a time of reduced activity until each man has secured his winter supply of side-hill salmon.

The forester, through his new growing forests, wages a continual war on pollution. That bracing air is not accidental; it is oxygen rich from being close to a major producer of the vital ingredient that enhances the air we must breathe to sustain life. The new forests, while growing wood, also consume carbon dioxide, one of the chief ingredients of industrial and domestic pollution. Thus the new forests help to cleanse the air and to renew the oxygen supply which is vital to all animal life. By comparison, an old forest produces more pollution than it does oxygen. The blue haze observed over conifer clad mountains is composed mostly of terpenes and cogeners, a natural pollution generated by old trees. It is true that it is natural; it is equally true that natural or not, it is still pollution.

Most foresters are highly dedicated men and women who are proud of their ancient profession and do an excellent job of maintaining the forests entrusted to their care. In Germany, France, Austria and Czechoslovakia, where the profession of forestry is an old and honored one, they are highly regarded members of the community, and deservedly so, for the care of those beautiful, park-like forests is entrusted to the skilled commitment of these men and women. In

America, their role is not as well understood and certainly not as well honored. That is a shame, because if anyone is deserving of respect, both for the depth of knowledge they must command and for the useful and honorable work that they do, often at great personal sacrifice, those are the foresters of America. A better understanding of their work and an increase in the respect that is rightfully theirs would be one of the greatest rewards I would reap from this book, for in the process of researching it, my path has crossed that of many foresters and I feel that my life has been immeasurably enriched by the contact. In the hands of these dedicated men and women it is safe to assume that America's forests will prosper, but only if they are given the chance to use the knowledge they have spent half a lifetime accumulating. Often times, legislation spawned by urbanites who think a Douglas fir is something from which you make a fur coat hampers these people in the performance of their duties to the point that some of them give up and quite unhappily make a much better living in some other occupation which they do not enjoy half as much. A forester doesn't take on his profession with the idea of getting wealthy: he never will, but he will become very rich in the spiritual values that accrue to a person who does a useful job and who knows that the beauty he is creating will bring joy to a host of people. That that beauty will be perpetuated long after he has turned to dust is simply frosting on the cake.

A new development, one that is very gratifying to loggers, is in the field of medicine. Recent research has indicated that the bark of the Pacific yew tree (Taxus Brevifolia) contains a substance, Taxol, which is the most promising specific to date against uterine cancer, a dreaded killer which every year strikes thousands of women. This development is especially gratifying because their industry can supply a remedy for a disease which conceivably could strike the logger's own family and because it makes use of a tree which up to this time had very few, if any, commercial uses.

Tough, resilient yew wood was formerly used for longbows. The cloth-yard shafts that decimated the flower of French chivalry at Crecy and Agincourt were propelled by yew longbows in the hands of English peasants, and up till recently, it was the preferred material for the venerable weapon. However, the demand for longbows is somewhat limited, these days, as well as for textile shuttles and wagon wheel spokes, other uses for this tough wood. Yew seemed to be a tree consigned to the dustbin of history, and, until the magical qualities of its bark were discovered, usually ignominiously consigned to the slash heap on logging shows. Now, it is the Cinderella tree, eagerly sought and for the first time paying its way out of the woods. In fact, environmental groups, alarmed at the interest which the lowly yew was receiving, tried to have it declared an endangered species. Fortunately, reason prevailed, and the research into its life-saving qualities continues. Yew seedlings are now grown in quantity in nurseries, so that new plantations of the slow-growing tree can be established and research into its growing habits are aimed toward producing a healthier, faster-growing tree.

It is gratifying to see the new uses to which wood and wood products are being put every day. The advent of the computer greatly increased the demand for paper, for this darling of the business world has a voracious appetite for it. At least a partial solution to this demand has recently put in an appearance on Northwest lands. A hybrid cottonwood, the result of intensive research, has been developed that grows to a height of forty feet in seven years. Planted in rows like corn and almost as closely spaced, it is harvested by machines that uproot it and turn the whole tree into chips which make a surprisingly good grade of computer paper.

Another thing that has seen a tremendous growth in the last eighteen years is the Christmas tree plantation. Already well established way back then, it has mushroomed into a multi-million dollar business that shows no sign of abating, although the market must certainly be reaching a saturation point, unless the planters can promote the idea that a family without at least two Christmas trees is underprivileged. A man with forty acres in Christmas trees with good contacts for selling them can live a better than comfortable life; and, like all trees, the supply is renewable.

The forests of America are many things to different people. To some, they are beauty and relaxation from the cares and worries of urban life, while others see them as the home of myriad wildlife species. They help stabilize our water supply and are the plentiful provider of the wood which is such an integral part of our everyday lives. Everyone agrees that forests should be managed somehow: the big argument arises over what form that management should take. Some will say that no management is the best management; let Nature take care of it! Others will point out that Nature, left to its own is often an ecological disaster and that intensive management by man is far superior. A third group sees a middle road as the best possible solution. As in any question that involves complex and often antithecal human emotions, there are no absolute solutions that will satisfy everyone. Fortunately, the diversity of America's forest system is such that, somewhere in it, almost everyone will find an ecological plan suiting their requirements whether those tastes run to recreation, conservation or timber.

The United States alone has over seven hundred million acres whose best use, according to modern technology, is the growing of trees. Presuming that man is the paramount creature on this planet and that he should be the central figure in our environment, the use of these acres should be directed toward the good of man and his environment, whether that use is in recreation or the food and shelter the forests have traditionally provided. Forests are so ingrained into the web of human existence that there is no question that we will always need them. Human life without them would be an impossibility since our Earth would be as inhospitable as the barren plateaus of the moon and as foreign. It remains for future generations to determine what will be made of this invaluable resource which, ever since the dawn of time in countless generations, has helped make this planet a viable home for man and enriched his life with its by-products.

The pragmatic view of a forest as a provider of raw

materials for our civilization is apt to be the recurrent and dominant feeling, yet there are moments when a different emotion engulfs a person, making the arguments of those who would never cut any tree seem almost logical. There are moments of peace and tranquility to be experienced in a forest that are unequaled by any other emotion; moments when a person feels one with Nature. It is a time when one may appreciate a breeze whose meanderings over hundreds of miles of pine and cedar have made it redolent with the spicy fragrance of their breath, when the sunlight filtering through a lacy canopy of gently-swaying branches weaves a pattern of light and shadow on the forest floor. The soft murmur of a gently-burbling forest stream invites one to drowse away a sleepy summer day, and the gentle footfalls of a browsing deer and the song of birds are the only sounds that disturb this arboreal Eden.

It is very easy, at such a time, to feel close to the forces of Nature that govern these gigantic plants, for they contain in principle the very essence of life. A person who feels this way may even come to a realization that has lived atavistically in man since he first emerged from his dark cave and wonderingly lifted his fact to the sun.

God lives in these trees.

On the Rochester, Washington, nursery of the Weyerhaeuser Company, two-year-old Douglas-fir seedlings are mechanically harvested to be used in replanting acres recently cleared of mature trees.

The forest of the future. It will be beautiful, productive, protected and harvested in time for the good of mankind.

This super tree, planted in a favored site, achieved a diameter of twenty-four inches in twenty-seven years, about half the usual time-span for such growth, an indication of what we can expect as more of these super trees come of age.

PHOTOGRAPHIC DATA

Unless otherwise noted, all lenses were capped with skylight filters. My primary film was my old standby, Kodachrome 25, although the 64 speed got quite a bit more usage in this book than it did in the first. My portable flash was a Vivitar 285 which proved quite adequate for my needs, even though I packed heavier, more powerful equipment which went unused, as were the zooms.

Lenses carried, in order of focal length were:

20mm Nikkor f2.8	58mm Nikkor f1.2
24mm Nikkor f2.8	85mm Nikkor f1.8
28mm Nikkor f2.8	105mm Nikkor f2.5
28mm Nikkor f2.	135mm Nikkor f3.5
35mm Nikkor f2.0	108mm Nikkor f2.5
35mm Nikkor f2.8	200mm Nikkor f4
Perspective control	300mm Nikkor f4.5
50mm Nikkor f1.4	43-86 Nikkor Zoom f3.5
50mm Nikkor f2.0	80-200 Nikkor Zoom f4.5
55mm Nikkor Macro f3.5	

Page	Shutter Speed	Aperture	Lens and Comments
Cover	1/8	f5.6	35mm f2 lens, 81B filter. Tripod and self timer.
2	4		81A filter , 35mm perspective control lens, tripod. The light is still a bit greenish: natural enough but an 85c filter gives a more normal (warmer) effect.
6	1/60	f5.6	with flash fill, tripod.
17	1/125	f5.6	50mm, f2 lens.
18	1/250	f4	50mm, f1.4 lens, overcast, areal.
19	1/125	f5.6	105mm lens, light overcast.
20	1/60	f5.6	105mm lens, flash fill.
22	1/250	f8	28mm, f2 lens.
24	1/30	f8	35mm perspective control lens, 81A filter, early evening.
26	1	f2	50mm, f2 lens, camera balanced on a convenient stump.
28	1/60	f4	50mm, 1.4 lens, overcast and light rain.
29	1/15	f4	28mm lens, handheld because I had left the tripod in the car!
32	1/60	f4	85mm lens, overcast and light rain.
33	1/30	f2.8	35mm f2 lens.
35	1/60	f4	50mm f1.4 lens, open shade.
38-39	1/125	f2	50mm f2 lens.
40	1/125	f4	105 lens, overcast.
42	1/250	f5.6	f 2 lens, Kodachrome 64.
43	1/250	f4	105mm lens.
44	1/250	f4	105mm lens, weak flash fill.
46	1/30	f4	35mm lens, heavy shade.
47	1/125	f5.6	50mm, f2 lens.
49	1/250	f5.6	50mm, f1.4 lens.
50	1/30	f4	105mm lens, heavy overcast and tripod.
50-51	1/250		50mm, f2 lens, f8 Kodachrome 64.
54	1/60	f5.6	50mm, f1.4 lens, weak flash fill.
55	1/250	f5.6	f2.0 lens.

Page	Shutter Speed	Aperture	Lens and Comments
56	1/125	f5.6	85mm lens.
59	1/250	f4	105mm lens.
60-61	1/125	f5.6	f2.0 lens, cloudy bright.
62	1/250	f4	105mm lens.
64	1/250	f5.6	50mm f1.4 lens.
67	1/125	f5.6	cloudy bright.
68	1/125	f2.8	35mm lens, raining.
69	1/15	f5.6	50mm, f1.4 lens, tripod.
70	1/30	f2.8	50mm, f1.4 lens.
71	1/125	f5.6	105mm lens.
72	1/125	f6.3	50mm, f2 lens.
75	1/125	f5.6	50mm lens.
77	1/15	F4	50mm lens and 81B filter.
78	1/15	f2.8	50mm lens, raining heavily, and heavy fog.
79	1/125	f8	50mm, f1.4 lens.
80-81	1/250	f4	50mm, f1.4 lens, aerial.
82	1/125	f2.5	105mm lens, Fujichrome Velva.
85	4 seconds	f8	35mm perspective control lens, tripod and 81B filter.
86	1/125	f4	85mm lens.
89	1/125	f8	50mm, f2 lens.
90	1/30	f11	50mm, f1.4 lens.
93 left	1/125	f8	35mm, f2 lens.
93 right	1/60	f5.6	35mm lens, pola screen.
93 bottom	1/125	f8	35mm lens.
94-95	1/125	f8	24mm lens.
96-97	1/250	f5.6	50mm, f2 lens.
99	1/125	f8	35mm, f2 lens.
100	1/60	f11	35mm lens, Kodachrome 64, light rain.
101	1/250	f4	50mm, f2 lens.
102	1/250	f5.6	50mm, f1.4 lens, light rain.
104	1/60	f5.6	50mm lens, pola screen.
105	1/30	f4	50mm lens, heavy overcast.
106	1/60	f5.6	50mm, f2 lens, pola screen.
109	1/125	f8	50mm, f2 lens.
110	1/250	f4	105mm lens.
111	1/60	f8	50mm, f2 lens, flash fill.
114	1/125	f4	50mm, f1.4 lens, good snow reflection helped the weak light.
115	1/125	f8	50mm, f1.4 lens.
118	1/125	f8	35mm lens.
119	1/4 second	f8	35mm perspective control lens, tripod.
120 bottom	1/125	f8	f2, 50mm lens.
121	8 seconds	f11	f2, 50mm lens, tripod and 81B filter.
122	1/60	f4	50mm, f1.4 lens, raining.
123	1/125	f8	50mm, f2 lens.
124	1/125	f8	50mm lens.
126-127	8 seconds	f11	f2, 50mm lens, tripod and 81B filter.
128	1/125	f8	35mm lens.
130	1/125	f5.6	50mm, f2 lens.
133	1/125	f5.6	50mm, f2 lens.
133	1/125	f5.6	50mm, f2 lens.
136	1/125	f5.6	50mm, f2 lens.
137	1/125	f5.6	50mm, f1.4 lens.
140	1/250	f8	50mm, f2 lens, Kodachrome 64.
141	1/125	f5.6	50mm, f2 lens.
142-143	1/125	f4	35mm, f2 lens.
144	1/125	f8	35mm lens Kodachrome 64.
147	1/125	f5.6	50mm, f2 lens.
148	1/125	f8	50mm, f2 lens.
149	1/125	f8	50mm, f2 lens.
151	1/60	f11	50mm, f2 lens, flash fill.
152	1/125	f4	50mm, f1.4 lens.
153	1/125	f5.6	50mm, f2 lens.
154	1/125	f8	35mm lens.
157	1/125	f8	50mm, f2 lens.
158-159	1/125	f8	28mm, Kodachrome 64.

Frame	Shutter	Aperture	Lens/Notes
160	1/15	f2.5	180mm lens, focused very carefully, and camera based on small stump.
161	1/60	f8	55mm Micro Nikkor lens, flash.
163	1/60	f4	50mm, f2, weak flash fill.
166	1/125	f5.6	50mm, f2 lens.
168	1/15	f1.2	55mm, f1.2 lens, this looks quite well-lighted but actually it was so dark here I had to use my fastest lens wide open and pray a lot, handheld.
169	1/60	f2.5	105mm lens, raining, and very poor light.
170	1/60	f4	35mm lens, overcast.

Frame	Shutter	Aperture	Lens/Notes
171	1/250	f5.6	50mm, f1.4 lens, aerial.
172	1/60	f11	50mm, f2 lens.
173	1/125	f5.6	50mm, f2 lens.
174	1/60	f4	35mm lens, taken immediately after a summer hailstorm.
177	1/125	f5.6	50mm, f1.4 lens.
181	1/500	f5.6	50mm, 1.4 lens, aerial.
183-184	1/60	f11	50mm, f2 lens.
185	1/125	f8	35mm lens.

Author's note: There was no question in my mind, when I undertook to revisit the timber country which had been such an exciting part of my life when I was a little bit younger, what photo system I would use to record this new adventure. Although I own far more camera systems than I will ever be able to wear out, I went back to the 35mm Nikon system which had served me so well on my previous foray into the woodlands. The renowned toughness of the miniature camera was well tried in that caper: when I got through with my first book on logging, I went to my camera distributor with two of the battle-scarred veterans of that war and was offered fifty dollars...for both of them...for parts.

Remembering that, I reached clear back into my equipment locker and came up with two only slightly less scarred, but completely functional, old FTNs which had languished on the back shelf while I flirted with newer and more handsome equipment. A new set of batteries, a few screws tightened, and we were ready to go to the wars. Somewhat grudgingly, I packed up those old veterans with a couple of only slightly newer F2s which had already survived enough battles to prove their worth.

Those rugged old cameras never let me down, even though they were exposed to rain, volcanic dust and the rugged beating any equipment used in logging invariably gets. Both those old FTNs still functional, and with inflation, I'll bet today they'd bring at least a hundred dollars...for both of them...for parts.